Making the News

D0220275

Making the News provides a rare, cross-national perspective on key features of journalism and newsmaking cultures and the changing media landscape in contemporary Europe.

Focusing on the key trends, practices and issues in contemporary journalism and news cultures, Paschal Preston maps the major contours of change. Adopting a multi-level approach, he examines individual as well as the broader industrial, organisational, institutional and cultural factors shaping journalism practices over the past two decades.

Moving beyond the tendency to focus on journalism trends and newsmaking practices within a single country, *Making the News* draws on unique, cross-national research examining current journalism practices and related newsmaking cultures in eleven West, Central and East European countries. The study included in-depth interviews with almost hundred senior journalists and subsequent workshop discussions with other interest groups

Making the News links reviews and discussions of the existing literature to original research engaging with the views and experiences of journalists working at the 'coal face' of contemporary newsmaking practices, to provide an original study and useful student text.

Paschal Preston is Head of the School of Communication and founder of the Communication, Technology and Culture (COMTEC) research unit, Dublin City University. Previous publications include *Reshaping Communications: Technology, Information and Social Change* (2001) and *Democracy and Communication in the New Europe: Change and Continuity in East and West* (1995).

Making the News

Journalism and news cultures in Europe

Paschal Preston

Routledge
Taylor & Francis Group

LONDON AND NEW YORK

First published 2009
by Routledge
2 Park Square, Milton Park, Abingdon, Oxon OX14 4RN

Simultaneously published in the USA and Canada
by Routledge
270 Madison Ave, New York, NY 10016

Routledge is an imprint of the Taylor & Francis Group, an informa business

Typeset in Baskerville by
Taylor & Francis Books
Printed and bound in Great Britain by
TJ International Ltd, Padstow, Cornwall

British Library Cataloguing in Publication Data
A catalogue record for this book is available from the British Library

Library of Congress Cataloging in Publication Data
Making the news : journalism and news cultures in contemporary Europe /
Paschal Preston.
    p. cm.
Includes bibliographical references and index.
1. Journalism—Europe. I. Title.
    PN5110.P73 2008
    079'.4–dc22
                          2008019122

ISBN10: 0-415-46188-X (hbk)
ISBN10: 0-415-46189-8 (pbk)
ISBN10: 0-203-88859-6 (ebk)

ISBN13: 978-0-415-46188-7 (hbk)
ISBN13: 978-0-415-46189-4 (pbk)
ISBN13: 978-0-203-88859-9 (ebk)

Contents

Contents

Illustrations

Figures

Tables

Boxes

Acknowledgements

Most books rely on the work and contributions of many persons in addition to the person named on the cover. That is especially the case here. Many sections of the text are informed by the work of partners in a multi-country research project: 'Media and Ethics of the European Public Sphere From the Treaty of Rome to the "War on Terror"' (eMEDIATE). The project was funded by the EU's Sixth Framework research programme (Priority 7: Citizens and Governance in a Knowledge-Based Society, Project number CIT2-CT-2004–506027).

Various section of this book draw upon research reports, workshop discussions and other contributions by my eMEDIATE project partners. Thus, I wish to acknowledge the help and contributions of partners in Utrecht (for research on the Netherlands and Italy), Paris (France and Spain), Budapest (Hungary), Ljubljana (Slovenia and Serbia) and Dublin (Britain and Ireland). So a big thank you goes to Jacques Guyot, Anikó Horváth, András Kovács, James Kaye, Primož Krašovec, Michal Krzyzanowski, Hagen Schulz-Forberg, Bo Strath, Jessika ter Wal, Ruth Wodak, Anna Triandafyllidou, Lenka Waschkova Cisarova, and Igor Zagar. And a special dedication is due to Andrej Pinter. However, the usual disclaimers apply, as responsibility for any errors, contentious claims and the rest reside with the present author.

I must especially acknowledge the various contributions of several colleagues involved in the research team and in supporting roles in Dublin City University. I want to thank John Horgan (my fellow coordinator till his retirement) for his inputs, support and advice in the first two years of the eMEDIATE project. I also express my appreciation for the valuable inputs of other members of the local DCU research team who worked on this project: Monika Metykova, Niamh Puirséil, Lughaidh O'Braonain, and Gary Quinn. Special thanks to Mami Ishikawa for her excellent work in sifting and sub-editing the various project reports and bibliographies, and to Pauline Jones for her diligent and patient work on the administrative aspects. All contributed to the successful completion of this project.

I also wish to thank the editorial team at Routledge, Natalie Foster, Paola Celli and Charlotte Wood, for their advice, patience and support in making this book possible.

Chapter 1

Journalism in a state of flux?

Explanatory perspectives

> A subject so complex as journalism can be treated with advantage from very different standpoints.
>
> (Carl Bücher, 1901: 215)

The Anglo-US model – hegemonic or in crisis?

To declare that journalism and newsmaking are in *a state of flux* and subject to deep, multi-dimensional changes in the first decade of the twenty-first century may be an understatement. We don't merely refer to the multiple innovations in the production and distribution of news enabled by the Internet and a whole cluster of other radical technological developments. Nor only to the growing array of news media 'products' and formats available on our television and computer screens, mobile handsets or other devices, all promising up-to-the-second, *mobile and ambient* news services in keeping with our brave 'new', 'knowledge-based' or 'networked' society. Nor are we only thinking of the more recent buzz around user-generated content, audience engagement in the co-production of news or even the evolution of a new species, citizen-journalists, threatening the privileged status if not the survival of the old professional sort. Certainly, these constitute important and much-studied aspects of the state of flux in newsmaking today. But they are also accompanied by other significant, if 'old', concerns to do with the qualitative aspects of news culture. We refer to concerns about the substantive or quality aspects of news culture, including journalism's changing roles and responsibilities towards its *public* – modern journalism's presumed raison d'être or 'god term' (Carey, 2007).

Here, we observe a growing sense that the Anglo-US model of journalistic values and newsmaking practices has become a universal standard for the remainder of the world. This appears to be particularly the case since the shift to a new world order marked by the end of the Cold War, the rise of WTO-based regulatory regimes for media and the USA's dominant role as the biggest 'bully' (Colin Powell) in the world's military playground. From a soap-box built from bits of chaos theory, one academic specialist proclaims that the old Anglo-US model has been renewed and is now performing in a manner that transcends criticism, thanks to new digital technologies and a 'more reflexive' cohort of journalists (McNair, 2006). Indeed, whilst there may be 'many ways of doing – or not doing – news' we note a growing perception that 'there is now only one approved mega-model', usually referred to as 'the Anglo-Saxon model' (Lloyd, 2004: 29). But even as 'the ideals of neutral professionalism' based on Anglo-American media history are widely proclaimed and accepted by journalists around the world, some research specialists find that this frequently occurs 'even where the actual practice ... departs radically' from such norms (Hallin and Papathanassopoulos, 2002: 176).

Equally significant, however, are the signs that this, apparently hegemonic, model is now experiencing a crisis in its homelands. For, just as the Anglo-US model of journalism is elevated to the dominant (if not universal) global standard, 'it is itself becoming the object of increasing internal criticism and questioning by some leading practitioners and researchers in its countries of origin' (Preston, 2006a: 3). In the USA, for example, academics and public intellectuals express serious concerns about the quality and political independence of the news media, especially in the context of the political regimes focused on war on terror and attendant restrictions on human rights and civil rights since 2001. There is a strong sense that the mainstream news media – not merely the populist neo-conservative outlets but also standard-bearers such as the *New York Times* – have failed to match the standards of independent and critical journalism they frequently presume for themselves or prescribe for others (Friel and Falk, 2007). In the USA and elsewhere, we also observe major concerns about a significant and long-term decline of public confidence in the news media institutions (Gronke and Cook, 2007).

Turning to the other side of the Atlantic, the past few years have witnessed intensive soul-searching on the part of (at least, some) senior journalists and media professionals concerning the role, operations and powers of the media in Britain. This is only partly related to the various consequences and fallout arising from a now-infamous early morning radio broadcast by a BBC journalist in 2003. The scope of the expressed concern extends way beyond public service broadcasting to address private sector news organisations, including the old print media. In recent years, senior working journalists as well as academics have proclaimed the need for a fundamental review of the British model of journalism (e.g. Lloyd, 2004; Rusbridger, 2005). For example, a senior editor on the *Financial Times* has argued the need for a major rethink and 'renewal of the values and tasks of free media' and that 'a real debate on what media do to our politics and civil society' is urgently required (Lloyd, 2004: 1). Others (e.g. O'Neill, 2002) have even called for more extensive forms of regulation of the print media in Britain. Such moves and proposals signal a somewhat unprecedented crisis given the proud and long-standing attachments to the ideals and self-image of an autonomous press in Britain – a tradition that dates back to the writings of David Hume in the eighteenth century. Such developments in its first country of origin, suggest that the Anglo-US model of journalism is in something of a pickle, if not facing a serious crisis.

For such reasons, then, we may take it that journalism and newsmaking are in a deep, multi-dimensional state of flux today. The prime task of this book is to map the key features and contours of such recent trends and to examine the major influences and explanatory perspectives which help us understand the sources and meaning of these developments.

This book is concerned with *describing* and *explaining* the key trends and issues in journalism and news culture in the early twenty-first century. It seeks to identify the contours and trends of multi-dimensional change now unfolding in journalism and newsmaking processes as well as the most compelling explanations of these trends – the alternative or optimal ways of understanding their sources and implications. To this end, the book provides a distinctive multi-layered approach to the influences on newsmaking and news culture. It also draws on a unique, cross-national research project examining the relevant research and current trends in news and journalism cultures in 11 European countries over the past 20 years or so. It adopts a multi-level approach to news culture and journalism practices in an effort to provide a rounded, inter-disciplinary account of the trends in this field. In so doing, it seeks to bridge the frequently encountered divide between journalism studies on the one hand, and media or political communication studies, on the other hand.

The book's agenda and its distinctive approach

At this point, it may be helpful to signal and summarise a number of distinctive features concerning the conceptual framework, research approach and resources that inform the following chapters. First, this book is framed around a distinctive multi-dimensional approach to understanding the influences on news culture and newsmaking processes. It explicitly recognises that the large and growing body of research on journalism and newsmaking is based on many different theoretical and methodological approaches. In this light, we have sought to develop a coherent, practical, yet reasonably comprehensive classification or pedagogic schema. The chosen typology aims to embrace the major concepts and explanatory perspectives on newsmaking. It is framed around five clusters of concepts associated with different explanatory perspectives or schools of research, each offering distinct but complementary ways of understanding the influences on journalism and news culture. This multi-dimensional approach is also inter-disciplinary in scope as it embraces research and concepts related to both journalism studies on the one hand, and the media and (political) communication studies field, on the other.

Second, this book has a distinct approach towards mapping the implications for journalism and news culture of digital technologies, new media and broader socio-technical developments variously referred to as the knowledge economy, network society or information age. These comprise a major set of issues, not least because digital technologies are multiple in form, and have a pervasive application potential, for example they are used extensively in both 'old' and 'new' news media (as explained in Chapter 2 and later). Thus, to understand the implications of the Internet for news culture and journalism, we need to address relevant trends and factors in both the old or mature media (newspapers, radio and television) as well as in online media and to consider the balance between *continuities* and *changes* on a number of fronts. It also means we must address the Internet as one significant node or sub-set of a wider cluster of new information and communication technologies (ICTs). The latter, in turn, may be viewed as a historically rare, major new technology system with a pervasive applications potential.

In negotiating this complex and challenging domain of inquiry, this book provides a distinctive approach centred on balancing contending viewpoints around a number of core issues. One involves recognising the specific features and significance of the Internet and other new ICTs whilst at the same time avoiding techno-centric approaches (or the seductions of the 'technological sublime') in analyses of newsmaking trends. Since quality journalism is not determined or tightly linked to technical factors, a second distinctive feature of our approach is to interrogate both *the commonalities* as well as *differences* between newsmaking and journalism culture in both new media and old media formats. A further and related feature of our approach in this regard is to address the balance between *changes* and *continuities* in the journalism and newsmaking landscape over the past 10–20 years. Here, we seek to introduce a nuanced understanding and distinction between *technology*-centred and *information* (e.g. information society or knowledge economy) perspectives on the wider structural changes now impacting on the newsmaking environment. The latter include, for example, the expanding role of various media services and 'soft communication' functions within our contemporary societal, economic and political systems.

Third, the book is informed by a relatively rare, cross-national study involving primary and secondary research in 11 countries, as described below. Finally, we may note that this book also seeks to engage with questions concerning the transnationalisation or 'globalisation' of news cultures today. In our cross-national study we sought to examine the forms (or extent) of any convergences in newsmaking practices and journalistic cultures across national cultural boundaries in Europe. Here the EU area may be taken as a 'leading-edge' site or test case for deepening trans-national economic and political integration at the world-region level. We examine whether and how these developments are being matched by a shared media culture or an emergent post-national public sphere across the EU region.

Thus, this text helps to address the growing interest in trans-national or cross-national studies of journalism and media cultures as it is based on a structured multi-country study that is relatively rare. The relevant international research and teaching literature indicates that cross-national and comparative studies of journalism and media cultures are becoming increasingly important, even urgent (e.g. Livingstone, 2003; Josephi, 2005). Many recent reviews of the relevant literature have argued that cross-national and comparative research on media and journalism, especially that which is systematic, theoretically informed and tailor-made, is now an urgent priority (e.g. Livingstone, 2003; Hanitzsch, 2005; Josephi, 2005).

Of course cross-national and comparative studies are much easier to prescribe than they are to perform or realise in practice. In part, this is because such studies pose many major practical, epistemological, and value-laden challenges for the researcher, resulting in a continuing paucity of texts based on purpose-built, multi-country research (Hanitzsch, 2005: 2). Besides, many of the recent cross-national or comparative studies of journalistic ethics and editorial cultures often comprise surveys of the declared principles of ethical codes, with little attention to their actual implementation or operational contexts (Himelboim and Limor, 2005). This book draws on primary research among journalists charged with interpreting and implementing the professional norms and codes in specific organisational, media sectors and national contexts. It also seeks to combine the primary research data with focused reviews of the specialised research literature produced in different national settings.

Fourth, as noted above, the book is informed by a carefully structured, cross-national study comprising two main aspects. One involves the findings from primary research, including in-depth interviews with 95 senior journalists in 11 countries in the West, Central and East European regions and from some subsequent workshop discussions with other interest groups. Co-ordinated by the present author, the primary research covered the following 'new' and 'old' EU member states: Britain, France, Hungary, Ireland, Italy, Netherlands, Spain, Sweden, Serbia, Slovenia, the Czech Republic and Slovakia. Our interviewees comprised experienced journalists or editors working in print and electronic media in these 11 countries. The semi-structured interviews also sought to address differences between different media, such as TV and press or private and public sector news organisations. The key questions framing our in-depth interviews, fieldwork and secondary research are indicated in Box 1.1.

In addition, this primary research was complemented by secondary research embracing a number of additional countries. This includes systematic reviews of the relevant international research on journalism trends and news influences, including the national literature in the countries covered by the primary research. The book's substantive chapters engage with the prevailing international research literature as well as drawing on key findings from primary research. In addition, some chapters are also informed by the proceedings of a series of seminar and roundtable discussions with media professionals, politicians and a range of key media user-organisations (representing social interests and non-governmental organisations) centred on discussions of the preliminary results of the research.

Box 1.1 Key questions framing the interviews and secondary research

1   What are the main features of journalism, its professional values, newsmaking practices and editorial cultures in contemporary Europe?
2   What have been the main trends of change in journalism and its news cultures over the past 15–20 years, including the key institutional, organisational and technological factors shaping these changes?
3   What are the key trends of change in journalists' relationship with their audiences and what are the key factors influencing such changes?
4   To what extent is there any singular European journalism culture or how can we best map a number of competing models (typologies or regionalisations) of journalism in EU countries?
5   To what extent is there an emergent (or growing) common European 'public sphere', especially when it comes to the news and the agenda of political issues related to the European Union area?

Five clusters of influences on newsmaking

Our five-fold explanatory frame: clusters of influences on news

As noted, this book is framed around a distinct multi-dimensional approach to understanding the diverse influences on news culture and newsmaking processes. The chosen typology comprises five explanatory perspectives or research traditions which offer distinct but complementary sets of concepts and ways of understanding the influences on journalism and news culture. In brief, our approach is based on our reading and reviews of the relevant international literature which reveal a number of competing but complementary explanatory perspectives (or levels of analysis) for understanding the influences on journalism and news culture. In designing our typology we have benefited from the prior schema of other authors who have sought to frame and summarise the relevant research into a number of categories. Particularly helpful in this regard have been the classifications proposed earlier by: Gans, 1979; Gitlin, 1980/2003; Shoemaker and Reese, 1996; Reese, 2001a; Schudson, 2000; Whitney *et al.*, 2004. Here, we identify and combine the major explanatory perspectives and related set of concepts into a five-fold typology. The resulting classification was deemed the most coherent and practical for presenting the research literature and our own research findings. Each of these five explanatory perspectives and clusters of concepts may be treated as highly complementary and even 'leaky' (see Figure 1.1).

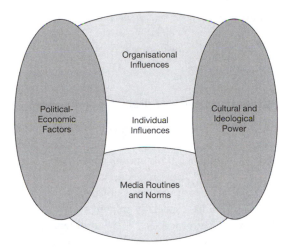

Figure 1.1 Five domains of influences: making the news

Individual level influences and professional values

Our first explanatory perspective and cluster of concepts focuses on the individual level. This covers research focused on the personal characteristics, background and values of working journalists. It considers the role of professional values and codes of ethics, including journalists' own definitions and self-understandings of their professional roles and norms as influences on newsmaking practices. This first set of potential influences on newsmaking is probably the most familiar, partly because it resonates closely with journalists' traditional self-understandings of their profession. It fits with the modes of explanation or models of 'common sense' reasoning favoured by the wider institutions and culture in most, if not all, contemporary capitalist societies.

This strand of research includes many studies that seek to describe the individual characteristics of journalists as an occupational group. Such research has been the most common approach to conducting research on professional issues (Whitney *et al.*, 2004). This is despite the paradox that the concept of objectivity implies that individual characteristics of journalists should have little if any influence on the output of their work. The research also includes many studies of journalists' beliefs and values, which have been undertaken on the assumption that such individual factors provide an adequate basis for explaining a perceived political bias in news content.

There are several reasons why individual level explanatory models are so popular. First, such perspectives closely match journalists' self-understanding of their professional roles and autonomy. This is manifest, for example, in the popular genre of journalists' biographies, and it links to a continuing tendency to frame journalism as linked to the literary domains of knowledge work. Second, the marketing and promotional campaigns of news and other media organisations have a growing, if long-established, tendency to emphasise the role of individual journalists, especially celebrity or 'star' reporters. Third, such perspectives are readily accepted because they are pervasive features of the wider institutional, discursive and cultural setting in contemporary societies.

Media industry routines: institutional practices and norms

Our second analytic approach is focused on media industry routines, the typical and taken-for-granted (but patterned) institutional practices and norms that frame and shape daily newsmaking. This cluster comprises concepts and insights on the routines of newsmaking and professional journalistic practices, usually based on sociological and ethnographic studies of newsrooms and their relations with certain external institutions, especially related to news sourcing. The concept of *routines* refers to the patterned sets of institutional practices and norms which frame or guide how individuals work and function within the complex settings that characterise industrial, urban and capitalist social formations. It embraces the shared procedures, rules and norms that are ongoing and highly structured, but often naturalised and taken-for-granted. However, these also comprise essential conditions for the performance of collaborative work in a modern society marked by large-scale organisations as well as deep social and technical divisions of labour.

Here, newsmaking is seen as a complex and time-pressured process requiring the coordinated and patterned activities of large numbers of individual workers to produce the news on a daily or hourly basis, within a specific configuration of time, space, norms, technologies and other resources. The practices, autonomy and influence of individual newsworkers are viewed as *situated* or conditioned (both constrained and enabled) by the operations of sector-specific or occupational procedures, rules, practices and norms. Here, the primary explanation of news culture shifts away from the dispositions, beliefs or personal characteristics of individual newsworkers and towards the operations and features of industrial routines and other institutional factors. These include the configurations and allocation of human and technical resources, time-based factors, patterns of relations with sources, professional norms, and news values.

Such institutional approaches to newsmaking routines recognise that individual journalists do not work alone in making the news, and they do not apply rules that they invented themselves. Concepts such as routines tend to emphasise the conditioning influences of prevailing procedures, norms and practices in the media industry. This explanatory approach suggests that individuals do not possess complete freedom to act on their beliefs and attitudes. Rather, they must operate within specific configurations of material, normative, social and technological resources to perform their roles in the newsmaking process. These may be perceived as constraints, but they can also be viewed as enabling. Indeed, they concern the very social roles or pre-conditions that enable professional newsworkers to have relatively privileged access to the production of news culture.

Both the institutional and the organisational (our third) perspectives tend to emphasise that newsmaking is a social process. Like most modern media or cultural production, it involves the collective and coordinated efforts of many different persons, skills, roles and functions. Because of the inherently ephemeral nature of the news 'product', its increasingly short life-cycle, and its informational role, news production requires a more complex and highly geared organisational structure compared to other segments of the media sector. Furthermore, most journalists are not 'their own master' in the sense of being self-employed, or owning and controlling the tools, technical instruments or other resources required to perform their newsmaking roles. Rather, they tend to be direct employees or freelance agents of the capitalist enterprises (firms) and other *media organisations* that comprise the newsmaking industry.

'Crucial containers': organisational influences on news

The third category concerns those newsmaking processes and influencing factors operating at the level of specific media organisations (e.g. print and television, public and private media organisations). Here the news organisation is viewed as a crucial container or context that serves to socialise, situate or otherwise steer journalists and their newsmaking practices in important respects. In essence, explanatory perspectives focused on the organisational influences on newsmaking tend to emphasise how the immediate working environment operates as a 'crucial' conditioning context shaping the production of news (e.g. Lloyd, 2004).

While news organisations may share and contribute to certain common (industry-wide) newsmaking routines, norms and procedures, they also tend to define and implement them in highly specific ways. Such specificities are linked to the distinctive sets of strategic goals, values, and policies of each news organisation. The overall direction of the organisation's goals and structures are decided by its owners and higher-level executives, since most industrial organisations are marked by a hierarchical structure of power and influence, however formal or informal its manifestation. Like other social groups, news organisations are also marked by conflicts over goals and values, especially between journalistic norms and criteria (such as news quality) and those related to managerial or economic performance (such as profit or revenue maximisation).

Thus, the organisational perspective examines the influences on newsmaking arising from the goals, policies, hierarchies of status and power structures, conflicts and practices of the formal organisations in which the work of most journalists is situated. These factors include firm-specific, departmental- or medium-specific editorial policies and their attendant sets of newsmaking routines, norms, and procedures (e.g. 'house-style') which inform the daily working practices of most journalists.

For example, Warren Breed's (1955) seminal study, *Social Control in the Newsroom*, alerts us to the ways internal organisational power may be expressed less by formal policies or channels than by informal mechanisms, such as the dynamics of small groups, peer group pressures, and other factors mobilising loyalties to the team spirit. The insight that organisational power may be exercised informally and only periodically, implicitly rather than overtly, poses many challenges. It suggests that journalists learn and internalise the subtle rules and anticipate the boundaries of organisational policies and values. As a result, organisational power and influence may be difficult to research when it is expressed in forms of self-censorship that are more effective than direct censorship. Clearly, these issues pose difficulties for research since empirical work focused on the visible, formal expressions of organisational power may be missing out on the real story – that centred around the informal exercise of power, such as self-censorship. For example, even if journalists rigorously follow professional ethical codes to avoid or declare all conflicts of interest, this may not be matched by more powerful organisational actors, such as owners and top-level executives, when it comes to external corporate or financial interests or other inter-elite linkages.

There are many links or spillover concepts shared by the explanatory approaches highlighting the organisational and institutional influences on news-making. While institutional researchers may refer to 'media routines' to indicate patterned procedures and norms that tend to be largely shared across the news *industry*, we should note that these may converge or collide with the *professional* standards and norms of journalism, one specific *occupation* within the media sector. In terms of this occupational dimension, journalists' professional norms may be seen as comprising two basic types: *technical norms* that largely deal with the operations and efficient performance of news gathering, writing and editing; and *ethical norms* that concern the journalists' obligations to the professed ideals of responsibility, impartiality, accuracy, fair play, and objectivity (Breed, 1955).

For some, the development of professional journalism 'establishes norms of conduct for journalists' that reduce the need for news organisations to put in place elaborate rules and regulations for staff (Soloski, 1989: 213). In addition, such professional norms may facilitate news organisations in the selection and recruitment of journalists, and enable them to employ experienced workers by minimising the need for expensive and time-consuming training. Yet, shared professional norms do not eliminate the challenges completely, for two reasons. First, these norms can provide journalists with a certain autonomy or power base that can resist heavy-handed interference by management. Second, if professional norms yield much power or freedom then news organisations may respond by developing new procedures to further limit the professional autonomy of their journalists (ibid.).

Political economy factors and influences on newsmaking

Our fourth and fifth explanatory perspectives focus on broader, macro-level influences and conceptual issues. Political economy approaches to communication, media and newsmaking tend to engage with state-based and economy-based influences in an integrated or holistic manner. They draw on strands of modern social thought, dating back to Smith, Ricardo, Marx, Mill, Cairnes, Polanyi and others, which engage with questions concerning the production, organisation and distribution of goods, wealth and power in society. This approach tends to define the scope and characteristics of the 'economy' and 'market' (as well as their relation to the state and political factors) in ways that are significantly different to the influential modern discipline of 'economics'. Beyond such high-level characteristics, however, we find many different definitions of the precise meaning and scope of political economy influences, with abundant variations in the news and communication studies fields.

For some, the political economy perspective on newsmaking and its outcomes tends to focus on 'the structure of the state and the economy, and to the economic foundations of the news organization'; at the same time, it is attentive to the various 'constitutional regimes' and 'institutional forms' that frame the operations of the media whilst recognising that 'both state and market' may limit free expression (Schudson, 2000: 171, 181). Golding and Murdock suggest that 'critical political economy' differs from mainstream economics in four main respects: first, 'it is holistic'; second, 'it is historical'; third, it is 'concerned with the balance between capitalist enterprise and public intervention'; and finally it goes beyond the technical issues of efficiency 'to engage with basic moral questions of justice, equity and public good' (Golding and Murdock, 2000: 72–73).

Thus, political economy research tends to address the high-level or 'macro' influences on news and questions concerning the role and responsibilities of the media to 'the public' – often defined in terms of citizenship rather than consumers. This agenda includes the normative issues related to the autonomy of the media, the independence of its editorial and journalistic work, and its watchdog role vis-à-vis the other major institutions and powers in society. The political economy perspective sheds light on the systemic and highly patterned ways in which news media and newsmaking may be influenced by their relationships to the key institutions and seats of power (political, economic, military, discursive or other forms) in the wider society. Thus, the issues of media ownership and control patterns, their relation to the definition and making of the news agenda, the role and influence of advertising and other economic interests have all been part of the political economy research agenda. So too have the evolving characteristics of the public sphere, and the pressures on journalism and political communication arising from deepening commercialisation. This strand of research has also paid much attention to the specific roles and operations of different media sub-sectors, especially that of public service broadcasting.

Just as we observe particularly strong conceptual overlaps between research highlighting the media routines and organisational layers of influences on newsmaking, the same applies to the political economy and cultural layers. In its narrow sense, political economy research addresses how material resources such as wealth and property, as well as symbolic resources are organised, controlled, and distributed by market and state institutions. Applied to the fields of communication and newsmaking, this approach spills over to questions of the sources and nature of power in the complex of economic, political and ideological relations within the advanced capitalist societies in which news and newsmaking is situated. At this point, it overlaps with the holistic conceptual frames and analyses favoured by cultural studies approaches to media and newsmaking. In sum, we observe considerable conceptual overlaps 'between the "ideological" level and the political economic work' influenced by the British cultural studies tradition (Whitney *et al.*, 2004: 400; Gitlin, 2004: 309).

'The cultural air we breathe': cultural, ideological or symbolic power

In an earlier review of the various filtering processes or influences on newsmaking, Richard Hoggart (1976) identified one as 'the cultural air we breathe'. He invoked this pithy phrase to embrace those influences related to 'the whole ideological atmosphere of our society', which in turn tells us how 'some things can be said and others had best not be said' (Glasgow Media Group, 1976; cited in Eldridge, 1995: 8).

The image of 'the cultural air we breathe' looks beyond the newsroom to evoke the surrounding atmosphere of prevailing ideas, ideologies and discourses that permeate journalists' working environment and news content, including its language, forms and 'feel' in a given societal context. This has certain links to the *structure of feeling* concept proposed by Raymond Williams, another pioneer of the British cultural studies approach to media. The latter is defined as 'the culture of a period ... the particular living result of all the elements in the general organization' and where 'the arts of a period' including their 'characteristic approaches, and tones in argument' are of major importance (Williams, 1961: 64–65). Even if the structure of feeling is not held by all members of any society, it is shared by 'very deep and very wide' segments 'precisely because it is on it that communication depends', even though it is not learned in any formal way (ibid.: 65). In this sense, news now contributes one, albeit rapidly changing, dimension of 'the arts' and ideas of a particular community or (modern) time period. Viewing the forms and patterns of communication as lying at the centre of the fabric of society, Williams observed that it was impossible to discuss communication or culture in society without addressing the issues of power. Williams noted that 'there is the power of established institutions and there is increasingly the power of money' with the latter imposing certain patterns of communication that are becoming very influential in society (Williams, 1989; cited in Eldridge and Eldridge, 1994: 99).

This fifth perspective tends to approach news influences in terms of whether and how the symbolic content and meanings in the news media may be linked to the broader patterns of social and cultural power. It is concerned with the content, framing, and forms or language of the news stories that are told. It is also concerned with the tendencies for some stories and experiences to remain untold as a result of the unequal structures of discursive or ideological power.

The latter type of analysis is often based on critical theories of ideology that view power in society as highly concentrated or unequally distributed among social and other interests. For example, it may examine how unequal power relations in society can be exerted through the typical operations of media to systematically reproduce certain sets of ideas and values and thereby help to engineer mass consent to the established social order. Thus, the news media may contribute to the process of *hegemony*, which concerns 'the maintenance of domination through means other than violence of direct state control' (Barnhurst, 2005: 241; see also Glasgow Media Group, 1976; Gitlin, 1980). Such explanatory perspectives tend to interrogate several key assumptions underpinning liberal and neo-liberal theories. This includes approaches to news based on various pluralist models whereby power is seen as widely distributed in modern capitalist societies – or at least balanced by its circulation among competing institutions or interests, and so avoiding any significant patterns of concentration.

We might view the cultural and ideological influences as moving beyond organisational and institutional factors towards deeper and wider layers of shaping forces within which the news is 'constructed' by the situated interactions of human actors. This fifth explanatory perspective is concerned with certain broad sets of values, assumptions, beliefs or 'cultural givens' within which everyday interaction is located, although these usually fall outside the gaze of studies focused on organisational or institutional factors. It draws attention to how journalism may be influenced by the 'unquestioned and generally unnoticed background assumptions' through which news in any society 'is gathered and within which it is framed' (Schudson, 2000: 192). Much like the air we breathe, such cultural givens are usually invisible, taken-for-granted elements in any given setting. Yet, they form essential components of meaning-making processes in community life and human interaction. These cultural givens 'cannot be extrapolated from features of social organisation' at any given moment of study; rather, they are usually uncovered by 'detailed historical analysis' or, we might add, by cross-cultural studies (ibid.: 189). While the general 'cultural air' may be partly shaped by the societal or political economy setting of its ruling groups and institutions, it also forms a key conditioning context in which such institutions become established. Thus, cultural influences also possess their own specificity (ibid.: 192; Gitlin, 2004: 309).

The interplay of influences: convergences and spillovers

Even if journalists are frequently depicted, especially in media representations, 'as independent, morally virtuous, and acting in the name of the public good' (Berkowitz and Limor, 2003: 784) that is only one of many factors shaping news culture or guiding their daily working lives. As we will see, there are significant sets of research indicating how the daily practices of journalists and other newsworkers are deeply embedded in multiple layers or (often conflicting) sets of powerful influences. Some of these are more immediately manifest or visible, for example in the case of tensions between journalists' professional ideals or ethical values on the one hand, and the profit-motivated concerns related to the business and financial pressures operating within increasingly commercial news organisations on the other. Other domains of the research also point to less visible or silent forms of power and influence shaping news cultures, including some which may appear as somewhat remote from the newsroom setting. Other examples include influences that are regarded as somehow natural, universal or beneficial features of the contemporary newsmaking environment. We will explore these issues in the following chapters, but the key point to note for now is that the various layers of influences are best seen as deeply interrelated when it comes to a rounded understanding of the daily practices of making the news.

Although this typology (and book) may appear to isolate the research perspectives highlighting each of these five different layers of influence in separate chapters, it must be understood that this is for pedagogic and expositional purposes only. In the daily work practices of journalism and newsmaking, these layers of influence are always operating simultaneously, even if some are more directly manifest or visible than others. In essence, all these layers of influence may be viewed as highly interactive and dialectically related – and often operating in tension – when it comes to the multiple actions, selections, treatments of events or other decisions undertaken in the daily work routines of newsworkers. Thus, although Chapters 3 through 7 will separately focus on one or other of these five sets of influence on news, we must note at the outset that these shaping factors are best understood as operating simultaneously in daily newsmaking practice.

Furthermore, it is important to note that many of the prior studies of newsmaking processes also tend to recognise or engage with the role and influence of two or more of these influences, if only implicitly. Thus, the reader should not regard these five sets of influences on news culture as discrete or mutually exclusive. Indeed, we expect that the reader will discern that these categories are not watertight capsules of knowledge, but should be understood as marked by multiple leakages or spillovers. Whilst many important studies of the newsmaking process tend to focus on one particular category of influences, this may well be justified by the need for selectivity when designing and undertaking any single study, especially if empirically based. But, even if they highlight only one particular set of factors, many researchers may also recognise the potential role and influence of other factors even if these fall outside the gaze or scope of any particular study. In like manner, we expect that the reader will critically engage with the claims and counterclaims advanced by the research on the five categories of influences as summarised above – and in so doing, arrive at their own understanding of the most compelling combinations of factors and influences which best explain the contemporary newsmaking process and news culture.

Outline of chapters

The following chapter (Chapter 2) provides a brief overview of the evolution of organised newsmaking and journalism. It also sets out the conceptual framework for understanding the strategic implications of new digital technologies and the changing role of information and knowledge services in the contemporary period.

Chapters 3 through 7 draw on our research findings to examine the key trends and issues in journalism and newsmaking, focusing on each of the five explanatory approaches and clusters of potential influences on newsmaking in turn. These chapters will be directly informed by the unique research resource described earlier. In each case, the chapter's theme and key sub-topics will be examined and discussed in light of: (i) examples of classic or seminal studies in international research literature related to each explanatory perspective and its core concepts; (ii) reviews of the more recent research literature addressing the trends and forms of unfolding changes, including those related to digital technologies and knowledge economy developments, as well as reviews of relevant literature from the 11 countries studied; and (iii) our primary research findings, especially those arising from our in-depth interviews with working journalists in those countries. Where relevant, we will also consider issues that emerged from subsequent discussions at workshops with non-media professionals and consultations with other key actors.

Chapter 8 considers key aspects of the changing character and role of the audience and its relation to newsmaking practices, including its increasingly multicultural composition. Chapter 9 examines the forms and extent to which we are witnessing a common European news culture and the patterns of coverage of common topics and issues. The final chapter will seek to identify the key issues and trends whilst also noting some implications.

Chapter 2

Evolution of organised news and journalism in Europe

> Journalism emerges, first, through a long and complex process, particular to each society, in which fact and fiction need to be separated and reporting and social commentary distinguished from other forms of writing.
>
> (James Carey, 2007: 12)

Organised news: its evolution and institutionalisation

This chapter provides an overview of the evolving meanings and role of news-making and journalism, as well as the wider media landscapes and socio-technical environments in which they have been embedded. It seeks to provide a histori-cally grounded and nuanced platform of concepts and ideas to help frame the more detailed analysis of contemporary developments in subsequent chapters.

First, this chapter considers the role of different forms of news, especially everyday and organised news, indicating how this book is primarily concerned with organised or professional news services. Second, it outlines the changing forms and roles of organised news in pre-modern (briefly) and in modern times, and third, it addresses the emergence of an orientation to 'the public' as an important feature, if not 'god term' (Carey, 2007: 12) for journalism and news-making in the modern era.

Fourth, this chapter sets out to establish an initial conceptual frame to aid understanding of the extent, forms and drivers of the flux and change in news media today, especially the role of technological innovations, such as the Internet, which feature prominently in recent analyses of newsmaking. This is an impor-tant, if tricky, theme because we live in 'technology tempered times' (Preston, 2001) and a culture which tends to favour technology-centred explanations of changes in journalism. Whilst it may be true that 'the history of journalism is in many ways defined by technological change' (Pavlik, 2000: 229), the precise role of technological innovation in shaping change in newsmaking is one of the least developed areas of journalism studies (Schudson, 2000; Boczkowski, 2004b).

For example, many textbooks still tend to treat technological change in rather simplistic if rigid fashion by framing the relevant issues in terms of whether its presumed 'effects' on journalism or media cultures are deemed to be positive or negative. Whatever choices students make in response to such framing, they are directed towards a deterministic bind of erroneous assumptions that technology has autonomous or discrete powers to shape journalism or media culture. Such framing of the issues fails to consider the distinctions between causal or necessary relations and what may be contingent or coincidental relations between new technologies on the one hand and specific new developments in journalism on the other hand. These approaches ignore the long history of research rejecting such deterministic views of technological innovation, including that on the radical variability or flexibility of most new communication technologies when it comes to their application and use in specific sectors, social contexts, organisational or cultural settings.

Like some others, we propose that analyses of journalism and newsmaking have much to gain by engaging with the large body of recent research focused on the relations between technological and social change (Boczkowski, 2004b; Carey, 2005). For these reasons, this chapter advances a particular socio-technical model for understanding the co-evolution of technological and social change and applies it to the field of journalism and newsmaking. This enables a historically grounded and non-deterministic approach which also acknowledges how technological innovation may play a role in enabling or providing incentives for other patterns of change. This schema also identifies how the current cluster of digital media and information technologies is now poised to play a central role not merely in journalism, but also (for the first time in modern industrialism) in the overall patterns of socio-technical change. It also provides us with a conceptual platform for understanding the expanding scope of news-related activities and journalism in the modern era and which helps to inform our explorations of current trends in the following chapters. In sum, this chapter introduces theoretically and historically grounded ideas that serve to better inform the detailed investigations of the current trends and change factors in news and journalism to be addressed in the remainder of this book.

News: a pervasive feature of social life?

As a particular category of information or knowledge, news is a *ubiquitous* feature of human social formations. Drawing on historical, anthropological and other comparative evidence, many of the early communication theorists argued that news is pervasive, universal – and indeed, essential – feature in the formation and continuation of social life. Whether in the most simple, small-scale societies, or their much larger and more complex contemporary equivalents, news plays a key role in the maintaining and sustaining community life. For example, news enables society's members to monitor their environment, identifying any threats, opportunities or other changes to which they may have to adjust. News also supplies people with the gossip and chit-chat that helps to keep personal and social life lubricated as well as serving to define or revise social norms and regulate what counts as deviant or unsocial behaviour (McQuail, 2000; Gans, 2007).

We must observe a distinction between 'everyday news' on the one hand, and systems of organised news, produced by specialist occupational or 'professional' groups on the other hand (Gans, 2007). Whilst also acknowledging certain commonalities between these two categories of news, the differences tend to outweigh the similarities. Everyday news tends to be primarily concerned with information about people's immediate or micro environments, while organised or professional news tends to address more distant domains and issues of concern to larger-scale groups. Oganised news is produced by specialists embedded in the social division of labour and a major portion of such news concerns influential, if elite, sections of society. Most significantly, however, we observe that organised news and professional journalism are primarily concerned with the 'formally organised or public world' (ibid.: 163) whilst everyday news tends to concern itself with 'private worlds' such as the affairs of family, friends, immediate colleagues in work or leisure pursuits.

Having noted this important distinction between these two basic categories, we may now better identify our object of study. We are here primarily concerned with regular and systematically 'organised' forms of news and related newsmaking practices.

Furthermore, we may also observe that whilst everyday news may be a pervasive feature of all human communities, organised or professional newsmaking activity is not universal. Rather, the latter comprises a relatively recent feature when viewed in the longer-term history of European societies. Yet it is one that has grown and developed significantly over the past two centuries or more to play a distinctive, and increasingly important, role in the very fabric and operations of what we may variously define as modern, liberal, democratic, or capitalist societies, especially in the Western hemisphere. In this light, organised news has come to play a highly significant role in informing the understandings, decisions and actions of individuals in the performance of their roles as workers, citizens and consumers as well as in sustaining and lubricating the functioning of the modern economy, society and polity. Indeed, according to one evolutionary theorist, such is the social role of news media in the contemporary era that 'whatever we know about our society, or indeed about the world in which we live, we know through the mass media' (Luhmann, 2000: 1).

But it was not always so. To get a better grasp of the role, specificities and evolving changes in organised news, a brief historical detour is required at this point, even if this runs up against the grain of journalism culture and certain characteristics of 'news as a form of knowledge' – its tendency to be highly time- and place-specific (Park, 1940; Carey, 2007).

A 'long revolution': news and public communication

The evolution of news and its communication in Europe up to c.1600

We find competing historical narratives on the evolution of news and journalism based on differing conceptualisations of the sources, role and features of news media, many displaying the peculiar moods and tempers of the time and place of their creation. Given that we currently live in 'technology tempered times', recent historical accounts of news and newsmaking are often framed around the evolution of the technologies that facilitate the exchange of symbolic and/or material goods.

The latter kind of narrative usually starts with Johann Gutenberg, the goldsmith from Mainz, Germany, who is credited with the introduction of moveable type printing in Europe circa 1440, more than two centuries after its invention in China and Korea around 1234. The point here is not to deny that Gutenberg's initiative comprised an important early moment in the story of modern newsmaking as we note that the technique was quickly imitated and diffused across Europe. But framing the history around the technical means by which the exchange of news or symbolic goods is facilitated tends to privilege certain factors whilst neglecting others, especially institutional innovations often linked to social and political movements (Preston, 2001). At the extreme, it leads to the kinds of blinkered, technological-determinist histories (à la Marshall McLuhan) which hold the printing press and subsequent technical innovations as the primary roots of modern democracies, the system of territorial states or even nationalism. A focus on technical systems tends to produce highly stilted accounts intoxicated by 'the technological sublime' (Carey, 1989).

A societal or information-centred (rather than technology-centred) historical approach provides a more satisfactory starting point to understand the evolution of news within the context of long-term societal developments. The production, framing, and exchange of symbols and meanings have been at the heart of all forms of human society and culture. Thus, information and knowledge, including the specific forms of 'news', have been central features of all types of social formations, despite the confusions caused by contemporary discourses that seek to define our present-day advanced capitalist formations as 'information' or 'knowledge-based' societies (Preston, 2001).

Viewed in this light, *organised news* comprises a specific knowledge form that long predates the modern technical means of its production, recording, storage, and distribution. In this historical perspective, the institutional roles and other features of organised news services have changed much in line with broader socio-economic and political developments, of which technical changes are but one dimension. Indeed, such a perspective suggests that technology tends to be a dependent variable rather than a determinant in the evolution of social roles and forms of information (including news). Only certain configurations of political-economic or societal developments tend to generate both the demands for and the capacities to produce organised news services as well as novel technical innovations capable of handling expanding arrays and flows of information (Bücher, 1901; Beniger, 1986; Preston, 2001; Gandy, 2003a).

To draw on European history, it was only after Roman supremacy had spread across all the Mediterranean countries and beyond, that we find the first system of organised news production and distribution. Following the establishment of the military monarchy and of administrative centralisation in Caesar's time, Rome became the site of the first organised news services. This comprised handwritten newsletters delivering news from the capital to the elites in the provinces. That early system of organised news in Europe disappeared following the fall of the Roman empire. During the so-called Middle Ages, the prevailing political and economic organisation was not capable of sustaining an organised news service. However, signs of the revival of organised news services begin to emerge again in Europe from about 1200 AD, initially centred on the powerful institution of the Catholic church which had begun to develop systematic networks for internal communication. The twelfth and thirteenth centuries witnessed expanding moves towards regular, organised messenger services for letter-based news transmission, centred on traders and merchants, monasteries, universities and the Catholic church. By the 1400s, this had developed towards a comprehensive system of local messenger bureaux for the epistolary exchanges amongst traders and municipal authorities (Bücher, 1901). It is notable that some of these handwritten, letter-based tidings of the fifteenth century frequently bore the title or heading of 'newspaper' (*zeitung*).

Thereafter, the expansion of trade and early forms of capitalist production dating from the Renaissance period, alongside changes in the cultural and symbolic orders associated with the Reformation, combine to play a role in expanding the scope of organised news services in Europe. In broad terms, the growing systems and flows of organised news developed alongside the traffic in commodities: 'with the expansion of trade, merchants' market-orientated calculations required more frequent and more exact information about distant events' (Habermas, 1962/1989: 16). In sixteenth-century Europe a certain 'species of news agency received definite form and organization as a business'. Such news bureaux first emerged in the major urban centres in Italy, especially Venice and Rome, followed by the urban centres of Germany, Austria, and the Netherlands (Bücher, 1901: 225). It is no accident that the early modern systems of organised news production (and embryonic forms of journalism) were first developed as a business in Venice. The city was then the key node of the trade networks between the East and West, as well as the seat of a government that organised the first political news service and consular system in the modern sense. Venice formed an ideal location for the collection, editing and distribution of important news items from all lands of the (then) known world. Alongside the official news system organised by the city's political authority, the Venetian Rialto became home to 'an independent news-bureau that made a business of gathering and distributing. … news' to interested elite groups (ibid.: 227).

Evolution of news and newspapers in the seventeenth century

So far, we have outlined a historical story of organised newsmaking and journalism that is quite different to the usual techno-centric narrative framed around the adoption of print technology. Indeed, we can see that at about the same time in several European countries, the *handwritten newspaper* arises as an important medium of news publication, even if one clearly confined to the elites. It is quite striking that the regular production and circulation of these written newssheets continue to expand after the introduction of printing in Europe in the mid-1400s, yet their development was in no way dependent on the (then) new technology. Indeed, in an early example of cross-media 'convergence', some of the early printed newspapers adapted themselves to the pre-established system of handwritten news. They were produced in the form of two printed and two unprinted pages, 'thereby enabling their subscribers to send them to others, enriched with additional notes in writing' (Bücher, 1901: 234).

From the early 1600s the European-based colonial and trading empires expanded in intensity and spatial reach, creating new levels of prosperity in the major urban centres as well as growing requirements for organised news services. The growing traffic in both commodities and news 'manifested their revolutionary power only in the mercantilist phase in which, simultaneously with the modern state, the national and territorial economies assumed their shape' (Habermas, 1962/1989: 17). Print-based news publishing services, including weekly printed newssheets, begin to emerge in many of Europe's major urban centres from the early 1600s. They addressed an expanding audience thanks to increases in trade, money incomes and because literacy levels were improving. But it took another half-century before the first daily newspapers appeared in Europe.

In the early stages, print periodicals were no match for the newsletters and private correspondence which contained detailed and current news about 'Imperial Diets, wars, harvests, taxes, transports of precious metals, and, of course, reports on foreign trade' (Habermas, 1962/1989: 20). As the main recipients of such private correspondence 'had no interest' in their contents becoming public, only 'a trickle of this stream of reports passed through the filter of these news letters into printed journals' (ibid.: 20). At this early stage, the periodical press was systematically made to serve the interests of the state administration as 'many of the early intelligence (news) agencies, gazettes and advertisers were taken over by governments or carefully moulded and monitored' (ibid.: 22).

News and social revolutions in the eighteenth century

In the eighteenth century, the pace and patterns of change accelerated, culminating at the century's end with political revolutions in France and America, the first stages of the industrial and urban revolution in Britain and the emergence of a new political form or force in the shape of a critical 'public' or 'public sphere' (Habermas, 1962/1989). The deepening social changes associated with the onward expansion of capitalism, trade and territorial state-building in eighteenth-century Europe brought about multiple shifts in the role and forms of organised news. So too did the ideological changes associated with the Enlightenment and related social and political movements. One aspect here, comprised a significant growth in the role and scale of print-based newspapers.

Second, news itself increasingly becomes a commodity rather than a private service, one that is available to the growing segments of the new middle classes alongside the older elites with the material resources and literacy capabilities to purchase and make use of it. Third, in line with fundamental changes in the form and function of public communication, the production of organised news becomes increasingly orientated to 'the public' – and the latter becomes enshrined as the 'god term' for modern journalism (Carey, 2007). As a new political force and form, 'the public' was often presumed to embrace all subjects of the territorial state. But in practice it comprised certain bourgeois strata including the 'capitalists', the merchants, bankers, entrepreneurs and manufacturers, as well as jurists, doctors, pastors, officers, professors, and scholars, located in a hierarchy reaching down through schoolteachers and scribes to the 'people' (Habermas, 1962/1989: 23). Whilst this new 'bourgeois' stratum may not be real 'burghers' in the traditional sense, they comprised 'the real carrier' of the new public, 'which from the outset was a reading public' (ibid.: 23). The political public sphere makes its first appearance just as members of this new public 'readied themselves to compel public authority to legitimate itself before public opinion' (ibid.: 24). In many important respects, the 'industrial' (or socio-economic) and political 'revolutions' at the close of the eighteenth century were linked to the inauguration of the liberal model of democracy and the political public sphere as key aspect of the, as yet 'unfinished', project of modernity (ibid.).

Decoding the 'technological sublime'

Unpacking technological versus other factors

Our brief historical tour suggests that the trajectory of organised news production in pre-modern Europe was neither technology-led nor one of linear growth. It further suggests that the enabling factors comprise changes in the socio-economic organisation and political order, including the intensity and spatial scale of trade and other economic activities. It indicates that the (print) technology factor only came into play at a relatively late stage in the process of organised news production in early modern Europe. We also observe the role of social innovations and political movements from the late eighteenth century in embedding the concept of 'the public' at the heart of journalism and organised news production.

This truncated if history-friendly account of organised news production in pre-modern Europe helps to construct an alternative and more nuanced approach compared to those celebrating print technology as the sole or key driver in such processes. These considerations now lead us to the thorny, but vitally important question of specifying how best to conceptualise the role or influence of technological innovation in the evolution and growth of organised news, or in reshaping newsmaking practices and news culture. A related question is whether or how the role and influence of technological innovation may have grown over time, especially given the apparent expansion and ever more pervasive presence of new communication systems and networks in our contemporary societies.

Beyond the 'technological sublime'

Whilst techno-centric approaches to journalism and news have a long history, the past decade has witnessed a veritable surge of research literature focused on the features, role and transformative 'potential' of the Internet and other new/ digital information and communication technologies (ICTs). This interest has also been manifest in the practices and discourses of formal political institutions. Such concerns can be linked to a more general increase in attention to 'technology matters' within political studies and an ever more pervasive techno-culture since the early 1980s (Preston, 2001).

Here, we must (reflexively) observe that we live in 'technology tempered times' (ibid.). By this I mean not merely that we are now surrounded by an increasing array of technologies in the conduct of our work and, especially, in our 'everyday' lives outside the workplace settings. I also refer to the way in which modes of thinking and discourse (political, journalistic, academic) have become much more highly inflected with technology-centred ideas and attentive to technology factors (ibid.).

The late James Carey addressed the tendencies towards utopian or millennial rhetorics underpinning much of contemporary analyses of the implications of the Internet for journalism. In interrogating the widespread optimism which resurfaced in the years surrounding the new millennium, he criticised those rhetorics of 'the technological sublime' which 'cultivated a wave of belief in the magically transforming power of technology' (Carey, 2005: 444–45). He also noted to note how the latest wave of the 'technological sublime' rhetorics suffers from several fatal flaws.

As an alternative to such rhetorics, Carey invokes the critical research spirit of the earlier US intellectual movement known as pragmatism, largely because it 'taught us to be absolutely deadly on bunkum, on pretension, on abstractions' (Carey, 2005: 447). He proposes a renewal of the spirit of pragmatism, suggesting two particular strategies to advance his proposal in terms of research in the journalistic field. First, there is a pressing need for more nuanced, historically and empirically grounded studies of technological innovations (such as the Internet) and their linkages to broader patterns of socio-economic and cultural change, including user-based studies. Second, the really interesting discoveries may well be made by identifying and addressing 'subtle social shifts taking place, relatively unnoticed' (ibid.: 443).

Carey's alternative perspective with its proposed two-pronged research strategy resonates closely with the approach and plan of this book. The second aspect is addressed in Chapters 3 through 6 where we engage with detailed empirical studies enabling attention to any 'subtle social shifts' taking place in newsmaking routines and practices. We begin to address the first aspect in the section immediately below whilst addressing more empirical material on relevant recent trends in later chapters.

Socio-technical systems: re-connecting the Internet

In essence, we are pointing here to the benefits of a socio-technical systems approach for a well grounded, strategic understanding of the dynamics of multi-dimensional change currently unfolding in the newsmaking environment. Such an approach to the co-evolution of socio-economic and technological developments framing the environment in which the newsmaking and public communication is currently situated may be rare, but it is not entirely novel. Indeed one of the first ever studies of the evolving role of the public sphere in Europe also adopted a rounded approach explicitly linking together technological, socio-economic and political changes (MacKinnon, 1828). But unlike MacKinnon, we can now approach this task with the benefit of many subsequent and well grounded accounts of the co-evolution of technological and social innovations in the information and communication fields (e.g. Hall and Preston, 1988; Preston, 2001). Today, we can also borrow from a considerable body of prior research concerned with the complex linkages between technological innovation and social, political and cultural change on the other hand, even if the fruits of this neighbouring research field are often neglected in journalism and media studies texts.

Thus, this book will combine analyses of 'subtle' shifts, such as changes and continuities in newsroom routines and journalism practices as well as attending to broader institutional and socio-technical developments (Preston, 2001; 2005). For the latter, we adopt an empirically and historically well-grounded socio-technical systems model which bestows several advantages with respect to our concerns in this book. In particular, it harmonises with our multi-layered approach to the influences on newsmaking by explicitly addressing the importance (and relative autonomy) of institutional, organisational, political and social factors in shaping and mediating the precise uses, applications and implications of radical technological innovations such as the Internet or new ICTs more broadly. Furthermore, in line with a core objective indicated in Chapter 1, this approach also facilitates our concern to address both the *continuities* and *changes* that may be evident in journalism and newsmaking processes.

Innovation, digital media and newsmaking: a long-wave view

In essence, a long-wave systems model recognises that there are several different categories of technological innovations, ranging from *incremental* or minor innovations to *radical* (e.g. the telegraph, radio, television, Internet) to *major new technology systems* (MNTS) which comprise clusters of interrelated technical innovations (e.g. the electrical technology system at the turn of the last century or new ICTs today). The successive series of one or more MNTS involve incentives for significant change in products and processes in a range of sectors if not the total economy, as well as the rise of entirely new 'leading-edge' industrial sectors. They also provide a history-friendly schema for periodising the major phases of socio-economic development in capitalist modernity (Hall and Preston, 1988; Preston, 2001).

This long-wave model also emphasises that innovation is a multi-dimensional process, within which the technological aspect is but one moment or dimension. In sum, past clusters of (radical and/or major) technological innovations can be seen to have only produced economic or social benefits when they were accompanied by 'complementary' sets of institutional, organisational (or managerial), social and policy innovations. These 'complementary' or 'matching' innovations are not directly inscribed or determined by the characteristics of the new technical innovations. Rather they must be discovered by a process of trial and error by the relevant groups of producers or users in application sectors and other related spheres of activity, a process of *social learning* that may take some time. Eventually, when an appropriate, complementary set of institutional, organisational, social or policy innovations is discovered and established, this then forms a new *socio-technical paradigm*. Whether particular national or regional economies, sectors or spheres derive benefits from investment in radical new technology systems will be largely determined by the patterns and extent to which they discover, adopt or creatively appropriate the relevant new *socio-technical paradigms* (Preston, 2001).

In light of this model, we can map the evolving role of media and communication technologies in relation to other major technical innovations in industrial modernity. For example, we can identify today's digital or new ICTs as one of those historically rare, major new technology systems with a pervasive applications potential, with the Internet forming one sub-set or sub-cluster within this interrelated family or wave of radical innovations. Furthermore, we observe that in all previous long-wave periods, the leading technical systems were concerned with the processing, handling or moving of material goods. Today (and for the first time), one of the two leading-edge MNTS comprises a cluster of technical innovation that is focused precisely on the handling, processing, storing and distribution of information (including news).

Furthermore, we observe another highly significant first in the long-run history of major socio-technical change in industrial capitalism: one of the 'leading-edge' or dynamic growth sectors comprises information services, including the media. Furthermore, we observe that a set of information or knowledge services (including news and other media services) have been designated as a 'new frontier' for industrial growth and exploitation. These unfolding developments are often framed around the concepts of 'information society' or 'knowledge-based economy' in academic and especially in policy discourses. These must be primarily understood as examples of unfolding policy, economic and institutional innovations rather than as an immediate expression or result of any inherent technical logics.

But as in the past, any latent or potential benefits of these new clusters of radical technological changes in information-intensive industries will only be realised if they are met and accompanied by new *socio-technical paradigms*. More specifically, this means that whether, where and how new ICTs are now enhancing or otherwise enabling change in the performance of journalism or newsmaking processes, will not be determined primarly by technological factors. Rather it depends on a range of new institutional, organisational, professional, social or policy innovations or practices. This includes the forms and extent of creative or stylistic innovations on the part of journalists, authors and designers and other creative specialists in media 'content' domains. Indeed, as we will see, even users may have the potential to harness or 'appropriate' the new possibilities afforded by digital technologies for institutional and social innovations in the domains of newsmaking.

In brief, this history-friendly systems model helps in framing and mapping the historical specificities and evolving role of new ICTs and digital media in the present era. It also enables the recognition of certain continuities, if only in the sense of locating contemporary developments in relation to past patterns of radical techno-economic and institutional change. This historically grounded, framing schema may be further fleshed out to trace key moments in the evolution of the modern news media (e.g. Preston, 2001).

Immediately below, we will briefly illustrate some key aspects of these processes and shifts in the modern era, as well as some of their implications for organised news and journalism. In subsequent chapters, we will examine, in greater detail, the more 'subtle' shifts (Carey, 2005) and other interplays between technological innovations on the one hand, and the institutional, organisational, professional, policy and cultural dimensions of current innovation processes in newsmaking on the other.

Capitalism, modernity and organised news

We paused our narrative of the evolution of organised news and journalism in Europe by noting how the political and industrial 'revolutions' at the close of the eighteenth century marked the inauguration of liberal democracies and the political *public sphere* as key aspects of the (as yet 'unfinished') project of modernity (Habermas, 1962/1989). The ascendancy and ever-expanding sway of capitalist industrialism marks a fundamental turning point in the production and distribution of news, as in most other aspects of the socio-economic and political order prevailing in pre-modern Europe. Indeed, the most distinctive – and only permanent – characteristic of capitalism is change: faced with its intrinsic expansive drives, 'all that is solid melts into air'. To the extent that it is unbound from the ties of the decaying old communal order, capitalism is free to pursue its devotion to innovation and change, a feature recognised equally by liberal proponents, from Adam Smith to J. S. Mill and Joseph Schumpeter, and by critics such as the Karls Marx and Polanyi.

Indeed, the fact that constant change is a prominent and permanent feature of modern capitalism can only be good news for the business of producing and supplying news. From the late 1700s, the future prospects of the newsmaking business are further amplified by the capitalist industrialism's intrinsic dynamic towards ever-expanding production, trade and finance, and towards deepening divisions of labour which in turn promotes the commodification of information. This is especially so if information can be captured or 'fixed' on some material medium, as Adam Smith observed from the heartland of the then leading 'high tech' economy of the late eighteenth century (Smith, 1776). Furthermore, modern capitalism's orientation towards dynamic change also extends to the technological domain, including innovation in the technical devices, networks and systems to support such newsmaking activities. In these and many other respects, the rise and subsequent pervasive growth of capitalist industrialisation introduces an entirely different dynamic to the domain of newsmaking compared to the pre-modern era (see Figure 2.1).

This is evident even in the early stages of capitalist modernity, (the first long-wave era, 1780s–1830s) even if the then 'leading edge' technologies and growth sectors still comprise basic material goods such as coal, textiles, iron and potteries, with 'steam power' and steam driven engines playing the role of the leading high-tech symbols of the period. Amidst the dynamic changes of this first stage of capitalist industrialism and urbanisation, we find that newsmaking and newspapers experience relatively rapid growth compared to the pace of change in pre-modern Europe. Yet, we must note that they only constitute a very small portion of the expanding new sources of employment and output in the economy as a whole in this period.

London, as the national political capital and centre of a vast colonial empire and trading system, was home to the most influential and the largest number of newspapers in Britain. In 1724, some 20 newspapers were produced in London, three of them dailies, but by 1792, the city was home to some 33 newspapers, comprising 13 daily and 20 semi-weekly or weekly papers. By 1810, the number of London-based newspapers had almost doubled to 63 and had grown to more than 90 by 1840. In Britain as a whole, the number of newspapers grew from 76 in 1775 to reach 180 in 1810, a number that more than doubled again by 1840. This period also witnessed a significant radical press in Britain – which often allied itself to the emerging labour and trade union movements – but it failed to attract financial support from advertisers which aided the expansion of more conservative papers (Curran and Seaton, 2003).

Despite such rapid growth in the numbers of British newspaper titles in this first long-wave era, the related quantitative trends in the USA proved to be even more striking. The number of newspapers published in the USA grew from 37 in the late 1770s, to some 359 by 1810 and reached more than 1,500 by 1840 (see Table 2.1). In the 1840s, it was estimated that aggregate daily newspaper circulation in the USA well exceeded that in Britain. One contemporary British observer conceded that 'no other country had so many newspapers and periodical journals' as the USA. Yet, he went on to claim, in the ethnocentric tones so familiar in much subsequent comparative analyses of journalism, that most of these publications in the USA 'are of an entirely ephemeral character, and very feebly supported' whilst few of them possess any 'literary merit' (Simmonds, 1841: 120).

'Leading-Edge' Growth Sectors

LW-1: 1780s – 1840s	LW-2: 1840s – 1880s	LW-3: 1890s – 1940s	LW-4: Late 1940s – 1990s	LW-5: ?
Textile Machinery - Cotton Potteries Beginnings of Trade in consumer goods	Railways & equipment Steam Engines Precision Machinery, Coal/Steel–based industries	Electrical & Heavy engineering Chemicals & Dyes industries Consumer Durables industries Clerical/White-collar jobs Minor role: New Media & Leisure industries	Automobiles Electronics Aerospace and Chemicals Finance Producer' services	Information as 'New Frontier' Digital Media e-Commerce etc

Major New Technology Systems and Infrastructures

LW-1: 1780s – 1840s	LW-2: 1840s – 1880s	LW-3: 1890s – 1940s	LW-4: Late 1940s – 1990s	LW-5: ?
Coal & Steam Power Early Mechanisation (eg Textiles sector) Iron Works & Casting New Iron Production technologies Canals/Turnpike Roads	**Railway Transport Steam-powered Factory & Shipping Precision Engineering tools/machinery New Steel & Coal production methods**	**Electrical Power/ Engineering/Machinery Chemicals & Dyes Steel & Heavy Engineering Urban Transport Systems Automobiles [esp in US]**	**Diffusion of Motorised Transport (cars) Electronics (telecoms, TV & computing) Aerospace Artificial fibres**	**New ICTs (e.g. Internet, 'ubiquitous' networks and media) & Biotechnologies**

Figure 2.1 Major new technology systems and leading growth sectors: a long-waves perspective

Table 2.1 Number of newspapers published in selected countries: c.1780–1840

Years	England, Scotland and Wales			Ireland	USA	France
	London	*Scotland*	*Total*[a]			
1775/1782	18	8	76	3	37	–
1809/1810	63	24	180	37	359	–
1828/1830	54	36	244	60	851	–
1833/1836	71	54	319	78	1,273	206
1839/1840	93[b]	70	388	90	1,555	–

Notes:[a] Total for England, Scotland and Wales
[b]The London data for the year 1839–40 include some (about 15–20) literary journals
  and the like so that approximately 90–95 (rather than 108 cited in source) may be
  treated as strictly newspapers.
Source: Author's estimates, based on various sources cited in the text of this chapter.

From an 'industrial' to a 'network' society?

Our very brief historical sketch serves to illustrate how the 'modern' political, economic and social revolutions from the close of the eighteenth century served to position the business of organised news on an entirely new footing. The Enlightenment, the rise of new capitalist and professional classes and the diffusion of liberal democratic ideas all helped to accord the news media a special role with respect to the public. The rise and subsequent pervasive growth of capitalist industrialisation introduces an entirely new dynamic to the organised newsmaking and distribution compared to the pre-modern era. Capitalist industrialism's expansionary logics and intrinsic orientation to change also means that the news media continue to expand their roles throughout the successive long-wave periods of the nineteenth and twentieth centuries (Preston, 2001).

During the second long-wave period (1840s–1880s), railways comprised the single most significant technical innovation and symbol, but the 1840s also witnessed the invention of the electrical telegraph. The latter was soon rapidly deployed to meet the signalling needs of railway services (the immediate social prompt for its invention) and applied to 'strategic' (military and political), financial, industrial and trade related information functions as well as more general news services orientated to 'the public'.

The subsequent third long-wave era (1890s–1940s) witnessed the first unfolding of many major technological, socio-economic, institutional and cultural innovations which the often seen to comprise the very symbols of modernity. These included electrical power, lighting and (sub-) urban rail services, telephony, truly *mass media*, the advent of mass production and consumption, the automobile, as well as universal adult voting rights (in Britain and many other countries) and, of course, modernism in the sphere of high culture. Whilst many historians have labelled the decades surrounding the turn of the last century the age of imperialism or monopoly capitalism, for media specialists it may be characterised as the first 'multi-media age'. It witnessed a swarm of radical technological innovations offering the capacity to record and reproduce sounds, music and moving images. Advances in photography and printing facilitated a much greater emphasis on the visual content and forms in print media, both in news coverage and in advertising.

Furthermore, these decades also witnessed the beginnings of truly 'mass media', at least in the advanced capitalist economies as the 'mature' medium of newspapers now became an everyday commodity for most households in countries such as the USA and Britain. But we must also note that social and institutional innovations played a major role in shaping the modes and forms in which the period's technological innovations were applied and socially embedded. These included the important role of the trades unions and socialist movements in pressing for reforms of both income and working time standards. The latter in turn helped to shape the new modes of mass production and mass consumption in this period, including those related to the expanding array of media services and products (Preston, 2001). Trades unions and professional associations also played a role in enhancing the working conditions and status of journalists. Indeed, we also observe that the third long-wave period witnessed the first emergence and consolidation of the modern 'news paradigm' in the USA, Britain and European other countries (Høyer and Pöttker, 2005).

But does the current state of flux and change mean that organised news and journalism matters are about to experience yet another revolutionary or dramatic new turn? As we noted above, for the first time in industrial modernity, a cluster of information and communication technologies are now poised to play a central role, not merely in news and other media sectors. They are now positioned as a 'leading edge', major new technology system in relation to the overall economy. Furthermore, information-based services, which include news and journalism amongst many other specialist activities, are now being defined as major growth sectors or a 'new frontier' for industrial development and employment growth. These unfolding developments are often (if, misleadingly) framed around the concepts of 'information society' or 'knowledge-based economy', especially in recent policy discourses.

In the following chapters we will examine our own and others' research on the interplay of technological and other factors in shaping change in news and journalism in the contemporary era. This includes consideration of the detailed and 'subtle social shifts' (Carey, 2005) that may be unfolding in newsmaking and the broader environment of journalism over the past 10–20 years. In the final chapter, we will attempt to sketch out the main contours of an emerging new socio-technical paradigm in the early twenty-first century, including those related to technological, organisational, institutional and policy innovations. We will seek to indicate its main implications for current and emerging features of newsmaking and journalism culture.

Chapter 3

Individual influences on news

Journalists' values and norms

Paschal Preston and
Monika Metykova

Introducing 'Mr Gates': individual influences

David Manning White's seminal 'gatekeeper' study examined how a certain Mr Gates, the wire editor of a morning newspaper in the USA's Midwest, set about rejecting or selecting news stories over the course of a week. White sought to understand why and how this individual wire editor made the 'complicated' set of decisions in selecting certain news stories sent by the news agencies whilst having to reject most of those received. The aim was to better understand how such individual editors or 'gatekeepers' play a crucial role in the news production process (White, 1950/1999: 66).

Clearly, White's study focused on the individual 'experiences, attitudes and expectations' of individuals in 'power' positions in the newsroom (White, 1950/1999: 66, 72). It starts from the view that there is a series of gatekeepers involved in selecting whether news items are 'in' or 'out'. News stories are transmitted from one gatekeeper to another in a chain of communications, 'till finally we come to our last gatekeeper, the one to whom we turn for the purpose of our case study' (ibid.: 67). Mr Gates, a man in his middle 40s with approximately 25 years' experience as a journalist, is responsible for the selection of national and international news which will appear on the front and 'jump' pages of his newspaper (ibid.: 67). Usually he also makes up these pages and copy-edits and writes the headlines for the selected stories.

White monitored and analysed the various stories in the form of wire copy that came across Mr Gates' desk over a week-long period in February 1949, largely relying on the editor's stated reasons for selection and rejection. White found that this key gatekeeper's weekly agenda of 'extremely complicated' decisions involved selecting one-tenth of the copy (or about one-ninth of the stories) sent by the news agencies whilst rejecting nine-tenths of the copy received (White, 1950/1999: 67). In drawing conclusions from his study's data and analysis, White emphasised the role of subjective and individual factors in shaping the news selection process:

Through studying his overt reasons for rejecting news stories from the press associations *we see how highly subjective, how based on the gatekeeper's own set of experiences, attitudes and expectations the communication of 'news' really is.*

(White, 1950/1999: 72; emphasis added)

White's study has been much cited by subsequent researchers and reviews of the literature. For example, Howard Tumber (1999: 63) deems it important for its 'insight into the subjective nature of the news production process' and for indicating the key role of the judgements, experiences and tacit knowledge of senior journalists involved in the news process. However, White's key conclusions, highlighting subjective and individual gatekeeper factors, have been questioned by many later studies (e.g. Whitney *et al.*, 2004). Subsequent analyses of White's own data have led to significant reinterpretations of the key meanings and conclusions to be drawn from this study. Some have emphasised how White's own evidence points to organisational and institutional influences, yet this is largely neglected in his analyses and conclusions. Despite such criticisms, many subsequent researchers acknowledge the value of empirical research methods pioneered by White and his contemporaries. Zelizer (2004: 52–53) notes that, although White's approach favours individualist and psychological explanations, his study helped open the way for more sociological, institutional and organisational forms of research on journalism.

Overview: scope of this chapter

In this chapter we commence our substantive inquiry by examining those explanations of newsmaking which emphasise the values, characteristics and orientations of individual newsworkers. In essence, research on individual-level influences tends to address 'the characteristics (e.g. gender, ethnicity, attitudes, political or ideological biases, practices) of individual communicators or homogeneous small groups of communicators' in order to explain the patterns or continuities in news content (Whitney *et al.*, 2004: 402). Here then, we are primarily concerned with the research perspectives focused on the characteristics and backgrounds, values and beliefs of journalists as major influences on making the news.

Studies of journalists' characteristics, values and ethics

Models of journalists' roles, responsibilities or identities

First we consider some attempts to identify the overall role of journalists, or models of journalism, in modern societies, since these are assumed to frame the personal and professional orientations of individual journalists. Many view these issues as particularly challenging because of the diversity of journalistic activities, journalism's status as an 'indeterminate occupation' (Tunstall, 1971), and the

difficulties in defining both journalism and 'news' (Zelizer, 2004: 29). Such surveys suggest that working journalists tend to view the role of journalism in terms
of two sharply contending models: on the one hand, that of a mirror reflecting,
supporting and reproducing society's values and goals, and on the other, that of
a tool or hammer the mission of which is to help reform or redirect society along
a specified path of development. The first tends to suggest a conservative or
independent mission for journalists and news media, whilst the second points
towards a more radical and committed role orientated towards transforming
society.

In one much cited example of contrasting conceptualisations of journalists'
roles in society, Cohen (1963) distinguishes between two basic models. The
first comprises a 'neutral reporter' role and the second concerns a 'participant'
role (Weaver, 1998; McQuail, 2000; Whitney *et al.*, 2004). Weaver and Wilhoit
(1996) have proposed a three-fold classification of journalists' roles. The first
comprises the *interpreter model*, invoking a role centred on the analysis and
interpretation of complex questions, including the scrutiny of claims made by
the government and their policies. Then there is the *disseminator model*, which
focuses on the journalistic roles and values involved in getting information to the
public quickly, alongside efforts to develop the largest possible audience. The
third comprises an *adversary model*, focusing on critical investigation of both government and business, even if the role of adversary of business or economic
power received very low support from journalists in the USA (Weaver and
Wilhoit, 1996, cited in Weaver, 1998: 406–8). Other recent surveys of such
models include Zelizer's (2004: 29–31) five-fold typology of 'metaphors'
mapping how journalists tend to define, think about, or 'reference' their own
occupation.

Personal characteristics and backgrounds: do they influence content?

The most radical versions of individualism tend to imagine and celebrate individuals as free-floating, autonomous actors whilst ignoring or denying their situated contexts or membership of different social or cultural groups. Those models
apart, most of the research considered here assumes that the personal or
background characteristics (e.g. class, gender, age, ethnicity, etc.) of working
journalists are likely to have a significant influence on how such actors view or
report on the world around them. Indeed, there has been a significant strand of
research focused on individual journalists ever since the early decades of the
twentieth century (e.g. Rosten, 1937/1974; Weaver, 1998). Such research has
centred around three specific issues: first, examining the individual characteristics
of journalists; second, exploring whether or how these may influence news
decisions and thus news content; third, the extent to which journalists may
possess characteristics which differ from the general public and which may be
influential in terms of newsmaking (McQuail, 2000; Peiser, 2000; Whitney *et al.*,
2004).

But whether, how or how far the personal characteristics or orientations of journalists are translated into actual influences on news content seems less clear-cut. The available evidence suggests that the role of personal and background factors may be considered a relatively minor influence on news content (Shoemaker and Reese, 1996: 78–79; McQuail, 2000: 266–67; Whitney *et al.*, 2004). Yet the view that the personal characteristics of media workers comprise a major influence on news content and forms persists. This is evident in many contemporary debates concerning bias or inequalities in news output, including those related to gender and news.

The gender case

Feminist and other critics have pointed to strong correlations between the low numbers and status of women in news media and the under-representation or stereotyping of women in the news. Much of the early feminist research tended to assume a rather straightforward 'sender–message–receiver' sequence, whereby the media were conceived as 'transmitting particular messages about gender (stereotypes, pornography, ideology) to the wider public', according to Liesbet Van Zoonen's review (1994/2002: 47). Such views assumed or suggested that an increased number of women media workers would lead to a more balanced media product (ibid.: 47).

The numbers of women employed in the news media have grown significantly in recent decades, albeit from a very low base. Yet there is little firm empirical evidence to suggest that the growing number of women news-workers has made a significant difference to news content. Some studies in the USA suggest that the (relative) growth of women journalists and news-makers in recent decades has been accompanied by greater attention to 'women's issues' in newspaper editorials. But that does not mean that women editors automatically privilege or respond favourably to women's issues as professional norms or organisational routines continue to play a constraining role. Indeed, many women journalists and editors tend to evaluate the agenda of potential issues in terms of prevailing professional criteria and news values, deemed to be gender-neutral (Shoemaker and Reese, 1996: 78–79; GMMP, 2006).

Others have argued that distortion in media production should not be understood as a direct derivative of the sexist inclinations of male media professionals nor of the malicious intents of capitalist male owners. It 'cannot be seen as a simple black box' transmitting the patriarchal, sexist or capitalist values of its producers, according to Van Zoonen (1994/2002: 47). Rather, it is better characterised by 'tensions and contradictions' between not only individuals with different professional values and personal opinions, but also 'between conflicting organizational demands such as creativity and innovation on the one hand and the commercial need to be popular among a variety of social groups on the other hand' (ibid.: 47).

These considerations do not, of course, undermine the value and justice of arguments for much greater gender equality with respect to roles in newsmaking or other media fields. For example, the Global Media Monitoring Project recently found that women's points of view are rarely heard 'in the topics that matter' and that 'there is not a single major news topic in which women out-number men as newsmakers' (GMMP, 2006: 3). Such studies suggest that gender equality in the newsrooms, as well as in news output, is still a long way from being realised. In this light, we can conclude that any quantitative shifts towards gender equality in the newsrooms comprise one necessary, but not sufficient, step towards achieving significant changes in news content.

Journalists' personal values and beliefs as influence

The individual backgrounds, values and personal beliefs of journalists tend to feature prominently in popular and media-based discourses concerning the key influences on the reporting of news and current affairs. In reviewing such research from Germany and other countries, Peiser (2000: 244) observes that it tends to indicate that journalists are 'somewhat more liberal and more likely to lean to the left than to the right', relative to the general public. Furthermore, the relevant research suggests that journalists perceive themselves to be more liberal than their news audiences (ibid.).

One highly influential research report published in the USA during the 1980s argued that journalists working in the leading ('elite') national media were pre-dominantly left-leaning, radical, alienated from the prevailing national belief system and highly critical of America's world role (Lichter et al., 1986). The findings of these right-leaning authors were challenged by some of those engaged in sociological and institutional research. For example, Herbert Gans argued that even if journalists held such personal beliefs or values, these are effectively neu-tralised by the prevailing professional values, newsmaking routines and norms and organisational constraints in US media. Only in the relatively rare cases where a highly opinionated editor wields strong influence, through ownership or part-ownership of the media organisation, can personal values and beliefs be translated into effects on news values or content (Gans, 1985; McQuail, 2000).

The research evidence suggests that the potential scope for individual media workers to exert personal influence tends to vary according to the profile and status of the media worker, the type of media organisation and/or genre. The bad news for journalists is that the relevant research suggests that non-news genres tend to provide greater scope for expressing personal beliefs (McQuail, 2000). Other relevant variables that influence the degree of personal influence include the extent to which the media organisation enjoys a healthy commercial and financial record. High-profile 'stars' or celebrities tend to enjoy relatively privileged degrees of freedom to express personal opinions and beliefs compared to the rank-and-file, even within news organisations (Shoemaker and Reese, 1996).

Journalists' professional values and codes

Another strand of research has focused on journalists' professional values, orientations and related occupational codes of ethics, addressing whether and how these may serve to influence newsmaking and media content. In journalism, as in other occupational settings, socialisation refers to the processes by which new entrants encounter, learn and internalise the norms, values, rights and obligations attaching to their roles or status, as well as the associated technical or instrumental competencies essential to role performance. One of the pioneering examples of such research was conducted by Breed (1955). He described the socialisation process in the case of newspaper journalism whereby new entrants learn and internalise the practices and expectations of the employing organisation by means of observation and on-the-job experience. Socialisation related to the values and norms of specific media organisations usually is effected via informal rather than formal policies, and is supervised by news managers or senior supervisors and editors in newsrooms. Much of the relevant research suggests that newsworkers' professional values and ethical orientations tend to be formed or shaped by socialisation processes mainly located in work-based experience and learning by doing, as we will see in Chapter 5. Formal professional education and training, based in journalism and communication schools, also plays an increasing role in more recent decades.

The research literature also suggests that professional values and competencies tend to embrace both normative and ethical dimensions, as well as technical or instrumental aspects related to the ability to perform the role of journalist (Im, 1997; Soloski, 1989). For example, despite the occupation's keen attachment to the goals of objectivity, questions of values and ethical judgements inevitably present themselves in the course of the journalist's work practices in covering newsworthy events. Some researchers note that journalists cannot seriously pursue the professional goal of being 'objective' when covering news events: they cannot proceed without values because 'reality judgements are never altogether divorced from values' (Gans, 1979: 38).

Research on professional values and norms also attempts to ascertain how journalists themselves identify the most significant occupational values. There are considerable methodological challenges in such research, as the meanings and evaluations of specific professional values (e.g. objectivity) are highly dependent on the context and on how they are defined and understood. The major findings from such surveys of working journalists tend to reveal 'objectivity' as the single most important professional value, especially in the case of the USA-based journalists (Weaver, 1998). Objectivity as a core value is often seen to match up closely with the neutral model of journalism and the notion of 'balanced' or even-handed reporting preferred by many news organisations – some of which, indeed have specific employee guidelines designed to limit the influence of personal beliefs on reporting. Others suggest that this preference for 'objectivity' also neatly matches the master logic of commercial media organisations, as partisanship might put off the potential appeal to advertisers or audiences (McManus, 1997; Weaver, 1998; McQuail, 2000). Other key values revealed by such studies include keeping the public up-to-date with news/information. Another value much cited in such studies is that of investigative journalism alongside the 'watchdog' role (Weaver, 1998). The provision of analyses of events also features as a prominent value for journalists in many countries, but it seems to be relatively less important for journalists in the USA (ibid.: 466–67).

Do online journalists perceive their roles in similar ways? This is a tricky question because it has been subject to more speculation than grounded research so far, and because trends towards greater newsroom integration are blurring the boundaries. One study by Deuze and Dimoudi (2002) in the Netherlands suggests that the most important values for online journalists comprise giving people a chance to express their view, reaching the widest possible audience, standing up for the disadvantaged and developing interests of the public. Later studies challenge this finding and so this remains a question subject to conflicting views, as we will see below and in later chapters.

Ethical codes and journalists' roles and responsibilities

The role and implications of journalistic codes of ethics represents one important sub-set of the research agenda surrounding the journalists' professional values and norms. Indeed some researchers point to the many parallels between the history of the professionalisation of journalism over the past century and the history of professional codes of ethics (Hallin, 1996; Deuze, 2002).

Within the journalism occupation, there are significant divisions regarding the legitimacy and utility of formal professional codes of ethics, even if many journalists do subscribe to the importance of being ethical. Keeble (2005) identifies four highly divergent sets of attitudes amongst journalists towards the role, relevance and legitimacy of formal codes of ethics. Rather similar divisions may be found in the academic field of journalism and communication studies. Deuze (2005: 449) suggests that journalists' approach to 'a sense of being ethical' tends in turn to 'legitimise' journalists' claims to the position of being (free and fair) watchdogs of society. For others like McManus (1997: 5), contemporary journalistic codes of ethics 'hinge more on fantasy than fact: the idea that journalists control what becomes news'. He argues that, even if journalists' influence over news may have grown during the twentieth century, 'it has never surpassed the influence of owners' (ibid.: 5). He mobilises evidence to argue that their authority has eroded as media firms seek to maximise returns to investors with the result that 'as journalists' autonomy recedes, national ethics codes become less relevant to practitioners and more publicly deceptive' (ibid.: 6).

Recent research highlights other tensions that journalists face between their professional ideals and the profit-motivated organisational goals that 'keep news organisations in business and financially viable' as Berkowitz and Limor (2003: 784) put it. These authors argue that journalists' professional values, attitudes and practices, including ethics, are increasingly affected by their working realities. As news organisations become ever more embedded in commercial concerns and pressures, organisational life increasingly becomes shaped by economic concerns (ibid.: 783; see also Hallin, 2000). However, other authors take a more favourable stance in relation to the role and potential influence of formal codes of ethics. For example, Belsey and Chadwick (1995) start from the observation that the question of media quality is important, given the close connections between media and liberal democracy. They argue that the legal route to media quality is necessary, but not sufficient to ensure quality: it 'needs to be supplemented by the ethical route, understood as a competence to deploy ethical consideration in professional practice' (ibid.: 461). Although codes of ethics have their limitations, the ethical route is indispensable, albeit one in need of further exploration.

The deepening internationalisation of the media and communication sector – and of the journalism studies field – has also impacted on professional codes of ethics. One important moment here was the adoption of the *Code of Bordeaux* by the International Federation of Journalists in 1956 (Nordenstreng and Topuz, 1989). More recent decades have witnessed many other efforts at developing supra-national codes of ethics, both at the world-region (e.g. European Union) and international scale (Laitila, 2005). The recent research also includes efforts to compare journalistic codes of ethics at the world-region and international levels. Hafez (2002) has undertaken a comparison of codes of ethics in Europe, North Africa, the Middle East, and Muslim Asia, focusing on those laid out by journalism associations. The study compares journalism codes from Europe and the Islamic world 'in order to revisit the widespread academic assumption of a deep divide between Western and Oriental philosophies of journalism that has played a role in many debates on political communication in the area' (ibid.: 225). Hafez's study suggests that there are rather strong convergences around the notion that standards of truth and objectivity should be central values of journalism. The most significant differences between the West and many Islamic countries are to be found in the status accorded to freedom of expression. Hafez's study points to several differences between Western and Middle Eastern/Islamic journalism ethics, including some neoconservative (Islamist) trends in societal norms. Yet Hafez concludes that, in overall terms, formal codes of journalism ethics have become a sphere of growing universalisation over recent decades.

Himelboim and Limor (2005) investigated some 242 codes of ethics from around the world, examining differences in role perception based on geography, economics and the level of freedom of the press. They borrow the term 'USA-made ethics', to describe how 'journalists and media organizations around the world adopt western and mainly American norms and ideals' resulting in a journalistic model centred around the roles of being 'neutral, detached from society and defensive toward the loci of power' (ibid.: 16). Himelboim and Limor (ibid.:17) argue that the codes of ethics very rarely promote roles 'such as serving as democratic watchdog' and the scrutiny of public institutions or other centres of power.

The Internet and journalists' roles and values

Online news: from marginal to 'mainstream'

As a major new technology system, digital ICT devices and networks have opened up multiple new opportunities for change in the news media landscape, not least by lowering the start-up costs for new kinds of online and specialised news services. In little more than a decade, the widespread diffusion of the Internet (with its World Wide Web overlay) has witnessed the online production and delivery of news move from the margins to a central role in overall land-scape of news media. Estimates suggest that there were more than 3,000 online newspapers, 3,900 online magazines and more than 13,000 news sites of all types in the USA by 2007 (Williams and Franklin, 2007). Furthermore, many journalism researchers now claim that online news media have 'moved from the periphery to the centre of US politics' since the 2004 election cycle in the USA (Singer, 2005: 173; Robinson, 2006). Some claim that online media have now become as important as the old media of print and television in performing the typical activities of US electoral politics such as generating revenue for candidates and mobilising supporters or votes (Singer, 2005; Robinson, 2006).

Thus, we observe a growing consensus that online journalism's role has become mainstream or 'normalised' when it comes to producing and supplying news and other aspects of political communication, especially in the USA (e.g. Gans, 2003; Singer, 2005). It is clearly the case that online news has become a significant platform amongst younger and other audience groups, especially in the USA where print media such as newspapers have had a marked decline in recent decades and where established media institutions are marked by low levels of public trust (Gronke and Cook, 2007). At the same time, however, it is important to avoid the 'substitution error' by assuming that new media usage necessarily displaces that of old media. This is not merely a case of remembering that many 'mature media' organisations play a major role in online news domains. Even in the rather exceptional case of the USA, television as well as newspapers continue to play a significant role as news sources and we must bear in mind that major segments of the population still remain on the wrong side of the 'digital divide' (see Table 3.1).

The recent journalism and media studies literature abounds with signals that the news production and distribution processes are currently undergoing multi-dimensional changes – processes in which the Internet and other digital tech-nologies are deemed to play crucial roles (e.g. Kopper et al., 2000; Pavlik, 2001; Boczkowski, 2004a; Klinenberg, 2005a). This applies to the domains of orga-nised, professional newsmaking and to those of everyday news (Gans, 2007). Pavlik's review, for example, proposes that digital technologies pose implications

Table 3.1 How the public learns about the presidential campaign in the USA, 2000–2008

Respondents who say they 'regularly learn something from':	Campaign years (all ages)			Aged 18–29 (2008)
	2000	2004	2008	
Local TV news	48	42	40	25
Cable news networks	34	38	38	35
Nightly network news	45	35	32	24
Daily newspaper	40	31	31	25
Internet	9	13	24	42
TV news magazines	29	25	22	21
Morning TV shows	18	20	22	18
National Public Radio	12	14	18	13
Talk radio	15	17	16	12
Cable political talk	14	14	15	12
Sunday political TV	15	13	14	4
Public TV shows	12	11	12	6
News magazines	15	10	11	8
Late-night talk shows	9	9	9	10

Note: Top 15 sources of such news only shown above; for others, see original source.
Source: Pew Research Center (2008) 'Internet's Broader Role in Campaign 2008'.

for newsmaking and journalism in at least four ways: first, the way journalists do their job; second, the nature of news content; third, the structure and organisation of the newsroom and news industry; and fourth, the nature of relationships between and among news organisations, journalists and their many publics (Pavlik, 2000).

Characteristics of online journalists

As noted earlier, there are many conceptual and empirical issues which make it difficult to draw any strong lines between online and older news services. For example many 'mature media' organisations are active players in online news domains and these have been moving towards more integrated newsrooms in recent years. One national survey of online journalists in the Netherlands reported that in 2002, some 47 per cent of online journalists were found to be employed by newspaper organisations and 20 per cent by broadcast organisations, with 27 per cent working for 'online only' media, and with one-third of online journalists declaring that this was their first job in journalism (Deuze and Dimoudi, 2002).

Such surveys suggest that the personal profiles of online journalists may not differ very much from their predecessors in other news media, as most online journalists tend to be male, aged between 26 and 35, and highly educated (e.g. Deuze and Dimoudi, 2002). In addition, some 95 per cent of respondents reported having full editorial freedom from their parent media organisations, such as newspapers, with respect to the online edition. Yet, only one-quarter of respondents said they had 100 per cent original content on their own website, suggesting that repurposing of content was a common practice (ibid.: 92). According to this same survey, online journalists produce up to a maximum of 50 per cent original content and 'almost all of them are reading and answering their emails (97 per cent)', some 91 per cent research the Internet for stories, and some 78 per cent are involved in rewriting 'shovelled' texts (ibid.: 92–93). Such findings may now be dated by the move towards more integrated newsrooms in recent years.

The Internet and journalists' professional status and roles

The idea that the Internet and/or online journalism may be reshaping the inherited model and role of journalism is a common theme in much of the recent research, and it also appears to be shared by many journalists working in online news services. For example, the survey by Deuze and Dimoudi (2002: 96) suggests that the 'media logic' of online journalism is to create a more interactive relationship with the audience, but other studies challenge such claims as we will see later.

The popular idea that the Internet, alongside the falling costs of digital authoring tools, enables more and more people to participate in media production and publishing is viewed as both a threat and benefit to professional journalists' role and status. On the one hand such techno-economic developments tend to erode the professional journalists' traditional (monopolistic) roles as gatekeeper of news and as watchdog of the public. Some accounts of a more participatory media system speculate in terms of the imminent death or decline of 'the people formerly known as the audience' (Rosen, 2006). Others discuss whether and how the Internet may enable politicians to deliver information directly to the public without a 'gatekeeper' control by journalists (Kopper et al., 2000). Singer argues that online journalism poses fundamental challenges to the notion of 'professionalism' even if noting that the latter is merely an ideological construct based on the idea that 'only certain people in society are uniquely entitled to fulfil a prestigious occupational niche, such as providing information' (Singer, 2003: 139).

On the other hand, these same techno-economic features of the digital media are seen to enhance journalism by supporting new participatory and democratic forms of news and public affairs reporting, discussion and analysis. For example, Pavlik (2000) highlights the potential role of new ICTs to change relationships between the professional journalists and their audience. He suggests that the newsmaking process is becoming 'much more of a dialog between the press and the public' as email 'has become a vital and instantaneous link between readers and reporters' (ibid.: 234). Other researchers have addressed the potential of the Internet in terms of the possibilities for a new or second phase of 'public journalism' (Nip, 2006). Some, including Robinson (2006), argue that blogging, and especially j-blogs, pose one key difference to traditional journalistic norms. Because 'readers are key sources in the blog world', and because bloggers routinely use readers as both sources and as co-authors, as a consequence 'audience agency is changing' (ibid.: 75).

Others have warned against the limits of analyses focused on extrapolations from the apparent technical or techno-economic features of the Internet. These suggest that the Internet's potential to support more participatory forms of political communication should be viewed as 'vulnerable' or dependent on considerable additional resources (time, energy, finance) to be realised in practice (e.g. Blumler and Gurevitch, 2001). Others emphasise that any compelling understanding of the Internet's potential in this regard will require in-depth studies of applications and uses by final users, local and voluntary citizens' organisations, public interest groups and detailed analyses of any 'subtle social shifts' that may be unfolding (e.g. Carey, 2005: 444). To date, there continues to be a dearth of ethnographic and other detailed studies of users relative to the swarm of speculative accounts of digital news culture.

User-generated content: audiences as co-producers of news?

The recent surge of interest in user-generated content (UGC) online sites (such as YouTube, Flickr, Wikipedia) appears to support the presumed blurring of the distinctions between professional media producers and media audiences or consumers. Many established media firms have invested heavily in such sites in recent years, not only by buying-up innovative start-ups but also through newspapers and broadcasting organisations developing major UGC sections on their web pages. Amongst the 'mature' media operators in Europe, broadcasters tended to be more readily able to embrace the challenges of online news media provision and new facilities and formats offering audiences the opportunities for feedback and comments. But many major newspapers have also moved rapidly in recent years to provide new facilities offering opportunities for various forms of audience-generated comment (Hermida and Thurman, 2007; Örnebring, 2007).

A study of 12 British newspaper websites undertaken in November 2006 found that all but one were providing 'tools for reader participation' (Hermida and Thurman, 2007: 4). It also observed a significant increase in the opportunities provided for readers to contribute content compared to another survey some 18 months previously (Hermida and Thurman, 2007). This study found a wide variation 'in the opportunities users have to contribute to the professionally edited publications studied', with three of the twelve newspaper sites requiring users to register in order to participate. It also found variations in the use of moderation, with eight of the sites 'exercising a high degree of control on contributions by fully moderating' (ibid.: 4). The same authors also report that the number of blogs had increased significantly (from 7 to 118) between April 2005 and November 2006, 'although there were wide variations in the nature of the blogs and how often they were updated' (ibid.: 5).

Despite the growing commercial interest in such developments, there has been relatively little independent academic research on the features or implications of these developments, such as what is being produced and what is being consumed in the expanding UGC services linked to established media such as newspapers. One recent study by Henrik Örnebring addresses this lacuna by examining the provision of UGC in two tabloid newspapers, the *Sun* (UK) and *Aftonbladet* (Sweden). Both of these newspapers have quite extensive systems for customisation and production of content and they are 'generally considered to be very successful in terms of their online presence' (Örnebring, 2007: 1, 19). The findings suggest that both the level of *control* the users have over the UGC production, and the *types* of content they produce are fairly limited in scope. The general finding is that users are mostly empowered to create content that is orientated towards popular culture and personal/everyday life issues 'rather than news/informational content' (ibid.: 19). Direct user involvement in the gathering, selection and production of news is minimal, and when it occurs 'it is not displayed in the same way as articles produced by the regular journalists of the paper' (ibid.). Readers' photographs of breaking news events comprise 'the only reader material that is given similar status' to that produced by the news organisations' professional staff (ibid.). Whilst further studies along these lines are urgently required to monitor the evolving patterns of UGC services, Örnebring's (2007) work suggests that any proclamations of the death of the audience are to be treated as highly premature.

Online journalism, professional values and ethics

The more recent literature includes work concerned that established journalistic values and professional norms are coming under heavy pressure from online news services based on very different sets of values. For example, Singer (2003) has argued that online journalism may pose fundamental challenges to the notion of 'professionalism', not least because the number of online journalists who produce 'original' online content is very small even if the number, role and status of online news services have grown rapidly. This leads Singer to pose the question about 'professional' qualifications and specificities: 'if journalism is about reporting but most online journalism is not', then one must ask 'what is the requisite set of knowledge or skills and how does a professional acquire them?' (Singer, 2003: 150). We will return to such issues by exploring studies of new online practices, routines and skills and their implications for journalists' values in the following chapters.

Nuancing the technology relation in newsmaking

When considering the growing literature on recent shifts in newsmaking values, norms and practices we must be wary of techno-centric perspectives and deterministic views or claims about the relations between technological and social change in news media firms (Boczkowski, 2004b: 198). As noted in Chapter 2, many conceptualisations of 'technology's effects' and understandings of the overall innovation process tend to advance 'the notion that technological developments generate editorial effects' (ibid.) by relying on highly deterministic assumptions.

As many recent contributions focus on the 'effects' of digital technologies on newsmaking practices, they tend to limit our understanding of the complexities of the phenomena under study. In particular, they neglect the often varied 'adoption processes' that shape whether and how very different 'effects' may be manifest in different newsrooms or other locations, even where the same technologies are being adopted and used (ibid.: 199). In the case of changes in media production, for example, 'technological innovation should be viewed as mediated by the political–institutional role' allocated to particular departments or occupational groups, their economic and organisational characteristics as well as 'corporate aims with regard to survival and growth' (Ursell, 2001: 176). If organisational change is tending towards multiskilling and multi-media news production, and 'the pursuit of novel news markets is seen to convey a potential to compromise journalistic performance', these trends may be underpinned by technological developments but not essentially shaped by the latter (ibid.). In this light, responsibility for any compromise in terms of news values or reporting standards is seen 'to be borne by political and corporate executives, not by technology' (ibid.).

Trends in news and journalists' values: eMEDIATE findings

We now move on to consider some relevant findings from our in-depth interviews with 95 experienced journalists and editors based in 11 countries, focusing on their views of the dominant trends related to journalistic values in contemporary newsmaking practice.

Dominant values in contemporary journalism and news

In summary terms, our research revealed little variation between journalists in terms of the key values related to journalism and newsmaking across the 11 countries studied. Indeed our interviews with senior journalists found that impartiality, objectivity and balance, fairness and accuracy, seeking the truth, were the values accorded the greatest importance in all countries, even if journalism did not always achieve these standards in practice. Other values mentioned included the importance of adequately contextualising news and avoiding voyeurism (e.g. ter Wal, 2006a). As well as identifying these key values, our interviewees also highlighted the importance of certain professional best-practices such as getting as many sources as possible; checking sources and citing them correctly. In essence, such findings come as no surprise. They resonate with a certain universalisation of declared professional values revealed in prior research and they closely match other aspects of our reviews of the relevant research literature earlier in this chapter.

Even though most journalists regard these professional values as important, many acknowledge that external factors (such as ownership, commercial or competitive pressures) made them difficult to apply in everyday practice. Our interviewees point to tensions between holding these values in the abstract and applying them in practice. The pressures are generally perceived to be top-down, arising from competitive or commercial factors or from ownership structures, although our interviewees did not cite explicit examples of owners directly forcing an editorial line on journalists. Rather, the relationship between ownership and control structures and the maintenance of journalists' professional values and autonomy with respect to news output is perceived and understood as subtle and indirect. The general constraints of working in a commercial or capitalist system were cited by some informants as important background influences. These include the growing competitive pressure to maintain circulation, produce news as a saleable commodity, and the implicit threat to employment that hangs over journalists employed on short-term contracts.

Most of our interviewees identified accuracy as the single most important value when asked to identify the key values in contemporary journalism. In many respects, such findings closely resonate with prior empirical studies. They indicate the conceptualisation of journalists as neutral professionals who seek to report on events in an impartial or balanced manner (the analogy of the mirror or messenger), as well as watchdogs who act as a check on government power. All our interviewees tended to nominate very similar basic professional journalistic values and implied or claimed that they adhered to these.

Yet, accounts of their own or colleagues' work experiences often suggest a more complex situation. First of all, it appears that professional values are applied selectively according to particular media contexts or the type of medium. Our interviewees, for example, associate the tabloid press with regular breaches of professional values, while public service media are understood as having a remit more firmly orientated towards fairness and objectivity, as one Irish journalist put it (Horgan, 2006). Moreover, it is clear that the public service ideal (independence from the state as well as the market) has a close affinity with journalistic values and professional 'myths' long-favoured in European or Western cultures. Yet many journalists acknowledge the existence of external pressures on professional values within both public service and private media.

The major factors identified by our interviewees as constraints on professional values included competition with other media, growing commercial or economic pressures, celebrity culture and tabloidisation, as well as use of official sources. For example, one Italian journalist pointed out that 'the double nature is inherent to journalism, a conflict of interests between ethics and the news as a product to be sold' (ter Wal and Valeriani, 2006). A senior editor at the London-based Sky News identified the 'getting the story first and getting the story right' as a major if not dominant influence in British journalistic practices (Preston, 2006a).

Competing for stories and getting them out before the competitors are important factors also for public service broadcasters.

A journalist from the Czech public service television argued that news values tend to be dominated by 'the overestimated importance of having an interesting topic' and that 'only after that does the journalist ask how to process this objectively' (Cisarova, 2007a). Thus adherence to professional values is often difficult or challenged by the working environment. Journalists from former communist countries, as well as from Italy and Spain, appear to be most pessimistic about the overall state of journalistic culture in their countries. Slovak and Czech interviewees gave examples of unethical conduct or referred to cases when political and economic interests interfered with professional ethics. One interviewee suggested that the worthy journalistic ideals of 'seeking truth [...] or an effort to find out how it is, disregarding whether it will cause me problems' tends to be 'almost non-existent in Slovak journalism' (Cisarova, 2007b). At the same time, although these interviewees may seem very pessimistic, they implied or asserted their own professional integrity, claiming to have been able to stick to professional values despite the unfavourable circumstances.

In contrast to the concept of neutral professionalism, some of our interviewees considered the role of journalists in shaping social values. The notions on this subject, however, ranged widely and we cannot identify a clear geographical or other pattern in this case. Some interviewees argued that media played key roles in society as they 'must serve democracy' as one French journalist put it (Guyot et al., 2006) or act as 'a counter power, defend the weak, but above all defend the local and regional community' according to one Spanish interviewee (ibid.). Hungarian, Serbian and Slovenian interviewees expressed the opinion that, although media cannot shape social values per se, they can have an educational influence and stimulate positive values. Several of our interviewees advanced the view that journalists bear social responsibility, suggesting, that 'information is a social good, not just a mere product', as one French journalist put it (ibid.).

Recent changes in journalism and news cultures

Our interviews suggest a widespread view that competition, commercialisation and market-centred policies have become incresingly powerful influences on journalism's values, norms and practices over the past 15 to 20 years. In the older EU member states, with well established market and liberal democratic media systems, this comprises an acceleration and strengthening of longer-term trends. The pressures of commercialism are a more recent development in the former communist countries, as their media systems have transitioned from a state-controlled to a free-market media system, even if now increasingly under foreign ownership and often subject to external managerial direction.

Concerns about the growing role of economic (commercial and competitive) pressures and the resulting potential tensions with professional ideals featured strongly in responses to the question on key changes in the journalistic culture over the past 15 to 20 years. The prevalent opinion among our interviewees was that professional values as such had not changed significantly. However, the application or interpretation of these values may have been influenced by changing practices related to increased competition, and the growth of infotainment and celebrity culture as well as technological and managerial change. Managerial and commercial changes in combination with technological innovations such as the Internet were seen as leading to a speed-up in working practices, an increased reliance on external sources and more office-bound working patterns. In considering technological changes and their influence on professional values, many of our interviewees referred to the increased speed of news gathering and publishing. There were concerns about tendencies towards a more flexible handling of professional values as journalists might have less time or opportunity to check their sources or to ensure they had sufficient sides to a story before publishing it.

Several journalists expressed strong concerns about adherence to professional values in the face of recent developments. 'Commercial competition, which is extremely hard competition, in the traditional media sector, combined with the arrival of the Internet, increased the level of competition, through immediacy, speed. On the other hand, the values linked to professional exactness, checking the news, have passed.' (Spanish interviewee; cited in Guyot et al., 2006)

For journalists working in the former Eastern bloc countries (Czech Republic, Hungary, Serbia, Slovakia and Slovenia) and also to a lesser extent, journalists working in Spain, the most important changes are seen to arise from political changes. Interviewees from the five former communist countries described the initial enthusiasm after the fall of communism and the special circumstances under which journalists worked. Serbian interviewees pointed out that journalists in their country now operated in a more politically open context while some Slovenian interviewees suggested that the opposite was the case. They noted that during the second half of the 1980s, journalists in Slovenia had played an important role in the wider campaign for democratisation. As many of these values have become reality in the period after 1991, journalists have had to adapt to a situation where the government was no longer the 'internal enemy'. They now face the challenge of finding a balance between criticism and support for the new government (Zagar and Zeljan, 2006a, 2006b). There were somewhat similar problems expressed by the Hungarian journalists, who contrasted the optimism shared among journalists after 1989 (that they would enjoy 'absolute freedom' after the regime change) with the realities of their lack of resources and a continuing culture of secrecy among the political, bureaucratic and business worlds (Kovács et al., 2005). A Czech journalist raised a similar point in arguing that the 'creative' enthusiasm of the first years after the fall of communism in 1989 had now disappeared from journalism. Czech journalists are now more careful, less prone to be wooed by politicians or companies. However, in his eyes, the end result seems to be that journalists are unable to recognise any good cause and so are unwilling to support anything (Cisarova, 2007a).

For many Spanish editors, the most significant changes comprise a greater degree of public debate, and this was associated with the changing role and practices of news media in the Spanish transition towards democracy. As one interviewee put it, Spanish journalism has now reached a stage of 'maturity and independence' following 'the strengthening of the institutional state and […] the democratic normality of political changeover between parties' (cited in Guyot *et al.*, 2006).

Individual influences as context dependent?

In this chapter, we considered the prior research base addressing how the individual characteristics and professional values of journalists may operate as influences, and then turned to the more recent literature engaging with the implications of the Internet. We then considered some relevant findings from our own primary research.

This individual-level approach resonates closely with the occupation's myths and journalists' self-understandings of their role in making the news. As one prominent US newscaster once put it, 'News is what I say it is. – it's something worth knowing by my standards' (David Brinkley, cited in Golding and Elliott, 1979: 118). This kind of approach is found wanting by sociologists and other researchers concerned with institutional factors and industrial routines in shaping the patterned processes of newsmaking. They suggest that most individual journalists most of the time do not wield the powerful or autonomous influence on the news agenda implied by the quotation from Brinkley above. Rather, journalists' newsmaking practices are strongly shaped by the industrial routines and institutional factors within which they are situated and perform their roles. For them, the 'obvious weakness' of individual-centred explanations 'is that the news changes very little when the individuals who make it are changed' (Golding and Elliott, 1979: 118).

In the next two chapters, we will turn to studies and explanations of newsmaking focused on institutional and organisational factors rather than the individual characteristics and values of journalists. We will consider how the daily practices and norms of journalists are patterned and shaped in daily work by industrial routines, the role of organisational factors, including informal socialisation and control processes in the work place, and other, wider sets of influences on newsmaking. Along the way, we will reflect further on how institutional and organisational factors relate to explanations centred on the individual characteristics and values of professional journalists as key influences on newsmaking.

Chapter 4

New news nets

Media routines in a 'knowledge society'

All the reporters in the world working all the hours of the day could not witness all the happenings in the world. There are not a great many reporters ... Yet the range of subjects these comparatively few men manage to cover would be a miracle indeed, if it were not a standardized routine.

(Lippmann, 1922: 183)

From a 'famine' to a swarm of 'institutional studies'

In the early 1970s, Herbert Gans, a prominent American sociologist and occasional journalist, complained of a 'famine' within US-based communication research as regards 'institutional studies' of the production of news and of media culture more generally. By the end of that decade, however, any such famine had been replaced by the proverbial feast as a swarm of innovative institutional studies advancing new theories, empirical methods and approaches appeared on both sides of the Atlantic.

Much of this swarm of new work was strongly influenced by recent developments in institutional or organisational sociology (Hirsch, 2000). However, some key ideas about media routines and patterned processes of newsmaking had been signalled in much earlier studies. These include pioneering analyses of the growing industrialisation of news, such as those of Wilcox (1900), Bücher (1901) and subsequent Progressive Era studies in the USA that invoked the idea of newsmaking as 'a standardized routine' (Lippmann, 1922: 183) or spoke in terms of the 'news factories'. The 1960s had seen some important new work such as Gieber's (1960) study of newsroom routines that frame the 'task-orientated' activities of individual newsmakers and Galtung and Ruge's (1965) seminal study of news values. Indeed, Hirsch later acknowledged that his (1972) study involved a 'depoliticized exploration' of what the Frankfurt School had earlier characterised as the 'culture industry' or the industrialisation of culture (Hirsch, 2000: 356). Thus we note a relatively long tradition of research on news production drawing on institutional and sociological perspectives, often focusing on factors and tendencies 'encapsulated in the idea of news as a manufactured product' (Whitney *et al.*, 2004: 402). Clearly, the new wave of institutional studies in the 1970s was not starting from a blank sheet.

Media industry routines: institutional views of news

Key features of institutional approaches to newsmaking

For sociologists and anthropologists, institutions are not ready-made entities as they involve dynamic, process-orientated activities, procedures, norms, routines, and roles. Institutions comprise regulative, normative, and cognitive structures and activities 'which provide stability and meaning to social behaviour' (Scott, 1995: 33; cited in Hirsch, 1997: 1709–10). They are shaped and relayed by various carriers such as industry routines, cultures, and structures. Applied to the field of journalism and newsmaking, such an approach draws attention to patterned procedures, industrial routines, standardised practices and professional norms and roles that steer the information-gathering, selection and editorial activities that lie at the heart of 'making the news' on a daily or hourly basis.

The growing body of new institutional studies in the USA and Europe from the 1970s sought to describe newsmaking as the patterned outcome of the activities of diverse newsworkers who were coordinated and regulated by specific sets of media-sector routines, procedures, occupational roles and norms. Such routines and procedures are viewed as the immediate environment which *situates* (enables and constrains) the daily work activity and outputs of the majority of newsworkers. Here, the focus shifts away from individual newsmakers, such as the 'gatekeepers' highlighted in White's (1950) study. The analytical spotlight turns towards the patterned newsroom routines that frame and shape what Gieber (1960) defined as the 'task-orientated' activities of individual newsmakers. Indeed, Gieber's 1960 study had revealed little difference between newspapers in terms of story selection and display, suggesting a shift in explanatory focus towards the media industry routines, patterned procedures and processes.

Some influential studies: Tuchman (1978) and Gans (1979)

Two of the most prominent contributions to the 1970s' wave of institutional studies were those of Tuchman (1978) and Gans (1979). Both studies were based on almost a decade of detailed fieldwork and other empirical research on four separate news organisations in the USA. Tuchman's approach drew on the sociology of work and research addressing organisations which deal with unexpected events on a routine basis. She observed how 'news work thrives upon processing unexpected events', especially those 'events that "burst to the surface" in some disruptive, exceptional and hence newsworthy manner' (Tuchman, 1973: 111). Whilst many prior researchers had 'the control of work' as a dominant theme, Tuchman was attentive to those who had noted how 'quickening urgency' is often 'the essence of news' (Hughes, 1940: 58; cited in Tuchman,

1973: 111). The key question of how management and workers impose routines upon their work poses particular issues when it comes to *non-specialised, unexpected events*. In such situations, Tuchman argued, 'without some routine method of coping with unexpected events, news organizations, as rational enterprises, would flounder and fail' (1973: 111). Her studies of newsmaking drew on two specific ideas from the sociology of work: first, 'routinization is impeded by variability in raw material', and second, persons categorise the objects of their work in order to control it (ibid.: 112).

Herbert Gans (1979) examined journalists in four news organisations (two major network news programmes and two newsweeklies). His study was designed 'to discover how they selected the news' and 'what they left out', and to study what US society 'tells itself about itself through the news' (Gans, 1979: xii). He conducted a content analysis of these news services (omitting controversial Vietnam War coverage, arguing that he wanted to focus on recurring patterns rather than episodic coverage). He identified enduring and topical values in US news, indicating that they largely reflected the core values of the society in which the newsmakers were socialised.

Gans analysed the factors shaping the selection and forms of news, emphasising routine procedures such as the use of sources, the norms of objectivity and suitability, the influence of commercial pressures, a certain disdain for audiences, and matters of censorship and self-censorship. His analysis suggested that newsworkers tended to insulate themselves from external and internal pressures through the routines associated with newsbeats and related specialist roles, as well as through peer-group support. Gans tended to emphasise situational constraints operating on news decision-making. At times, he suggested that the power of news sources comprised a primary influence, as they constantly sought to exploit or outmanoeuvre the media's routines and operations for their own ends. At one point, he proposes that the roles of journalists may often, if not primarily, involve 'summarizing, refining and altering what becomes available to them from sources' (Gans, 1979: 80).

Tuchman (1978) and Gans (1979) both suggest that the form of organisational control over newswork is generally consensual, with relatively little mention of overt editorial interventions or other efforts at control by management or owners. Tuchman found much less conflict between managers and reporters than she had expected. She described the relationship between newsworkers and editors as largely consensual, with control and coordination achieved largely through the commitment of both parties to the codes of professional journalism. Gans, meanwhile, suggested that, although media owners can intervene in the news, 'they do so only rarely' (Gans, 1979: 84).

Routines and news as 'constructed' reality

A distinctive feature of many 1970s (and subsequent) institutional studies embracing 'the idea of news as a manufactured product' comprised an emphasis on news as a 'construction of reality rather than a picture of reality' (Whitney *et al.*, 2004: 402). Molotch and Lester (1974), Tuchman (1978) and others emphasised how standard media routines and professional practices operate systematically to construct or manufacture very specific forms of social reality in making the news. They suggested that media routines and standard professional newsmaking procedures operate to promote highly specific, even if not consciously biased or distorted, ways of looking at and reporting events (Altheide, 1976; Shoemaker and Reese, 1996). Media routines and professional procedures systematically construct what counted as news, by selecting and promoting a highly partial range of daily occurrences or issues to the status of newsworthiness.

Tuchman also drew on the social construction of reality perspective to argue that the concept of 'distortion' should be regarded as 'alien to the discussion of socially constructed realities' such as news (1973: 129). She tried to distance her analysis from prior studies of news 'distortion' on the grounds that 'each socially constructed reality necessarily has meaning' (ibid.: 129). Indeed, she pointed out distortion was itself a socially constructed concept. Tuchman suggested that 'newsmen's typifications indicate that it might be valuable to think of news not as distorting, but rather as reconstituting the everyday world' (ibid.: 129). Tuchman advanced the notion of the 'news net' to conceptualise the newsmakers' imposition of order on the social world. The idea of 'news net' presented an image of a device designed to 'catch' news. Her analysis suggested that the 'newsbeat' was not only spatial and topical, but it was also a social process, 'a network of social relations' involving reporters and sources who frequented particular places or locations (Tuchman, 1978; McQuail, 2000: 281–82). Her study suggested that news was very much the product of the mobilisation of resources. Tuchman's 'news net' concept has been taken as more compelling than 'the mirror' metaphor of news culture which many journalists and social critics drew on to describe how news reflected the social world (Allan, 2004: 60–61).

Typology of key media routines shaping news culture

We now move to identify and consider several specific media industry routines or patterned practices that serve to frame and shape the production of news, according to various institutional and sociological studies since the 1970s. While these are presented separately here, many of them should be seen as interlocking influences on the definition and productions of news (see Box 4.1).

Key routines: resources, sources, news values

News resources and resource allocation as critical factors

Institutional approaches to newsmaking emphasise how resources – especially the numbers, allocation and roles of newsworkers – play crucial roles in the definition and making of news (e.g. Tuchman, 1978; Golding and Elliott, 1979).

Box 4.1 Major media industry 'routines' related to making the news

1 News resources and resource allocation as critical factors
2 Time factors in 'news nets' and newsmaking routines/procedures
3 News sources and 'privileged' suppliers: (in)forming the news net
4 Regular relations with/across other media as key routine
5 News values and definitional issues
6 News framing and newsmaking routines

To effectively source and manage the flow of potentially relevant information, management and editors organise newsmaking resources along certain locational and temporal grids. They organise and allocate reporters towards roles or locations that are deemed to generate good flows of information on 'news-worthy' events or occurrences that may be accommodated within production deadlines. For example, Tuchman (1973, 1978) indicates the importance of 'news nets' or networks of 'newsbeats', whereby reporters were routinely allo-cated to specific kinds of institutions where steady flows of information were generated (e.g. the courts, the police, the offices of politicians). The capacity of the news net depended on the fineness of the mesh and the strength of its fibre. Reporters and news agencies provided the larger mesh, while stringers supplied the finer mesh or strands of the newsmaking process. The news net also involved hierarchy. The news net had a very tight weave (allocation of news-making resources) in places where power was concentrated, such as in the Washington–New York corridor or the London–Paris–Berlin triangle. For Tuchman, the news net constructs an overarching frame on the occurrences or events to be reported through the configuration of allocated reporters, whilst status within the news net determined whose information was likely to be iden-tified and defined as news. In their pioneering cross-national study of broad-casting organisations in three countries, Golding and Elliott (1979) paid close attention to the levels and distribution of key resources, both human and mate-rial, within these organisations. They examined the struggles of news depart-ments against the claims of other departments and units over the allocation of resources, ranging from personnel, to studios, cameras and recording equipment, and to shares-out of budgets (Golding and Elliott, 1979: 300; Boyd-Barrett and Newbold, 1995).

Time factors in news nets and newsmaking routines

As a distinct form of knowledge, contemporary news is time-dependent by defi-nition. News production is 'so organized that its basic dynamic emphasizes the perishability of stories' (Schlesinger, 1978: 92). Newsmaking routines and norms are marked by 'an emphatic bias towards immediacy', and in the occupational mythology of newsworkers, 'time looms large among the wicked beasts to be defeated daily in the battle of production' (Schlesinger, 1978: 92). This research literature underlines how news production processes as well as 'the news itself' have to fit within the time available, 'with consequences for the kind of event that figures in the news and is most likely to have news value' (Whitney *et al.*, 2004: 404).

Institutional studies indicated a 'bias towards immediacy' across the media sector, but its intensity varied according to the medium, for example, television routines and norms are more obsessed than newspapers with the 'stop-watch culture' (Schlesinger, 1978). Schlesinger, Tuchman (1978) and others underlined how the temporal aspects of events were crucial in news selection processes, especially in broadcast media. Decisions about timing are crucial aspects of professionalism among journalists, editors and producers. Tuchman's (1978) account also emphasised how news work is organised to manage time as well as space, suggesting that it was precisely in defining and responding to time constraints that journalists played an active role in shaping the news. News routines also lead newsworkers to 'typify' potential news stories into different 'news type' categories, each of them with strong temporal dimensions. Tuchman (1978) suggests that, by applying these routine standards and time-related 'typifications', newsworkers actively construct a particular version of the news and impose a highly specific 'social reality'. In this light, pre-planned events 'make up a large part of routine news coverage', but pre-planning could have unexpected and undesirable consequences on accuracy and truth (Whitney *et al.*, 2004: 404).

Thus, institutional studies emphasise how temporal rhythms, in combination with the organisation and allocation of resources, play an important role in the definition, selection and production of news to meet specific schedules. Occurrences falling outside the production schedule are less likely to be defined as newsworthy and be covered. Media owners, executives, editors and journalists do not seek only timely or immediate news as close to the present as possible. They also seek convenient and manageable news as close to the deadline as possible. Such routines bestow special advantages to well placed sources who possess the knowledge and resources to time their own interventions and events in order to maximise the opportunities for access to coverage (Schlesinger, 1978; Schudson, 1978; Whitney *et al.*, 2004).

News sources and suppliers: (in)forming the news net

Most institutional studies of newsmaking pay close attention to sources and their interaction with the routines and procedures by which events come to the attention of news organisations and enter the news agenda. They highlight how newsmaking routinely relies on established, official sources, well resourced private individuals or organisations, as well as centralised news services. Such industrial routines and professional practice may lead to systematic biases in the flow of news or to the construction of a specific but patterned version of reality (Tuchman, 1976; Schlesinger, 1978).

Institutional studies emphasise how news managers and journalists tend to adopt patterned routines and strategies for organising the identification and assembly of potential news stories, largely based on the allocation of resources to different subject areas and newsbeats. Media industry routines involved in the sourcing and assembly of news stories are strongly centred on locations and agents where events deemed newsworthy are likely to arise. They lead news-makers to concentrate on the particular locations where such events are deemed to be located, and the kinds of people around whom it happens. The former typically include the offices of top politicians, parliaments, corporate head-quarters, stock markets, sport stadiums, law courts, tribunals, police or military headquarters. On a day-to-day basis, 'journalism is the story of the interaction of reporters and government officials, both politicians and bureaucrats' (Schudson, 2000: 184), although some might add economic and business elites to that list.

Thus, contrary to the image of the media as the public's watchdog, most news stories originate in the initiatives of non-media actors, especially those of wealthy and powerful institutions, individuals or organised interests. For example, McManus (1994) classifies the potential range of the media's news discovery strategies along a continuum of 'activity level', ranging from active to passive. His study of a television news station, estimated that three-quarters of news was 'passively dis-covered', some 20 per cent arose from moderately active discovery, but only 5 per cent from highly active means. Applying an economic analysis, McManus addresses how the more active modes of news search and discovery are likely to cost the news organisation much more time and money. Commercial news organisations will tend to minimise costs, thus leading to the prominent role of 'passively discovered' news (McManus, 1994; Whitney et al., 2004).

Privileged sources: powerful and resource-rich sources

Many institutional and sociological studies of the news suggest that powerful and wealthy elite groups tend to have privileged roles as news sources and influences. This is most widely recognised in the case of political elites, not least because of the way that journalistic resources, routines and day-to-day practices are pat-terned (Gieber and Johnson, 1961). One routine solution to the news organisation's need for a constant supply of raw material for news is to draw on a network of 'dependable sources' but this, in turn, leads to certain 'ties of interdependence with sources' and even opens the way to collaboration (Whitney et al., 2004: 403). Institutional studies suggest that news media and sources may often end up in dependent or collaborative relationships with elites orientated towards 'mutual advantage' rather than the good of the public.

Molotch and Lester's study (1974: 111) found that the news media should be viewed less as a catalogue of the important events of the day than as 'the poli-tical work by which certain events are constituted by those who happen to cur-rently hold power' over the media or ideas more generally. They emphasised that certain powerful sources play a major role in shaping or predicting what becomes a newsworthy or public event. In effect, certain groups tend to be in the position to 'make news' and possess 'habitual access' to the media as sources. Johnstone (1982: 1180) argued that some institutional accounts tend to neglect the external influences of powerful, wealthy, and well resourced sources on news definitions (or 'typifications') and newsmaking processes more generally.

Other studies have been increasingly attentive to the high proportion of news-related material supplied in the form of 'information subsidies' to the news media (Gandy, 1982). This refers to material that is produced and published by self-interested sources, either directly by their own employees or by using public relations, promotional, lobbyist, or strategic communication services (ibid.; Whitney *et al.*, 2004). Such influences comprise wealthy individuals, corporations, lobby groups or other types of organisations possessing the material (financial) wherewithal to hire 'professional' discursive resources and competencies (symbolic analysts) to produce subsidised news materials in order to promote their own interests. Furthermore, many of the public relations experts, lobbyists and strategists employed by powerful sources tend to be former newsworkers who well understand the routines, temporal and other constraints under which the news media operate (Johnstone, 1982: 1180).

More recent studies address the patterned influences on newsmaking arising from the rapid growth of specialist 'organisations, professions and skills' whose roles and functions are 'aimed at manipulating the media' (Curran and Seaton, 1997: 277–78; cited in Harcup and O'Neill, 2001: 277). Thrall's (2006) study of the ability of ordinary groups to make news suggests that the best predictor of an interest group's ability to use the mass media as a political tool comprises the level of resources (money, members, staff) they possess. Investigating the quantity and quality of news coverage received by a sample of 244 interest groups, Thrall (2006) found that the uneven distribution of resources led to heavy concentration of news on the largest and wealthiest groups as well as to important differences in how the media portray group actions.

Such trends seem to locate contemporary political culture, or *The New Public* (Mayhew, 1997) quite some distance from the level playing field of disinterested, deliberative and unsubsidised ('free') exchange of ideas that underpinned the liberal model of democracy and its attendant public sphere in the early modern era (Habermas, 1962; 1989). They suggest that the 'free market of ideas' may be increasingly subverted by the 'invisible hand' or 'subsidies' of the wealthy and powerful (Gandy, 1982; Gandy and Farrall, 2007).

Regular relations with other media: a key source as well as routine

Many institutional studies have observed a marked tendency for newsworkers from different (often competing) media organisations to engage in (a) the pursuit of the same kind of stories; and (b) collaborative sharing of news items, images or clips; as well as (c) discussion and other exchanges on how to interpret, highlight or frame the significance of particular occurrences. For Tuchman, 'the famed cooperation among reporters', tends to result in a shared selection of 'facts' and 'a common labelling of situations' (Tuchman, 1976: 1066).

The occupational myths of the news media have long accorded a privileged place to the idea of the 'scoop' or 'exclusive'. In practice, however, the pursuit of the exclusive is exceptional, as such stories comprise a tiny share of the total. Despite the industry's favoured myths, news organisations rarely come down on the side of investing resources in the long, detailed and risky empirical work required for investigative journalism – whatever the orientations and inclinations of the company's journalists to the contrary. Institutional studies reveal that the day-to-day work of newsmakers involves a striking routine reliance on other media. These tendencies towards 'pack' or 'copycat journalism' (or 'deep inter-textuality') are motivated in part by pressures to meet scheduling deadlines and news content targets. They may also point to *consistency* as another distinct, and unspoken, industrial routine and norm, whereby copycat newsmaking minimises risk and uncertainty in defining what is newsworthy (Shoemaker and Reese, 1996: 123–25). New managerial strategies and working routines in news orga-nisations may serve to amplify such tendencies (Laville, 2007).

News values and definitional issues

The idea of 'news values' has a long-standing role in efforts to explain how news is defined and produced along certain lines. Indeed, news values have played a particularly prominent role in the occupational discourse or myths of journalism, comprising the central norms or beliefs deemed to guide and frame newsmaking practices (Hall, 1973; McQuail, 2000). They have also routinely featured at the heart of journalism training and textbooks for several decades (Shoemaker and Reese, 1996). The concepts of news values and news judgement formed 'the sacred knowledge, the secret ability of the newsman which differentiates him from other people' (Tuchman, 1972). Yet, until the seminal work of Galtung and Ruge (1965) and the new wave of institutional and cultural studies of news from the 1970s, the precise meaning, role and operations of news values were poorly defined and understood.

Galtung and Ruge's (1965) study of foreign news in the Norwegian press 'led to the first clear statement of new values that influence decisions' (McQuail, 2000: 278). Their analysis of news values emphasised how selected occurrences or events were more likely to become news if they matched certain institutional and organisational criteria as well as privileged cultural and ideological values. The kinds of ideological news factors identified by Galtung and Ruge centred on particular values deeply embedded in Western, capitalist societies, such as those related to a materialist and individualistic value system or philosophy. Their model was an important starting point, if not major influence, on subsequent work on news values. For many, it remains the benchmark and may be 'regar-ded as *the* study of news values' (Harcup and O'Neill, 2001: 264).

Galtung and Ruge's model was centred around 12 major 'news factors' (for a recent summary, see Harcup and O'Neill, 2001). It had an orientation towards a gatekeeping approach and thus tends to assume that there is a given reality 'out there' which the news gatherers can simply select or exclude (ibid.: 265). For many other researchers adopting institutionalist or culturalist approaches to newsmaking, any such focus on external 'events' only tells part of the story as many items of news are not occurrences in the real world which take place independently of the media (Curran and Seaton, 1997). Institutional researchers produced many subsequent studies that interrogated the meanings, forms and roles of news values in the overall newsmaking process. Tuchman (1973, 1978) explored newsworkers' classifications of events-as-news, interrogating the basis for definitional categories such as hard, soft, spot, developing, and continuing news. She emphasised that newsworkers' own ways of defining categories (or 'typifications') tend to be inadequate and inconsistent. Golding and Elliott's (1979: 114) cross-national study of newsmaking in three different countries addressed how news values tended to be 'surrounded by a mystique, an impenetrable cloud of verbal imprecision and conceptual obscurity'. They suggested that news values tended to be used in two ways: first, they concern 'criteria of selection' and second, they concern 'guidelines for the presentation of selected items' (ibid.: 114). Golding and Elliott defined news values as working rules, comprising a corpus of occupational lore that explained and guided newsroom practice. The greater diversity of news values a story contained, the greater its chances of inclusion (ibid.: 115).

Drawing on prior typologies such as those identified by Golding and Elliott (1979) and Harcup and O'Neill (2001), we can identify a dozen of the more typical or persistent news values identified in the literature. The first four derive from considerations of the audience. The remainder arise from a mixture of the factors, including 'accessibility' referring to the news event's prominence and ease of capture, and 'fit' which concerns the degree to which it is compatible with production routines (Golding and Elliott, 1979: 116) (see Box 4.2).

Box 4.2 List of typical/persistent news values

1 Drama/surprise
2 Visual attractiveness
3 Entertainment
4 Importance/relevance/magnitude
5 Size
6 Proximity
7 Brevity
8 Negativity/bad news
9 Recency
10 Elites/the power elite
11 Personalities/celebrities
12 Objectivity, bias and ideology

News framing and newsmaking routines

The idea of news *frame* or *framing* builds on earlier concepts such 'principles of organization', 'frames' (Goffman, 1974), and the 'hierarchy of credibility' (Becker, 1967). Many institutional approaches to news production processes draw on Goffman's idea that a frame is needed to organise otherwise fragmentary items of information, not least the array of potential events that may be deemed newsworthy at any given time. Tuchman (1978) and others have linked the idea of news frame to the 'window' through which newsworkers view and compose their picture of the world (Whitney *et al.*, 2004: 405). The framing concept also has many overlaps with the notion of encoding and preferred meanings advanced by Hall and others in the British cultural studies tradition (see Chapter 7).

In institutional studies of news production, the concept of *framing* often refers to the ways in which news information is presented or 'framed' with a certain slant or angle, often in an attempt to connect one event with others that are seemingly similar. The concept suggests that newsworkers bring certain anticipated scripts or predefined viewpoints to their coverage of news events (Shoemaker and Reese, 1996). For example, one early sociological study of news – focused on the reporting of political demonstrations in London against the Vietnam War – indicated how media coverage, aligned with concerns of the authorities, can produce very specific and powerful framing effects (Halloran *et al.*,1970). In this case, the news media and these other actors combined to frame the protest events as violent and the work of foreign agitators, even when the actual levels of violence were relatively minor and much less than the media or authorities had anticipated.

Others have applied the idea of news framing in a broader institutional understanding of potential influences. In his study, *The Great Frame Robbery*, Gandy investigated the ways in which representations of public opinion 'have been used strategically in an effort to influence media policy at the national level' in the USA (Gandy, 2003b: 2). Gandy's study is particularly interesting because it examines policy framing around several significant changes in media and communication policy in the USA. One of Gandy's key conclusions is that 'public opinion plays a relatively insignificant role in the discursive framing of media policy debates' (2003b: 2).

In many applications, the news frame concept can be linked to the idea of news 'peg' or 'angle' as 'organizing otherwise fragmentary pieces of information in a thematic way', and so framing 'helps to connect apparently similar events into a connected whole' (Whitney *et al.*, 2004: 405). For many researchers, such news frames are rarely neutral, objective or value-free. One influential proponent of the concept, Robert Entman (1993), suggested that framing centres on news selection and salience, referring to the process by which journalists select topics, define the underlying issue, and interpret causes and effects. In a much-cited study, Entman (1991) examined two similar incidents, the shooting down of a Korean airliner by the Soviet forces and the downing of an Iranian airliner by the US Navy. He demonstrated how these events were framed in highly contrasting ways in the US media and thus led to quite different evaluative outcomes or meanings. The research by Entman and by others adopting the framing concept serves to illustrate how the struggle for power over media 'is often conducted initially as a struggle over definitions of events' (Whitney *et al.*, 2004: 406). More recently, Entman (2004) has proposed that frames become dominant through the close relationship between governing elites and news organisations, utilising concepts such as 'cascading activation' and 'substantive framing'. Furthermore, thanks to the popularity of the term, there are now many different concepts and models of framing to be found in the research literature (McQuail, 2000; 2005; Gandy, 2003a; Reese *et al.*, 2003).

Net effects: paradigm shifts in news routines?

The Internet, 'network society' and institutional innovations

Having reviewed some seminal studies, key concepts and insights concerning the role of industrial routines and institutional processes in shaping newsmaking, we now turn to focus on more recent research and developments. Here we consider whether and how new institutional and technological innovations may be combining to produce significant changes (or 'paradigm shift') in the patterned industrial routines and institutional practices involved in the production of news.

In terms of a long-wave system model, we are here concerned with the contours of any emergent new socio-technical paradigm that may be emerging in the newsmaking sector (Preston, 2001). How or to what extent are new ICTs (especially the Internet) and related institutional innovations leading to significant changes in the industrial routines and professional practices which structure and pattern the daily practices of newsmaking? To what extent are the new technological developments being accompanied by matching sets of institutional innovations, including new industrial routines, managerial strategies and professional practices involved in the production of news? And if they are, how does any emergent 'paradigm shift' in news media routines serve to prompt complementary or contradictory changes in professional norms, occupational codes and practices?

At a headline level, we note that news media organisations, like other knowledge-intensive services, may be located at the forefront of current 'network society' or 'knowledge economy' developments. They have been facing multi-dimensional innovations, of which the technological moment is perhaps the first or easiest aspect to identify (Preston, 2001). The concept of a new socio-technical paradigm highlights the multi-dimensional innovation process associated with major new technical systems. It also signals that the technological aspect is only the first or most obvious aspect. The concept helps to identify how the contemporary context of newsmaking also involves a range of equally important innovations to be negotiated, including product, process, managerial and institutional innovations (e.g. Saltzis, 2007; Nygren, 2007).

Like some other recent studies (e.g. Saltzis, 2007: 8–9) we suggest that major media organisations have been challenged to innovate in recent years along at least four major fronts (or in some combination of these directions). These four fronts comprise: (a) product innovations; (b) process innovations, including changes to established industrial routines and institutional patterns; (c) innovation in the internal division of labour and skill structures; and (d) the design and application of 'flexible' new ICT-enabled organisational systems for all aspects of news production and distribution, including marketing, administrative, financial and other support functions.

Major or modest changes in media routines?

Whilst the number of well grounded institutional studies of the relation between digital technologies and innovations in newsmaking routines remains fairly small relative to techno-centric speculation, we can identify some relevant examples. But we should not underestimate the difficulties in arriving at solid or well grounded studies of the role and implications of the Internet and related technological innovations for journalism practices or forms. It is extremely difficult to conduct 'real-time' studies of long-run, institutional and *social learning* processes or arrive at definitive statements on the distinctive features of emergent trends in phenomena still undergoing dynamic and multi-sided development. This applies even in the case of online journalism, which now has a 15-year historical record (Allan, 2005). The role, features and applications of digital systems in news production still 'remain in the early stages' of their potential developmental trajectory (Klinenberg and Fayer, 2005: 229). Their future direction will be determined not only or mainly by technical factors but by further institutional and social innovations (Preston, 2001), including those related to 'political economy, cultural conventions, and regulatory' factors (Klinenberg and Fayer, 2005: 229).

A useful starting point is to examine early examples of innovative online newsmaking practices and routines, particularly those related to important 'crises' or unexpected news events since the emergence of the Web. Such examples help reveal the gaps between unfolding practices and the 'potential' of the Internet to support truly innovative news services and forms to audiences in ways which transcend those that are possible or available through older technical platforms. In examining some early cases of news events where the Internet demonstrated its potential to support and deliver novel modes and patterns of newsmaking, Stuart Allan highlights 'the socially contingent, frequently contested nature of their lived negotiation' (Allan, 2005: 69). He concludes that despite multiple potential strategies for the production and presentation of news, online news sites have become very similar both in terms of appearance and 'in their preferred definitions of what counts as news and how best to report it' (ibid.: 80). Allan's conclusions include concerns that online journalism is becoming more closely aligned with the 'attractive wrapping' of television news. Yet, he wishes to reaffirm 'the reportorial ethos of the investigative press' as part of a stronger commitment to developing new ways of improving the quality of online journalism (ibid.: 80).

Many studies suggests that significant changes are currently unfolding in the industrial routines, institutional patterns and journalistic practices shaping news production in the early twenty-first century (Pavlik, 2000; Klinenberg, 2005a; Nygren, 2007). Some suggest significant changes are unfolding in the division of labour and in the mobilisation and allocation of 'human resources' in newsmaking, including trends towards the erosion of traditional boundaries between journalistic roles, on the one hand, and advertising and marketing on the other. For example, Klinenberg (2005a: 48) examines changes in jour-nalistic production routines and practices. Building on a 'multiyear ethno-graphic project' centred on news organisations that began with print media but now use advanced technologies to produce and distribute content across different platforms, this study seeks to explore how reporters and editors now confront and negotiate novel 'constraints of time, space, and market pressure under regimes of convergence newsmaking' amongst other issues (Klinenberg, 2005a: 48).

As noted in Chapter 3, the research literature abounds with robust claims concerning the power or potential of the Internet to transform journalists' roles and practices. But, we must be attentive to the *continuities* as well as *changes* in considering the forms and extent of any significant shifts in the institutional patterns and industrial routines framing news production (Preston, 2001). Some empirically grounded studies point to fairly modest sets of changes or a 'conservative revolution' when it comes to news production routines and prac-tices associated with the adoption of the Internet or new ICTs more broadly (Reich, 2005: 552). Reich (ibid.: 553) reports 'remarkable continuities' in news-work and news content and 'relatively similar' information practices in print and online newsrooms. That study suggests that the role played by new technologies in the production of news information 'seems neither revolutionary nor irre-levant, but rather a conservative revolution' (ibid.: 564). Reich finds that, despite major changes in the technical means of news production, there have been 'relatively minor changes' only in 'the journalistic methodology of produc-tion' (ibid.: 564).

In an exemplary study of three online newsrooms, all with access to broadly similar sets of 'new technologies', Boczkowski (2004b: 201) found very different outcomes in terms of the extent of changes in newsmaking routines. In one case, Boczkowski found that reporters' work 'did not differ much from what they did when they worked for print papers' whilst, in another, news design and production practices had changed quite dramati-cally (ibid.: 207). The crucial variable was not technology but much more a matter of differences in institutional and management strategies, including approaches to the design, resourcing and organisation of the online news service.

New news routines in a 'network' or 'knowledge' society

Blurring lines? New divisions of labour and newsmaking routines

Many of the seminal institutional studies of newsmaking reported that editorial professionals tended to perceive their own work and roles as operating somewhat autonomously from the managerial and business goals and functions (economic, marketing, advertising, etc., departments) of news organisations. However, several recent studies suggest that traditional presumptions concerning clear and distinct boundaries between the editorial and business functions of news media have been significantly eroded or may be no longer tenable (e.g. Pavlik, 2000: 233; Klinenberg and Fayer, 2005: 229; Nygren, 2007: 6; IFJ and ILO, 2006: v–vi).

For example, Pavlik (2000) argues that the changing technology and economics of online news are undermining the traditional separation of editorial and business functions in media organisations in the USA. Pavlik finds that the 'lines between advertising and editorial are blurring', including cases where 'banner advertisements are featured on many online newspaper front pages', a practice frowned upon in most printed newspapers (2000: 233). He cites other examples which raise 'troubling ethical concerns about the possible influence of advertising on editorial content' (ibid.). Drawing on Swedish research, Nygren 2007: 6) argues that 'financial motives are much stronger today in media companies than 5–10 years ago' and this corresponds to a relative weakening of professional norms and journalistic values. In his interview surveys of newsworkers, Nygren finds that now 'even newsroom editors talk about target groups and the portfolio the company offers the advertisers' as, more than ever before, 'everything is done to defend the position in the advertising market' (ibid.: 6–7). Nygren argues that 'journalism is more connected than ever to finance' as 'the old wall between the newsroom and the advertising and finance departments is ... crumbling' (Nygren, 2007: 7). Indeed, Nygren suggests that much the same applies to (the Swedish) public service companies where 'the finance department's influence is stronger, more production is done outside the company' and a growing proportion of the journalists are temporarily employed with lower salaries (ibid.).

Klinenberg and Fayer (2005: 229) suggest that the penetration of market principles and marketing projects into the editorial divisions of news organisations comprises 'one of the most dramatic changes in journalism' in recent times. They report that wider changes in the organisation and division of labour in news media are eroding the prior boundaries between editorial and marketing/ business departments. Corporate managers and advertisers are increasingly 'active participants in editorial decision making, and their interests now structure the form and content of news to unprecedented levels' (ibid.). Editors now have to 'work hard to produce more marketable and profitable products', as detailed market research is harnessed to ascertain the kinds of content that will appeal to specific categories of consumers; this, in turn, may lead to important qualitative changes in news organisations' offerings to meet market demands, according to Klinenberg and Fayer (2005: 229; see also Klinenberg, 2005a). Digital technologies have enabled media executives and corporations to take the principles of target marketing to new levels, making specialised media products for niche groups of consumers that can still be reached by advertising staff.

Furthermore, some recent studies examine how the changing institutional environment is forcing newspaper journalists to take on additional responsibilities for online media with different news cycles in the same work period (Klinenberg, 2005a; Klinenberg and Fayer, 2005; Ruusunoksa and Kunelius, 2007). The resultant increased workloads have consequences for the quality of news production, as editorial staff tend to have less time than before to check, research, report, or even to think about their work. The greater emphasis on throughput and efficiency in news organisations appears to be pushing journalists to rely on the most easily accessible information (online information), and aiming for the easiest-to-produce content becomes a more attractive norm compared to the more costly procedures involved in investigative-type journalism. Such studies suggest that digital technologies are enabling management to implement deep changes in news production routines and practices, 'but not according to the journalists' preferences – the goal is productivity, efficiency, and profitability' according to Klinenberg and Fayer (2005: 229; see also Nygren, 2007; Ruusunoksa and Kunelius, 2007).

New resources: more 'flexible' human resources

Newsrooms still organise their journalists according to newsbeats and news nets but it appears that the numbers of professional editorial staff (especially those who are full-time or on permanent contracts) have not been increasing in line with the ever-expanding flows of source information or media outlets. Whilst the media industry 'has undergone dramatic growth and change' over the last two decades, it has also seen significant changes in the structure of the labour market and in the organisation of work 'both within and outside the framework of the employment relationship' (IFJ and ILO, 2006: v).

In a global perspective, journalists are increasingly being employed in 'atypical and contingent employment relationships – casual employment, use of contract work and the rise of the use of triangular, ambiguous and disguised employment' (IFJ and ILO, 2006: v). According to the International Federation of Journalists, the global body of journalists' unions, employment in media 'has become more precarious, less secure and more intense' over the last five years, alongside a trend away from collective bargaining, and towards individual negotiations (IFJ and ILO, 2006: vi). Experienced senior journalists are being replaced by younger graduates who more often work on non-permanent, or 'atypical', employment contracts. One result is that 'journalists' average rate of pay appears to be declining in real terms, or at best, standing still, over the past five years' (IFJ and ILO, 2006: vi).

Whilst journalists and other editorial staff may be allocated to specific news-beats, to an increasing extent they must be prepared to move freely between print and/or broadcast, and online news production tasks in order to meet the demands of the new managerial and institutional routines (Klinenberg, 2005a; Klinenberg and Fayer, 2005). In the emerging new media newsroom, 'being flexible adds to employee value' as 'journalists have to become flexible laborers' who are skilled and willing to meet the varying demands of several media at once (Klinenberg and Fayer, 2005: 228). This emphasis on flexibility or inte-gration appears to be linked to a continuous 'culture of projects', involving a never-ending process of 'tackling change' as prominent managerial themes in negotiating new working practices and routines with editorial staff in con-temporary news organisations (Ruusunoksa and Kunelius, 2007: 12).

Utilising concepts such as new modes of production in newsmaking, Gunnar Nygren (2007) reports on a study examining strategic shifts in the daily work routines and production processes in eight different types of newsrooms in Sweden. The author demonstrates the applicability to newsmaking routines and practices of more generic concepts and practices such as lean-production, out-sourcing, flexible specialisation, differentiation and complexity, which help relate changes in newsmaking to those in other sectors (Nygren, 2007). This study is also of interest because it pays attention to the various layers of influence which lie outside the immediate newsroom setting, including the growing role of mar-keting, financial and other economic factors in the contemporary newsmaking environment (Nygren, 2007).

The changing division of labour in news media may have seen a relative decline in the role of some specific functions, such as sub-editors, but it also sees the creation or expansion of new kinds of roles, including those related to the monitoring of user-generated content (UGC) (Hermida and Thurman, 2007; Ugille and Paulussen, 2007). UGC developments are widely viewed as much more than an extension of prior roles of readers' letters to editor or ombudsman (see also Chapter 3).

News sources and suppliers: (in-)forming the new news net

Several recent studies point to significant changes unfolding in the industrial routines and journalistic practices related to news sources and sourcing (Pavlik, 2000; Klinenberg, 2005a; Ruusunoksa and Kunelius, 2007). In his survey of the literature, Pavlik (2000) highlights how journalists now have online tools to gather information or communicate with people. They are more likely to use online sources, e.g. a company website, if they cannot contact a source, e.g. reporting a breaking story outside of normal business hours. Also, more jour-nalists are going online for story ideas. There are also important differences between media production with analogue and with digital technologies, e.g. journalists can now edit video in the field; text input is also easier. Whilst Reich generally finds that changes in news production practices in the print media over the past two decades have been relatively minor and something of a 'conservative revolution', he emphasises to how use of the telephone 'has been displaced from its once central role by textual modes' (Reich, 2005: 562–64). He suggests that the shift to text may have important implications for the relationship between source information and the final version published in the news media. Textual data can not only speed up the transmission of information, it may also 'avoid friction between the proposers of information (sources) and those who decided what to do with it (reporters)' (Reich, 2005: 566).

A recent Swedish survey suggests that one in every two journalists leaves the newsroom every day for work purposes. But at the same time, 'many journalists say that in spite of the increasing mobile possibilities they spend more time in the newsroom now than 5–10 years ago' (Nygren, 2007: 5). This same survey suggests that 'the group of journalists that most seldom leave the newsroom are the online journalists – they use material collected by other journalists, sources on the net and the telephone to produce as much news as fast as possible' (Nygren, 2007: 5).

When it comes to the important routines related to sources or sourcing of news, some studies underline that the diffusion of the Internet does not appear to have enabled much change with respect to increasing the diversity of news sources. This seems to apply particularly to local and regional news media, which have relatively low, indeed 'shrinking', levels of journalistic and related financial resources in real terms, even if they are usually now owned by large and profitable corporations (Wahl-Jorgensen, 2007; O'Neill and O'Connor, 2007).

Speed up but quality down? Time factors and new news nets

Several recent studies indicate that the shift towards multi-platform newsmaking and the introduction of more complex content management systems are perceived by journalists as meaning ever shorter time cycles for handling news stories alongside significant increases in workloads. These shifts are often combined with a lack of appropriate back-up resources or training to manage the transition successfully (e.g. Nygren, 2007; Ugille and Paulussen, 2007).

For example, Nygren's study (2007: 3) suggests that journalists are 'hardworking people' as half of them work overtime at least one day each week and many work overtime 2–3 days per week'. This study also reports that journalists in the regional media produce 2–3 articles/items per day, 'but the most productive are journalists working for online media producing 5–10 items a day' (Nygren, 2007: 3). It suggests that the adoption of the Internet and digital production in newsmaking has made 'processes faster for all journalists' whilst the gains from technical development 'are used mostly to increase produced quantity, and not to increase quality' or develop new forms of expression (Nygren, 2007: 3).

Klinenberg (2005a) notes how digital technologies are enabling major changes in traditional news cycles and journalistic deadlines. The 'time cycle for news-making in the age of digital production is radically different,' as it has 'an erratic and unending pattern' that may be characterised as 'a news cyclone' (Klinenberg, 2005a: 54). The growth of 24-hour television news and the rapid emergence of instant Internet news sites 'have eliminated the temporal borders in the news day', creating an informational environment in which there is always breaking news to produce, consume, and react against (Klinenberg, 2005a: 54). Not only do journalists have to be reskilled to produce for several media at once; they are also facing time compression in which to do their work (Klinenberg, 2005a: 54).

Such integrated or coordinated newsmaking activities 'keep labour costs down and increase the output and efficiency of the production process' (Klinenberg, 2005a: 54) but they can push journalists to use the most easily available sources or even to 'pulling information off the Internet' (Klinenberg, 2005a: 55–56; see also Nygren, 2007).

'News values' and boundary issues

Business and economic influences related to profit-seeking, advertising revenue-seeking or other financial motives may be long-established pressures. But, for many practitioners and researchers, the balance between journalistic and financial motives has changed significantly in recent times, making the news media more like any other industry (Preston, 2001; Nygren, 2007). Recent empirical surveys of journalists indicate a strong perception that 'financial forces are getting stronger' and, as journalistic forces or factors shaping news media become relatively weaker, 'new media are developed from financial perspectives trying to catch new target audiences for advertisers' (Nygren, 2007: 8).

Some of these recent studies suggest trends towards ever closer integration of editorial and business aspects of media industry routines and norms which, in turn, pose significant implications for the professional values and standards defining or framing news culture. Corporate managers and advertisers are becoming more active participants in shaping editorial decision making so that professional discourses, norms and practices are increasingly permeated with managerial criteria and financial considerations. Such trends imply that commercial and other powerful interests are likely to structure the form and content of news to an ever greater extent (Klinenberg, 2005a; Klinenberg and Fayer, 2005).

The International Federation of Journalists (IFJ) has expressed concern about the consequences for editorial standards arising from unfolding trends such as the growing 'insecurity in employment' for journalists, 'changes in media concentration', pressure from external forces, as well as the growing role of industrial norms and discourses focused on commercial and business criteria, including a growing emphasis on the importance of advertising and sponsorship (IFJ and ILO, 2006: vi). The IFJ is concerned that these trends may be 'contributing to a decline in critical and investigative reporting', or 'leading to a creeping culture of self-censorship in the news media' or otherwise 'impacting on editorial decisions' (IFJ and ILO, 2006: vi). The IFJ warns that current industrial trends and norms may affect professional standards, and that they 'appear to be having a negative impact on the quality of editorial content' and 'may be jeopardizing the media's role as a watchdog for society' (IFJ and ILO, 2006: vi).

News formats and templates: digital media logics?

In certain respects, all kinds of journalism and media cultures must be based on some sort of format in order to operate effectively as public communication, especially when it comes to the organised production of news. In essence, formats such as the inverted pyramid have made it easier for both journalist and the audience to produce and consume news, not least in terms of material constraints such as time. Thus, notions such as 'templates' or 'story formats' are not new; 'in fact much of the professional values and skills have been and are materialized in such routines' (Ruusunoksa and Kunelius, 2007: 14).

In the contemporary setting, digital devices and systems afford both journalists and the wider public new creative possibilities for news story telling. However, some researchers are concerned that these new developments may prompt or lead to 'a greater need for formats in the daily production' in professional newsroom settings (Nygren, 2007: 4). New content management systems are being designed to provide more extensive or standard layouts which dictate that reporters write directly to the pages without sub-editing. This tends to make newspaper pages 'look the same every day' and in broadcast news 'the format leaves very little room for surprise' whilst online news seems to be characterised by 'the most well defined formats' (ibid.). At the same time, the same researchers observe that digital tools offer novel opportunities 'to create new formats and news types of content', for example 'photo galleries' and 'chat-sessions' (ibid.).

Once again, the question arises as to the gap between the potential of new digital tools and the actual practices of their appropriation in industry routines and managerial or newsroom strategies. A key question is whether or how new creative opportunities are being mobilised when the news organisations appropriate new ICTs in line with their institutional and managerial change projects. Do the new techno-managerial innovations and 'change projects' merely aim for integration or 'streamlined production' or can their practical implementation serve to advance the goals and values of good journalism? Ruusunoksa and Kunelius (2007) examine the implications of unfolding institutional innovations centred around streamlined news production, increasingly specific format and layout templates and more centralised planning in news organisations. They suggest that the overall outcomes of such shifts and trends are not yet clear but comprise pressing subjects for further research. Although driven by managerial logics of efficiency, these institutional innovations also seem to lie 'in an interesting tension' with the reality of reporters' practices, journalistic values and 'other ideals of the dominant ideology' of professional journalism (Ruusunoksa and Kunelius, 2007: 14).

Primary research findings: new news routines

Almost all of our interviewees perceived that the Internet and related technological changes were having a profound impact on the way journalists worked, and to a lesser extent, on journalistic values and culture. For the most part, the changes were regarded as positive, but many of those interviewed pointed to areas which had changed for the worse. The one aspect which was almost universally emphasised by our interviewees concerned the extent to which technology changes had contributed to a marked quickening in the pace of news gathering and dissemination, with some suggesting this had changed almost beyond recognition in a relatively short period.

In sum, we find that the interviewees from all countries indicated a strong belief that digital technologies were bringing about significant shifts in newsmaking practices and routines but had lesser implications for the values of journalism. As one French interviewee put it, 'values do not depend on technology', and that while technical innovations may impact on journalistic practices they should not affect journalistic values (Guyot *et al.*, 2006: 29).

Some interviewees, however, indicated the view that the Internet was having negative implications for the quality of journalism. The majority of our interviewees, tend to define the Internet as a mixed blessing. It was welcomed for providing ultra-quick information, but these benefits were offset by the fact that such information was often unreliable or of dubious quality. This mixed blessing viewpoint was expressed by some of the Dutch interviewees who observed that, whilst the Internet was very useful for accessing and researching official documents and related information, for other purposes it was to be regarded as a less reliable source and a less scrupulous platform or channel (ter Wal, 2006a).

This was echoed by journalists throughout the countries surveyed. The Internet is widely perceived as something of a 'poisoned chalice' not only in terms of the veracity of the information which it provides. Interviewees also identified the downside as manifest in the consequences of the Internet and email communication on journalists' working practices generally. As one journalist from a middle-market British newspaper noted,

> I think there is less going out and about. Everything's on email, on the telephone, and so much research is done on the Internet. There's much less leg work. This has also had an effect on the whole news agenda.
>
> (Preston, 2006a: 43)

This same British journalist argued that newsmaking routines had also become more reliant on information from news agencies and related services, leading to a more homogenised news agenda: 'In the old days you'd go out on the story and get a completely different angle from somebody else'.

This view was echoed by the political editor of the British tabloid, the *Sun*, who observed, 'I think they have handcuffed us to our desks'. However, this same informant did note how communication between journalists and their sources had become so much more immediate through the use of mobile phones and Blackberries than ever before. He also pointed to a recent vote in Parliament, when he had been sent the result by text message before it had been announced in the House of Commons (Preston, 2006a).

However, this state of affairs is capable of creating an increasingly elitist voice in journalism. As one Spanish journalist observed of life in the new computerised work environment: 'In the old times, people would be in bars, in cafeterias, in the streets ... [Now] we do not sound out the streets. We don't know what the citizen thinks. We live in capsules' (Guyot *et al.*, 2006, 40).

But if some print journalists feel as though technology has made them more detached and office-bound, some broadcast journalists argued that technological innovations had opened up the frontiers of reportage, allowing for greater coverage of international events. For such broadcasters, the main benefits include increased speed and accessiblilty as it was now much easier to get to foreign stories, with fewer staff required. One British television editor argued that it was now possible, for instance, to send a team of two out to cover a story in a remote location such as China, whereas in the past perhaps a team of twenty would have been necessary. It was also easier to put the story out using visual editing and visual production processes instead of tape and traditional craft editing, as well as the greater use of live feeds. As this interviewee put it: 'There's nowhere we can't get a live picture out of' (Preston, 2006a: 47).

If technological innovations were generally perceived in positive light by such television journalists, they also pointed to some down sides. One perceived outcome is that many broadcast journalists found themselves acting as 'one-man-bands' to use one Spanish interviewee's description. They now have to report and produce the packages themselves, a fact which put even more pressure on people who are already working to tight schedules (Guyot *et al.*, 2006). As was noted in the Dutch interviews: technology 'requires multiple skills of journalists who have to be able to do more than one thing, such as cutting the materials and maintaining an archive oneself'. This also affects the quality: 'you cannot do everything well, so there is less time to specialise and go in-depth' (ter Wal, 2006a). In sum, interviewees from most countries expressed concerns that the speed with which news can now be diseminated left less time for contemplation or analysis and more room for mistakes (e.g. Kovács *et al.*, 2005).

Moreover, as a British TV journalist put it: 'the speed with which you can get the stories back sometimes poses ethical questions [such as] what effect will this have on the ground', especially in cases such as the coverage of live sieges (Preston, 2006a: 42). Another ethical problem frequently associated with new technology concerns the huge amount of material now available through the use of digital photography and mobile phones and other devices owned by members of the public. This point was emphasised especially by two of the British broadcasters who noted the enormous volume of such footage which they had received from members of the public following the terrorist bombs on London's public transport system in July 2005. These developments posed new problems of ensuring the veracity of such footage, as well as issues concerning the ownership of the images (ibid.).

From watchdogs to mouse minders?

The research examined above indicates that industry routines and newsmaking practices and norms have all been undergoing significant, multi-dimensional innovation and changes in recent years. We can also observe that the features and sources of such innovations are not merely technological, but also economic, managerial and institutional in character.

The evidence points to multiple shifts and changes in most if not all the key dimensions of newsmaking routines identified in the earlier research literature, from resources to sourcing of news information, as well as contacts and relations with sources, time-related factors and relations with other media. The research also suggests changes in the internal division of labour within newsmaking industries and shifts in the relations between news professionals and other functions, as well as a greater prevalence of temporary or part-time employment contracts. The evidence from recent studies suggests that journalists are now responsible for more and more aspects of the overall news production process than ever before – at least concerning the range of newsmaking activities located within news organisations. There is a strong sense of increasing speed-up in the processing of news related information and in working practices, with less time available for checking and editing news stories originating with sources. Journalists appear to be much more office-bound as working practices become more screen-based and reliant on electronic flows of source information. Do such developments raise the spectre of the journalists' role shifting, as one informant put it, from that of 'watchdog' on behalf of the public to 'mere mouse minder' (Preston, 2006a) ?

Whether or not the multiple changes and institutional innovations considered in this chapter amount to a veritable 'new paradigm' in newsmaking routines, practices and norms remains an open question at this point. But it seems clear that the multiple shifts and changes in media 'routines' – the patterned practices and norms that frame the day-to-day performance of newsmaking *industry* – pose significant challenges for modern journalism's professional values, norms and codes of ethics as discussed in the previous chapter. In the next chapter, we move on to consider how these occupational norms and values relate to influences embedded in specific media organisations.

Chapter 5

From news nets to house rules

Organisational contexts

Paschal Preston and Monika Metykova

> Context is often by far the most important thing about news. ... The most powerful context is often that provided by the news organization for which the journalist works; in this sense, context is the network of assumptions, political beliefs, and moral position which the organization holds.
>
> (John Lloyd, 2004: 81)

House rules OK? Organisational factors

'The most powerful context ... the news organisation'

The quotation above, from a senior member of the *Financial Times* editorial staff, provides a rare practitioner's conceptualisation of the 'media organisation' as the crucial context in the making and framing of news[1] (Lloyd, 2004). Lloyd declares that the context is often 'by far the most important thing about news' as it 'will usually determine how the bare facts are given' (ibid.: 80–81). Although the news organisation for which the journalist works comprises the 'most powerful context', this factor 'is surprisingly often neglected' (ibid.: 81). As Lloyd indicates, once journalists have internalised the news organisation's 'line' or 'attitude', it tends to be reproduced continuously or 'almost unconsciously' (ibid.: 81) – an argument that resonates with the findings of several seminal studies on news influences as we will see below.

This chapter examines the research literature on news organisations as influences on journalism practices and news cultures. It also considers more recent work addressing technological and managerial innovations in news organisations. This chapter also briefly considers findings from our primary research concerning the influence of ownership structures and market forces.

Social control in the newsroom: informal 'house rules'

In a seminal and much-cited study of organisational influences, Warren Breed (1955) examined policy maintenance and social control in news organisations and how young journalists are socialised into the norms of their roles and tasks. Breed's research mainly drew on in-depth interviews with 120 journalists work- ing mostly in the northeastern region of the USA, as well as some other data. This classic study provides important insights on how the organisation's policy tends to be maintained and followed by news staff despite three empirical con- ditions: (i) policy sometimes contravenes journalistic norms; (ii) staffers often personally disagree with it; and (iii) owners and executives cannot legitimately command that policy be followed (Breed, 1955: 328, 335).

Breed (ibid.: 328) argues that 'every newspaper has policy, admitted or not' even if journalists often do not recognise the fact. In the newspaper organisations studied by Breed, when young reporters start work, they are 'not told what policy is', nor are they ever told. Several of the newspapers in his study had training programmes or 'style books' dealing with writing or literary style, but none provided training dealing with the organisation's policy. Yet Breed found that, on being asked, 'all but the newest staffers know what the policy is' with some declaring that they learn it 'by osmosis' (ibid.: 328, 335). In sociological terms, the new recruit becomes socialised, 'discovers and internalises the rights and obligations of his status and its norms and values', and learns to anticipate what is expected 'so as to win rewards and avoid punishments' (ibid.: 328).

As regards mechanisms producing policy maintenance and staff conformity in the news organisation setting, Breed identifies several key factors that appear to operate as the major variables. Of these key variables, Breed suggests that 'obligation and esteem for superiors', was not only very important, but also 'the most fluctuating variable' from newspaper to newspaper. Breed's study found that although the publisher's policy, in a given subject area, 'is usually followed' once it is established, this may not always be the case (ibid.: 335). In order to show that organisational control and policy are 'not iron-clad', this study also identified five conditions whereby 'staffers may by-pass policy' (ibid.: 335).

As regards the wider implications of his study, Breed argued that 'the cultural patterns of the newsroom' and its organisational setting produce results that are 'insufficient for wider democratic needs'. Breed suggests that any important change towards 'a more free and responsible press' must arise from pressures focused on the publishers and executives of media organisations who command 'the policy making and coordinating role' (ibid.: 335).

Interplays between organisational and institutional factors

In modern capitalist societies the means of communication, like most other productive resources, tend to be owned, controlled, allocated or managed by specific organisations in particular ways, even if this may vary somewhat according to sector or type of product. In the case of the news media sector, the majority of newsworkers (or 'human resources', in management speak) are employed in particular media organisations and the latter also own and control significant portions of the material resources required for news production and distribution. If professional journalists have privileged access to the means of public communication, this is generally because they are employed by (or have some other contractual relations with) particular media organisations.

Many studies of media organisations suggest that their overall goals and missions comprise key influences on news production, especially the kinds of high-level policies favoured by the owners and top executives (e.g. Breed, 1955; Sigelman, 1973; McManus, 1995). Some early studies of newsrooms suggested that newsworkers 'modified their own personal values in accordance with the requisites of the organization' (Epstein, 1973: xiv; cited in Schudson, 2000: 186). Such work was criticised by others for underestimating the counterbalancing role of professional norms (Schudson, 2000). Here, we will explore some of the ways in which the media organisation context engages with such professional values and the extent to which it comprises a powerful source of influence on news-making practices, as Breed (1955), Lloyd (2004) and others suggest.

Commercial, PSB and other media organisations

The dominant type of media organisation and alternatives

When it comes to different types of media organisation, the most basic conceptual distinction is that between 'public' (state-owned or state-funded) media on the one hand, and the private sector (commercial or market-based) on the other. Some claim, however, that although this fundamental distinction is 'vital', it may mask important differences within each category because it 'gives no purchase whatever' when it comes to assessing or understanding important variations in the types of media organisations and their roles (Schudson, 2000: 182). When we examine media systems beyond the dominant US- and European-centred horizons framing the official canon in this field, we also find many other 'hybrid' forms of organisational structures. Zhao provides several interesting examples in an analysis of the mixing of commercial and state-controlled media in contemporary China (Hackett and Zhao, 1998).

That said, however, in the USA and Europe, as in other advanced capitalist economies, the most significant organisations playing the role of producing news and other 'public communication' services are private sector organisations. The majority of these are straightforward commercial, profit-orientated organisations in terms of their overall corporate 'mission' or strategic goals. This majority of media organisations also derive almost all their income (revenues) from two sources: a large number of highly dispersed, fragmented and disorganised viewers and readers (or 'audience') and a much smaller number of relatively large or 'lumpy' customers in the shape of major advertisers. Furthermore, the very term 'news organisation' itself may be somewhat misleading today since much news is now produced by sub-units of a large media corporation which are not independent entities generating their own income, but accountable to larger parent bodies often engaged in many industrial activities.

Profit-orientated, private sector media organisations

A large and growing proportion of the media of public communication in Europe is owned, controlled and administered as profit-orientated, private sector, commercial enterprises. This has long been the case with the news media in the USA, where the local political culture has a strong anti-statist orientation and private ownership of media tends to be taken as a universal or naturalised norm – and where public service (broadcasting) media have played a relatively marginal role. Indeed, the majority of studies of newsmaking reported in the international literature have been focused on profit-seeking, private sector media.

But if profit-seeking represents the primary goal of most commercial private sector media, this is rarely expressed as the sole or key mission of news organisations. Rather, like other commercial enterprises, they also tend to possess (and operate through) certain organisational beliefs or 'myths', involving efforts to 'state in language of uplift and idealism, what is distinctive about the aims and methods of the enterprise' in question (Selznick, 1957: 151; cited in Sigelman, 1973: 133). News media organisations and their related professions tend to define their role in terms of 'dramatically stated symbols of their mission in society' (Sigelman, 1973: 133). For example, in terms of the 'reigning institutional myths' in US journalism two key aspects have been noted in this regard: the primary one of the news organisation's (and/or journalism's) public service function and 'the operational one of disinterested objectivity' (ibid.: 133–34).

In line with such tendencies, we observe that private sector media enterprises are frequently assumed to comprise the optimal or sole basis for a realm of maximum or absolute 'freedom' of expression. In contrast, publicly funded media organisations (such as PSB) are seen to be subject to constraints imposed by political interests or various other kinds of influences or restrictions. The default assumption (or assertion) in contemporary neo-liberal discourse is that market-based, commercial media organisations are autonomous of any special interests or influences and so afford the sole or optimal platform for maximum freedom of expression (Preston and Grisold, 1996; Preston, 2001; Staats, 2005). But it was not always so. Some of the earliest analysts of the expanding social role and industrial scope of the newspaper press in the nineteenth century were critical of both economic as well as political pressures on news media and political communication processes (Speed, 1893: cited in Sumpter, 2001; Wilcox, 1900).

Habermas's influential study provides a critical view of the role of profit-orientated, commercial media organisations and the increased reliance on advertising revenues in terms of the rise and transformation of the public sphere (Habermas, 1989). In this light, the concepts of media *freedom* or independence, as well as the *watchdog* or *fourth estate* role of the media with respect to the public sphere, the 'public' and its interests, have all been 'transformed', losing much of the radical democratic thrust and challenge to entrenched powers they posed in the early modern period (ibid.; see also Preston, 2001; Splichal, 2002).

One of the best known critiques of commercial news media in the USA context is Herman and Chomsky's (1988) *Manufacturing Consent*. These authors suggest that the media play a propagandistic role which serves to support the special interests of the elites who dominate the state and private industry. In turn their model has been criticised for relying on 'flat-footed functionalism' by Michael Schudson (2000: 180) and by many other US-based scholars. Yet, Schudson acknowledges that as most major media organisations are now owned by a few large corporations or else by the state, 'it would be a shock' to find them expressing radical ideas or thought. In this light, Schudson argues that the greatest research challenge is to examine and specify which 'structural or cultural features of the media' can serve to keep 'news porous, open to dissident voices' and genuine debate (ibid.).

Many other studies have examined how commercial news and other media tend to be increasingly concentrated in terms of ownership and control arising from powerful economic incentives (e.g. Bagdikian, 2000). The effects of such tendencies towards media monopoly or oligopoly on the diversity of news content have been much debated (e.g. Preston and Grisold, 1996; Schudson, 2000), as has the growing dependence on advertising revenue (McManus, 1995; McQuail, 2005; Staats, 2005; Picard, 2007).

In a number of works, McManus has applied economic concepts to examine how various market-based factors (related to advertisers, consumers, investors and news sources) may play roles in shaping news production in commercial organisations (McManus, 1995; 1997). His analysis suggests that newsmaking dominated by private sector interests 'fails to meet the minimum conditions' that economists have established as necessary for markets to benefit society (McManus, 1995: 301). This study challenges the conventional wisdom of the media industry and of neo-liberal discourse 'that the news content that best serves the market also serves the public best' (ibid.: 332). McManus argues that 'the autonomy of journalists is sharply bounded by more powerful actors within and without the newsroom' (ibid.).

PSB: public service broadcasting organisations in Europe

In many European countries, broadcasting services were originally established and institutionalised in the form of public service broadcasting (PSB) institutions for most of the twentieth century. This is one of the features of the European media landscape which distinguishes it from the US case. In general, PSB institutions, such as the BBC in Britain, have been constituted as public sector bodies with governance structures deemed to isolate them from direct interference from government or special political interests. However, the precise funding arrangements, modes of governance and mechanisms to insulate these PSB institutions from potential influence from state actors tend to vary by country (for a useful summary, see Garnham, 1990; McQuail, 2000; 2005).

Some researchers have defined PSB as providing an important platform for the maintenance or renewal of the public sphere ideal in late modern societies, especially given the increasingly commercial goals and orientations of other media (e.g. Garnham, 1990; 2000; Preston, 2001). Unlike commercially orientated and privately owned media, these PSB institutions were established with a very specific mission or high-level policy. This included obligations to 'educate, inform and entertain' the audience (as the first director-general of the BBC put it), and to treat listeners and viewers in terms of their identities as citizens as well as consumers, even if the range of views has tended to be restricted to establishment interests (Schlesinger, 1978). For others, the balance of evidence seems to suggest that the conservative effects of governance factors do not prevent fundamental criticism being reported or carried by PSB organisations (McQuail, 2000: 254–55). Clearly, questions of whether and how far the PSB institutions have performed in line with their declared goals and ideals, or under what conditions, or with what effects, are matters of dispute and subjects for empirical inquiry (Barnett and Curry, 1994; O'Malley, 1994; Leys, 2001; Curran and Seaton, 2003).

We also observe that PSB institutions have been subject to increasing pressures in more recent times in most of the older EU member states. This arises in large part from neo-liberal policy regimes favouring privately owned, commercial channels. Born (2003) examines the rise of numerous accountability and audit processes the BBC faced during the 1990s. Denis McQuail (2003) explores how public service broadcasting has become ever more subject to scrutiny in Europe in recent times just as its role has declined in relative terms within the overall supply of television broadcasting. Nevertheless, PSB remains an important part of the media landscape in much of Europe. Indeed, PSB has formed an important, if contested, part of the new media systems in many Central and East European countries since the fall of the Berlin Wall (Jakubowicz, 2004; Splichal, 1999, 2006).

The crisis experienced by the BBC in reporting controversial aspects of Prime Minister Blair's justifications for the Iraq War in 2003–4 served to underline just how sensitive relations between PSB organisations and government can be in times of crisis (McQuail, 2005). Yet, despite major upheavals enforced on the leadership and policy of the BBC following that controversy – and the subsequent report of the government-appointed Hutton Inquiry – the public service broadcaster went on to conduct 'a good war' in terms of its news coverage and balance. Indeed, by the usual professional standards, the BBC performed very well at least relative to establishment media in the USA, the leader of the so-called 'coalition of the willing' in that war. The BBC's coverage and reporting of the invasion and subsequent wars in Iraq seems to have been way superior to the fare offered by print and broadcast media in the USA. Indeed many US citizens, dissatisfied with the poor quality coverage offered by their local media, turned to the online news services of the BBC, and that of the *Guardian* newspaper, as alternative sources of news, especially for international affairs. It is interesting to observe that the online version of BBC News has been attracting more US-based users than the websites of US national domestic brands such as *USA Today*, Fox News and the *Wall Street Journal* in recent years (Thurman, 2007). Coverage of international news stories, including the ongoing war in Iraq, appears to be a significant factor in the relatively high levels of US-based audiences accessing the online news services of the BBC and those of newspapers such as the *Guardian* (ibid.).

Furthermore, despite the negative consequences of the government-appointed Hutton Inquiry for the broadcaster, the BBC seems to have gained public trust relative to the government. A survey conducted in 2004 indicated that 'the public were far more likely to trust the BBC to tell the truth (44 per cent) than the government (7 per cent)' even if nearly 30 per cent said they would trust neither (Gunter, 2005).

Private sector media: structures, logics, impacts

'Informal socialisation' and 'loose' control structures

Ever since Breed's seminal study, much subsequent research confirms that organisational influences tend to operate more through the informal group processes than they do through explicit or formal policies, house rulebooks or codes. Indeed, such studies suggest that the dynamics of small groups within an organisation serve to 'bring common beliefs and motivations into working realities'; in this way, young journalists 'learn how news "is supposed to go" in order to seem appropriate' with respect to the news organisation's particular set of goals or values (Berkowitz and Limor, 2003: 784).

Many news organisations provide little by way of formal training or socialisation of new staff members, nor indeed for mid-career retraining. Yet studies highlight the important role of informal socialisation (or training) processes within media organisations. Young reporters and journalists learn not merely the technical or craft skills of the profession from more senior or experienced staff 'on the job' as it were, they also become acquainted with, and internalise other tacit forms of knowledge, not least the particular news values and orientations prevailing in the employing organisation. Berkowitz and Limor (ibid.) argue that news managers tend to 'enforce behavioral ideals unofficially' because official policy in this direction 'would conflict explicitly with foundational beliefs of the profession'. News managers are likely to equate the success of the news organisation with the success of their own careers and thus 'tend to support the goals of non-news managers in the organization' (ibid.: 784).

Operations: exercise of (internal) control and power

News media organisations can be seen as 'crucial containers' shaping the news because they afford their employees (or contracted or freelance journalists) privileged access to the means of public communication whilst also controlling the array of material resources and setting the broad policy agendas which frame the newsmaking process. Like other capitalist enterprises, they seek to achieve their overall mission or goals through a variety of control mechanisms (symbolic and material incentives, formal and informal policies) to ensure that employees are 'singing from the same hymn sheet'.

The research on organisational control suggests that the precise configuration of managerial strategies for control over employees will vary according to the kinds of good or services produced as well as the particular categories of workers involved (e.g. Braverman, 1974). Unlike the various forms of 'direct control' adopted by management in the case of mass production and blue-collar work, the rather different managerial control strategy of 'responsible autonomy' tends to prevail in the case of professional or knowledge-intensive occupations (Friedman, 1977; Burawoy, 1985). Indeed, this latter managerial control strategy of 'responsible autonomy' seems to resonate closely with the important role of informal socialisation, small team or peer pressures, 'observability' (Sigelman, 1973: 143) and related control models reported in studies of news organisations. The 'responsible autonomy' model can also accommodate the occupational taboo surrounding explicit or overt managerial interference in the professional tasks of the journalist or editor (Breed, 1955; Sigelman, 1973; Im, 1997).

Some of the seminal studies of the organisational influences on newsmaking provide indications of how, in practice, the relative or 'responsible' autonomy of journalists can be accommodated within the imperatives of hierarchical organisational control and a coherent overall mission. Sigelman (1973: 144) explored how the measure of autonomy enjoyed by journalists in reporting local politics may be reconciled with 'the dramatic differences' between the political coverage of the two newspapers. This study examined the recruitment and socialisation of journalists as well as the control structures, defining the latter as 'a tension-avoiding process', one that 'ensures favourable performance without violating institutional mythology' (ibid.: 147). Sigelman found that the political news coverage and differing biases in the case study newspapers result from 'a particular matrix of organisational processes'; these processes 'commence in the recruitment of the reporter', carry on through his or her socialisation and 'culminate' in specific kinds of 'working arrangements' (ibid.: 149). Sigelman (1973) identified a number of working arrangements and practices in news organisations which operate as powerful influences on what journalist tells what news story and how it is told. Sigelman observed that many significant decisions about a news story can be made by others in the news organisation even before the reporter begins his or her coverage. The reporter's 'autonomy may realistically consist of little more than freedom to maneuver within the constraining bounds' of the given framework or assignment (ibid.: 147). Sigelman observed that reporters tend to perceive their roles in narrow technical terms ('more a feat of engineering than of architecture') so that they do not feel that their professional autonomy is jeopardised (ibid.: 147). News organisations' control strategies towards journalists tend to operate on the 'principle of minimum intervention' based on the reliance of informal and indirect mechanisms whilst minimising direct meddling in daily operations (ibid.: 148).

Thus, in contrast to Speed's study, Sigelman concludes that the relations between journalists and their news organisation may be more accurately typified in terms of harmony rather than conflict (ibid.: 148). Sigelman also observed that journalists in the newspapers he studied were 'fiercely loyal to their employers' and concludes that where such sentiments prevail 'the incidence of policy conflict is bound to be low' (ibid.: 144).

Incentives and controls: material and normative

Several reviews of the research literature on newsmaking complain that much attention has been paid to reporter–source relations whilst there is a relative lack of empirically rich studies of reporters' relations with editors and other senior management – especially as these comprise further 'crucial aspects of the social organization of newswork' (Schudson, 2000: 185). In part such silences in the research arise because the 'looseness' (Sigelman, 1973) or the 'informal' character of the control and power relations (Breed, 1955) in news organisations do not readily lend themselves to the usual empirical research methods. Here we must be mindful that, as Max Weber once observed, the exercise of power is often most potent precisely when its exercise is not manifest or visible.

Some studies provide indicative or 'suggestive' hints as to the myriad ways in which organisational incentives and control systems may operate as powerful influences, for example by encouraging reporters to 'engage in self-censorship when they have an eye fixed on pleasing an editor' or other senior staff (Schudson, 2000: 185). Management in news media, as in other enterprises, tends to rely on a mix of material and normative incentives to ensure that employees' working practices broadly conform to the organisation's strategic goals and mission (Breed, 1955; Sigelman, 1973). As Sigelman observed of reporters in his case study, the 'most obvious incentives ... are monetary and normative' (1973: 144). In news organisations, the usual material incentives of salary and promotion to posts with superior pay and status are complemented by other incentives related to the allocation of high-status newsbeats or specialist correspondent roles.

The role of material incentives in news media seems to differ from other sectors or knowledge-intensive professional occupations where organisational control strategies centred on 'responsible autonomy' also prevail (Friedman, 1977; Im, 1997). In the case of many high-tech occupations, such as software designers or developers, the employer organisations have long complained of a certain 'skill shortage' and a persistent deficit in the number of suitably qualified staff. The opposite is the case with journalism and newsmaking occupations where the job market is characterised by a long-standing oversupply of potential recruits to the ranks. Pierre Bourdieu and others have emphasised this as an important feature in understanding the play of material and normative factors in maintaining managerial control in the case of journalism (see Benson and Neveu, 2005: 42–45, 65–67,148–49). Several other recent studies have underlined the 'precarious' features of the working conditions of newsworkers, especially in the case of young recruits to the profession, whether working in the established or new media sectors (e.g. Bodnar, 2006; IFJ and ILO, 2006).

Organisational hierarchies and newsworkers' autonomy

Studies of news organisations also draw attention to the importance of hierarchies of status, power and position amongst different categories of newsworkers, as these lead to variations in the degrees of professional autonomy or discretion enjoyed in newsroom working practices. At the most obvious level, editors and other senior journalistic staff tend to possess much more discretionary power, as well as material rewards, relative to the majority of rank and file journalists. Foreign correspondents and senior staff assigned to the coverage of political affairs tend to spend much of their time outside the newsroom and so are seen to possess a relatively high degree of individual discretion in pursuit of their daily newsmaking practices. Another important distinction here comprises that between 'star reporters' and their rank and file colleagues (Breed, 1955; Sigelman, 1973). As Sigelman put it, 'without question', the star reporter 'enjoys more functional autonomy than any other reporter' (1973: 142). The relatively privileged position of the 'star reporter', especially one 'long on experience and expertise' is related to the 'possession of several resources' such as access to sources, accumulated knowledge (relevant experience and expertise), and 'irreplaceability' (ibid.: 142). Some studies also suggest that all reporters tend to be highly conscious of how the possession or lack of star status is closely linked to different degrees of professional autonomy and power vis-à-vis the organisation's policy or management preferences (e.g. see Sigelman, 1973: 142).

Role conflicts and tensions in media organisations

We can observe two contrasting sets of research traditions, orientations and findings in the literature on the forms and extent of conflicts within news organisations. On the one hand those such as Sigelman (1973: 146) reject the view that news organisations are 'antagonistic and inherently conflict ridden' and underline the normative and material mechanisms which tend towards the minimisation of conflicts between professional and organisational goals; similarly, Gans (1979) tended to find little conflict within newsrooms. There is another contrasting tradition, dating from Breed (1955) and Stark (1962), which tends to highlight the antagonistic and conflict-ridden characteristics of relations and processes in news organisations. In like vein, Bantz proposed that conflict be viewed as 'a crafted cultural norm' within news organisations, identifying five aspects of the organisational culture in newswork, which tend to 'normalize' the occurrence of conflict, particularly in television news (Bantz, 1985, 225–26). The incompatibility of factors such as professional norms and business norms result in conflict becoming 'ordinary, routine, perhaps even valuable' (ibid.: 225).

Internet, knowledge economy and organisational factors

Digital media: threat or boom for major media corporations?

One key issue in the recent research on techno-economic and organisational trends concerns the extent to which the established pattern (or matrix) of news media organisations as described earlier, is now vulnerable to the disruptive effects of radical new technologies such as the Internet. Much of the recent literature focused on the technical or techno-social characteristics of digital media tends to emphasise significant declines in the entry costs for would-be authors and publishers or start-up firms competing with existing media organisations. Such potential disruptive effects may be compounded by the evidence on declining public trust in the established media as well as falling audiences for certain segments. Indeed, many studies emphasise the potential of the Internet to enable radically new citizen-based information and communication services which are deemed to be undermining the traditional role and dominance of commercial media organisations or even professional journalism. But as noted in previous chapters, there is no consensus on the precise drift or key implications of the unfolding developments.

If in the first decade of the Internet, many 'mature media' became masters of the 'new media' content spaces (Preston, 2001), does the same hold in the era of Web 2.0, and expanding arrays of user-generated content services or alternative media? For example, many researchers now argue that the Internet combined with greater user access and digital literacy now offers scope for multiple new public spheres as manifest in the growth of blogging, alternative news services, citizen-based journalism, and user-generated content online (e.g. Splichal, 2002; Cammaerts and Van Audenhove, 2005; Allan, 2006; Robinson, 2006; Reese *et al.*, 2007: 238, 240).

For some, the most important conceptual boundary in the blogosphere is between citizen-based media and 'professional' media, suggesting that there is ample scope for new kinds of media organisations and services centred on citizens or audiences. Some emphasise that participants in citizen-based media do not require formal training or employment, or major investments, only 'a motivated individual or group willing to speak to a public' (Reese *et al.*, 2007: 239). Robinson (2006) proposes that the j-blog is 'the corporate answer to the internet, and to independent bloggers' and that it is forcing journalism to define a new identity (Robinson, 2006: 79).

Some empirical studies suggest that new organisational innovations alongside the further application of digital systems are eroding the monopoly or privileged access to the public sphere held by journalists since early modern times. Nygren suggests that the journalism profession 'is less unique than 10–15 years ago – a change that has been faster than the media realize' (Nygren, 2007: 8). In this view, the news media landscape is increasingly defined around niche or specialist cultures, genres and target groups whilst mass media aimed at large-scale national audiences decline. This implies 'a fragmented media world with smaller audiences and bigger differences between various media' leading to multiple kinds of journalism 'offering new professional roles' (ibid.: 8–9).

Integration, multiskilling, and convergence or 'shovelling'?

Even if investors and executives remain uncertain about the optimal business models for digital news media, there is now a much greater emphasis on the authoring and design of media content for multiple platforms and requisite new skill sets or competencies. Some British newspaper editors advance the view that the days when journalists worked with just a notebook and pencil are over and that they now have to be comfortable working in 'at least five media, keyboard, sound, stills, and moving pictures, podcasts and hyperlinks' (Williams and Franklin, 2007: 2). The survey of online journalists by Deuze and Dimoudi (2002) suggested that some 90 per cent of respondents agreed that developing additional technological skills was a necessary precondition for the online journalist.

As noted in Chapter 2, the full diffusion or appropriation of digital technologies can be expected to mean multiple changes in the managerial strategies and division of labour in news organisations. This includes the creation of new specialist roles and skill sets for journalists alongside the erosion of others (Nygren, 2007). For example, Ursell (2001) suggests that managerial strategies have appropriated new production technologies to reorganise the working arrangements and practices in broadcast news by 'creating a new species of editorial worker and server manager, an occupational hybrid of journalist and computer expert' (Ursell, 2001: 187).

The trend towards the integration of newsrooms has been a long-term feature of management-led strategies in large media organisations, but it has been intensified in recent years and centred round ideas such as 'multiskilling', flexibility and multi-platform or 'integrated' news production. This trend is linked to industrial practices and managerial or policy discourses surrounding the growth of online news services as well as the increasing diversity of distribution channels and platforms enabled by digital technologies.

In response to the management-led shifts towards newsroom integration, journalists are now expected to become 'more versatile' while their jobs become 'rationalised and re-designated' (Saltzis, 2007: 9). The increasing importance attached to 'multiskilling' in managerial discourse and organisational practices means that 'a journalist with interchangeable skills is more valuable than one without' (ibid.). However, it appears that the full-on technocratic vision of a seamlessly integrated multimedia newsroom has yet to be realised in practice anywhere as the degree and forms of newsroom integration are heavily dependent on 'financial, managerial and cultural' factors (ibid.). In general terms, it seems that the larger and better-resourced organisations are better able to derive benefits from moves towards closer newsroom integration – and to negotiate the considerable costs and managerial or socio-institutional obstacles involved in such moves (ibid.; Quinn, 2006; Erdal, 2007a; Ruusunoksa and Kunelius, 2007). But even amongst well resourced national newspapers in Britain with successful online sites, significant variations are found due to different organisational and managerial cultures, for example in terms of the forms and approaches to 'multi-skilling' or integrated newsrooms (Saltzis, 2007: 9–10).

The growing emphasis on 'multi-skilling' or 'flexibility' is closely linked to increasing workloads, throughput or productivity and ever decreasing news cycles, as noted in Chapter 4 (e.g. Klinenberg and Fayer, 2005; Erdal, 2007a). It is also associated with a 'culture of projects' or a continuous process of 'tackling change' as prominent managerial themes in designing and negotiating new working practices with editorial staff (Ruusunoksa and Kunelius, 2007: 12). Recent Finnish studies suggest that newspaper managements now seem to 'react to change pressures *by constant organisational reform projects* such as new layout development projects, structural changes in the newsroom, reorganisation of journalists' positions and the like (ibid.). One unsurprising consequence is a certain kind of 'project weariness' apparent among newspaper reporters as the numerous management-led reform projects tend to neglect those professional values and editorial goals of most concern to journalists – 'in an ironical vein, one respondent put it like this: "journalistic development soon needs a project oF its own"' (ibid.: 13).

Business and marketing versus journalistic values?

Various changes in organisational structures and strategies over the past twenty years appear to be narrowing the presumed separations between the business and editorial functions in commercial news media, and so eroding the autonomous space or potential for journalism and news cultures that are independent of economic influences. For example, Hallin (2000: 221) observes important shifts in the organisational structures and strategies of media in the USA since the 1980s whereby the prior (or 'modern') model of journalism is increasingly giving way to concepts such as 'total newspapering'. He cites the example of one prominent US newspaper chain – hailed as having been highly successful in terms of profit-making and other commercial criteria during the 1990s – where managerial strategy at one point promoted a campaign to 'get every Knight Ridder employee thinking like a marketer' (ibid.). News organisations are now utilising the Internet and other digital technologies to 'push the principles of targeted marketing to new levels' so that they can develop new tailored news services orientated towards niche audiences of interest to advertisers (Klinenberg and Fayer, 2005: 224). Although there are variations in the extent and intensity of such shifts across media organisations, the general trend points towards increasing tensions between 'the cultures of journalism and marketing', and this is manifest in a news agenda moving away 'from traditional public affairs and towards lifestyle features and "news you can use"' (Hallin, 2000: 221). We'll revisit these issues later in this chapter.

Social control in digital news nets/beats

Earlier, we've noted how Breed's seminal study emphasised the importance of informal channels and mechanisms for managerial control in newsmaking organisations, especially the role of peer groups and teams working within the newsroom setting. This insight resonates with the typical modes of managerial control, such as responsible autonomy, indicated by research on other professional or knowledge-intensive occupations and sectors (Im, 1997). The evidence from more recent studies suggests that informal modes of managerial control continue to be important, yet their precise forms are changing and they are being complemented by more formal, structured or explicit systems and normative controls compared to earlier decades (Im, 1997; Nygren, 2007).

Traditionally, editorial professionals tended to perceive their own work and roles as operating somewhat autonomously and separate from the managerial and business goals and functions (economic, marketing, advertising, etc. departments) of news organisations (as noted in institutional studies discussed in the previous chapter). However, many recent studies suggest that the traditional presumptions of distinct boundaries between the editorial and business functions of news media have been significantly eroded and are no longer tenable (e.g. Pavlik, 2000: 233; Klinenberg and Fayer, 2005: 229; IFJ and ILO, 2006: v–vi; Nygren, 2007: 6).

For example, Klinenberg and Fayer argue that the penetration of market principles and marketing projects into the editorial divisions of news organisations comprises 'one of the most dramatic changes in journalism' in recent times (2005: 229). They report that wider changes in the organisation and division of labour in news media are being accompanied by ever closer integration of editorial and business aspects of media industry routines and norms, posing significant implications for the (always delicate) balance between organisational goals and professional values in defining and framing news culture. In sum, these recent studies suggest that commercial and other economic considerations are becoming more powerful or explicit factors in shaping the norms and practices of news organisations. Compared to previous decades, working journalists are now socialised to be made more aware and mindful of the business aspects of the news organisation. Manifestations of this trend include managerial discourses emphasising commercial pressures, the importance of advertising interests and revenues, as well as marketing considerations in relation to newsmaking norms and practices (see also Hallin, 2000). This represents a significant shift in journalists' prior self-understandings, conceptualisations and ideals concerning the relative autonomy accorded to their professional roles, values and norms in shaping and making the news. These trends imply an erosion of the presumed boundaries and distance separating professional journalists from the business aspects and commercial functions of the news organisation (Klinenberg, 2005a; Klinenberg and Fayer, 2005; Nygren, 2007).

The shifting boundaries suggest a significant intrusion of norms and values related to economic or material (business, commercial and managerial) aspects of the news organisation into the professional space (of journalists' roles, values, norms) compared to earlier decades. This of itself seems to comprise a significant new feature of the informal processes of social and managerial control in news organisations. Its implications may be further amplified by the decreasing levels of job security and financial independence associated with other aspects of management strategies in news organisations in recent decades. As noted earlier, the International Federation of Journalists (IFJ) has expressed concern that as the media sector is becoming more commercialised, owners and executives are expanding the use of short-term or freelance contracts leading to growing 'insecurity in employment' for journalists (IFJ and ILO, 2006: vi). The IFJ is concerned that these trends, alongside greater dependency on advertising and sponsorship revenues, may be contributing to 'a decline in critical and investigative reporting' in the news media or 'a creeping culture of self-censorship' in editorial decisions (IFJ and ILO, 2006: vi).

The forms of social and managerial control are also changing due to techno-organisational innovations associated with more integrated or multi-platform production. These mean that 'multi-skilled workers are replacing well defined departments and specializations' and that journalists are expected to 'work more in teams than before' in order to handle more parts of the work process whilst also dealing with greater diversity of media formats (Nygren, 2007: 2–3). The work of journalists is also 'more concentrated to the newsroom, with less time "in the field" doing research' as there is a tendency to presume that the growing flows of information on the Net and in emails mean that journalists don't have to leave the newsroom as much as before (ibid.: 3). Within management discourses, the working culture in the newsroom is now often defined as heading towards a dominant mode of journalism that is 'more oriented to *product* and teamwork than individual producers and journalists' (Ruusunoksa and Kunelius, 2007: 13).

Recent studies indicate that *teamwork* comprises a major theme in the current wave of organisational innovations and change 'projects' aiming to reshape the working culture in newsrooms. The latter is sometimes defined as a specific case within wider change projects stressing integration or 'cooperation within the whole organization' (Ruusunoksa and Kunelius, 2007: 13). This teamworking theme is closely associated with the current managerial emphasis on concepts such as flexibility and multi-skilling reported in several studies examined earlier (e.g Klinenberg, 2005a). This organisational emphasis on teamwork is reflected in the recruitment of journalists whereby 'today we look for skills of cooperation … you have to accept that you are no longer the only person having a say on a story' (managing editor, cited in Ruusunoksa and Kunelius, 2007: 13).

These organisational innovation strategies are usually linked to new ICT-based content management systems but their implications are by no means confined to technical or practical changes in the news production process. Executives and news managers may define such changes in routines as necessary for handling the increasing flows of information alongside ever-shortening news cycles and the logics of multi-platform news production. Yet, such organisational innovations often involve new structures of control and modes of managerial discipline. For example, new managerial strategies for teamworking are often experienced as a diminution in professional autonomy or perceived 'sense of authority' by journalists compared to their prior capacities 'to choose news items, craft their perspectives and decide the story format' relatively free of managerial controls (Ruusunoksa and Kunelius, 2007: 13).

At the same time, we observe that the organisational change projects emphasising teamworking and greater emphasis on flexibility and interchangeable roles in newsrooms also tend to be in tension with other aspects of emerging new journalistic norms and practices. For example, the managerial discourse emphasising that journalists must be team players seems to contradict the growing demand that journalists must also be more readily able to play the role of public personality or celebrity on behalf of the organisation, whether in old media platforms or in new online blogging formats (Ruusunoksa and Kunelius, 2007: 13).

New hierarchies? Organisational and professional

Another theme in recent studies of news production concerns the potential development of significant new journalistic hierarchies related to product and process innovations in the news sector as well as the introduction of new production systems and other organisational or managerial innovations (e.g. Erdal, 2007a; Nygren, 2007; Ruusunoksa and Kunelius, 2007). Erdal (2007b) discusses emerging hierarchies associated with the expanding trends of news reproduction and republication. Others address the issues of hierarchy in relation to the growing role of integrated planning, the centralisation of editorial decisions, 'form-orientated planning', new formats or 'template journalism' within news organisations and their potential tensions with journalistic values and norms (e.g. Ruusunoksa and Kunelius, 2007: 14).

Recent studies suggest that journalism and news production is becoming a more complex or differentiated field than in previous decades thanks to the wider effects of the socio-technical and institutional innovations enabled by new ICTs (IFJ and ILO, 2006; Nygren, 2007). Growing differences in the status and role of journalists themselves have emerged as the new work force has been 'divided into a "core staff" who give the company its profile' and temporarily employed journalists, freelance or contracted staff as well as external workers related to production processes that may have been outsourced (Nygren, 2007: 7; see also IFJ and ILO, 2006). For example, surveys in

Sweden indicate that approximately 25 per cent of Swedish journalists 'work on temporary contracts doing much of the daily news' whilst at the same time a minority of 'journalist-stars' become high-profile personalities for their employing organisations and form an essential 'part of the companies' marketing' (Nygren, 2007: 7).

In addition, certain emerging shifts in the organisation and forms of journalistic work 'also make it more difficult to decide who is a journalist' as the boundaries between journalists and other professions, such as press officers, become even less clearly defined (Nygren, 2007: 7). Surveys of journalists indicate a strong perception that 'financial forces are getting stronger' as business criteria and economic considerations become more influential in all areas of media organisations. As professional values and journalistic factors shaping newsmaking become relatively weaker in the established media, emerging new media firms – often more strongly charged with financial perspectives – are now also competing for target audiences and for advertisers (ibid.: 8).

PSB news services and managerial innovations

In many European countries PSB organisations have faced a considerable array of financial and policy pressures in recent years linked to the broader shifts towards neo-liberal policy regimes and knowledge economy strategies (Preston, 2001). Indeed, as Sampson and Lugo observe, PSB has been the subject of discourses which often invoke *convergence* as a 'slippery term' to de-politicise the relevant policy debates and legitimate neo-liberal ideology and practices focused on media de-regulation, ownership concentration and private participation in the sector (Sampson and Lugo, 2003: 83).

Yet, PSB organisations have also been amongst the earliest and most successful 'mature' media organisations moving into online media domains in several EU countries, both in terms of audience or traffic metrics as well as investments in quality online news service offerings (Allan, 2006; Erdal, 2007a). For example, the BBC has one of the largest online news sites in the world and even small PSB organisations such as Norway's NRK has 'established itself as a major news source on the web' (Erdal, 2007a: 75). Over the past decade, many PSB operators have launched various integration projects in order to address the unfolding trends related to both 'convergence' of production and 'divergence' of media outlets and platforms (ibid.: 74–77). These projects have sought to reorganise news production activities in order to supply an expanding number and diversity of media formats and platforms for which PSB organisations now produce news (ibid.: 75).

According to the evidence presented in some recent studies, there seem to be many similarities in the forms and effects of techno-organisational change projects for news production undertaken in private sector media firms and PSB organisations (Quinn, 2006; Erdal, 2007a). Alongside trends in technical and managerial innovation, some recent research points to the increasing penetration of commercial media logics and news management practices in European PSB organisations (e.g. Nygren, 2007). Recent developments in one of the flagships of PSB 'best practices' in online news domains seem to signal a declining, if not marginal, role for 'public service' orientated organisational forms in the future online and broadcast news media landscapes of the knowledge-based economy in Europe.

In May 2006, the BBC (2006) framed its online activities as helping to 'build digital Britain', no doubt invoking such technocratic language as part of its efforts to alleviate the hostile pressures from the New Labour government which, if anything, have exceeded those of the Thatcherite era. In announcing the BBC's statements of programme policy, the director-general, Mark Thompson, declared that these efforts involved 'a new public purpose' (BBC, 2006). He argued that its current plans are designed to provide 'the best in information, education, entertainment and involvement', by introducing 'innovative services like the Creative Archive and pilots such as BBC iPlayer' service – implicitly adding a further dimension to the BBC's old mission to 'inform, educate and entertain' (ibid.).

Yet, once again we find that technocratic visions do not necessarily translate into the enhancement of newsmaking and journalistic standards. As noted earlier, the BBC's broadcast and online news services have been much accessed by audiences in the USA and elsewhere in recent years, especially with respect to coverage of Iraq and other foreign news. Data for the first nine months of 2007 confirm that the BBC's broadcast news services increased the numbers of domestic audiences, whilst its news website 'remains the UK's most popular online news site' attracting an average weekly reach of 13.8 million users globally (BBC, 2007a). Yet in the closing quarter of 2007, by way of response to the most recent spate of pressures from 'New Labour' policies, the BBC's decision makers announced a 'radical reform to deliver a more focused BBC' comprising a six-year plan, that in classic neo-liberal speak promises to 'deliver a smaller but fitter organisation' (BBC, 2007b). The plan involves downsizing, by shedding some 2,500 jobs by 2012 '*with the areas of News and factual production most affected*' (ibid.: present authors' emphasis).

We can only presume that Mr Thompson's scriptwriter was seeking to privilege the BBC's mission to 'entertain' its audiences (rather than 'inform' or 'educate' them) when he went on to claim that the proposed reform will mean a BBC 'more focused on quality and the content that really makes a difference to audiences' as well as one 'which is fully prepared for digital' (BBC, 2007b). Understandably, the BBC's staff involved in news and current affairs production immediately spoke out against this extraordinary manifestation of the technological sublime – and disregard of their professional performance and achievements in prior years. But they were just as quickly condemned to silence by strict orders issued from the BBC's hierarchy reminding staff that freedom of expression did not extend to the affairs of the (news) organisation which employed them.

Owner influences and organisational logics

The seminal studies suggest that, despite the prevalence of 'informal' and 'loose' systems of control, owners or top level management comprise the single most important and powerful actors in news organisations. For example, both Breed and Sigelman tend to concur that in any given subject area, the policy of the organisation (or publisher) 'is usually followed' (Breed, 1955: 335). Whilst the professional codes of journalists comprise the 'most significant' sources of leverage on publishers and management, such organisational studies highlight 'the weakness of these codes when policy decisions are made' (ibid.: 334). Subsequent research on news organisations tends to highlight the continuing prevalence of 'informal' and 'loose' systems of organisational control (or 'policy' implementation) in line with the managerial strategies of 'responsible autonomy' found in other kinds of knowledge-intensive services or professional occupations (Friedman, 1977; Im, 1997).

How did the issues of ownership and owner's influence feature in our in-depth interviews with working journalists? In essence, there was little by way of consensus among our interviewees regarding the influence of owners on news media output. The most striking feature of our findings is that there appear to be marked differences across national cultures in the extent to which ownership matters are explicitly recognised and discussed as a source of influence on news culture.

This is not very surprising but it poses tricky questions in light of the weak treatment of such issues in the prevailing research literature. The prior literature suggests that the issues of owner influences on news may be less readily or explicitly addressed by journalists or academic researchers in those news cultures where the modern (Anglo-US) model of journalism is most deeply embedded. This may be because the tradition of liberal thinking has long accorded priority value to ownership and 'private property' rights. This may account for the low priority attached to challenging economic as opposed to political or governmental bases of power and influence amongst US journalists (Weaver, 1998) or even media researchers. In other countries, such as France and some of the Eastern European cultures, there appears to be a much greater willingness to engage with ownership issues and their potential or actual role as news influences.

For example, most interviewees in the Netherlands expressed the view that ownership had no impact on their professional conduct (ter Wal, 2006a). On the other hand, five out of the eight Czech interviewees reported that they experienced pressures in the course of their work, exerted either by the proprietor or political actors (Cisarova, 2007a). Our Czech interviewees also addressed the supposed non-existence of an editorial line at the organisations for which they worked. They pointed out that this was in line with hegemonic professional standards (such as balance and objectivity) yet it was not necessarily regarded as a positive fact, 'we are all so scared that we're not supposed to have our own opinion that … it is not like that actually … and it is wrong of course … ' (ibid.).

Compared to their counterparts in Anglophone countries at least, French journalists have a stronger tradition of explicit concern and debate concerning the influence of ownership on news output. Indeed, in recent years there have been a number of trade union actions by French journalists opposed to proposed changes in newspaper ownership. Several of our French interviewees talked freely about the actual or potential threats of owners' influence or direct interference on news content. Some French journalists argued that it is downright naïve to believe that media are independent of owners' influence (Guyot *et al.*, 2006).

Interference in journalistic work from a proprietor can arise for financial as well as political reasons. A number of our interviewees, from a variety of countries, also acknowledge that owners may well be motivated by political interests as well as economic or industrial ones (Guyot *et al.*, 2006; Preston, 2006a; Cisarova, 2007b). Some of our Slovak interviewees, for example, point out that under Prime Minister Mečiar's government at the beginning of the 1990s they had to decide which political camp to join. But even later in Markíza television, owned by the then minister of industry Pavol Rusko, journalists were 'sold' to the owner and served Rusko's political and economic interests (Cisarova, 2007b).

Our interviews indicate that the nature of pressures or interferences is different in private and public service media (as observed also in Chapter 6). Several of our interviewees reported that they experienced economic pressures while working in private media and political interference when working in public service media. However, given the role of 'informal socialisation' and peer pressures, the relevant research literature alerts us to the difficulties in observing or finding explicit evidence of ownership influence. Very few of our interviewees acknowledge the existence of ownership influence in their present organisation, but several readily pointed to the actual or potential interference on news content in other media organisations in their own countries.

Some interviewees suggested that the most significant aspects of ownership influence may be implicit or indirect rather than direct. One of our Irish interviewees acknowledged that journalists might practise forms of self-censorship in order to act in what they presume to be the owner's interest – without the owner or his line managers ever having to demand such actions (Horgan, 2006). As noted earlier, hierarchies of status and power in the news organisation serve to determine who has what kind of influence on news output. But the exercise of power often takes rather subtle and intangible forms, given the informal mechanisms of managerial control in news organisations (Cisarova, 2007a).

Note

1 We may note, however, that Lloyd does not apply these insights in a consistent fashion throughout his book. Nevertheless, this work provides some insightful analyses of the current malaise of British media culture, although clearly one that is highly attentive to the views and perceptions of government ministers.

Chapter 6

Political-economic factors shaping news culture

Jacques Guyot

Subtle but pervasive influences

Histories of the printed press and occupational myths tend to emphasise that journalists in most European countries have long been concerned about interferences from political authorities in the editorial sphere. But over time, other sources of potential influence, including advertising, commercial pressures, competition and other economic pressures became matters of concern. As news evolved to become a big business, news desks have had to cope with different forms of political and economic influences, ranging from soft pressures to strict censorship.

On the whole, journalistic practices have been strongly marked by national historical situations and values linked to the particular context in which media were built and to the balance of power with political authorities. European democracies and Eastern regimes produced many national journalistic traditions and models, reflecting differing forms and degrees of media independence and editorial freedom.

If this era is not totally over, a period characterised by the logics of globalisation has opened up since the 1980s with the advent of neo-liberal regulation policies along with the end of state broadcasting monopolies, the decline of PSB models, the increasing role of advertisers, the exponential development of commercial audiovisual channels and, of course, the Internet. Even if political attempts to interfere with newsmaking activities have not disappeared, new factors linked to the capitalistic reorganisation of media have a more subtle and wider impact on journalistic practices, values and work. Among those factors, we can point out the structures of ownership and the forces of market, assuming they may influence journalism or even editorial content, especially when newsworkers have to report on sensitive issues.

This chapter will assess how journalists perceive the role of broader political economy and social factors in shaping their work and newsmaking practices. Two key research questions are considered here: first, the influence of the structures of ownership and market forces, and second, the way journalists deal with controversial issues.

A short introduction contextualises the emergence of the political economy in the field of communication and media studies, before moving on to a review of the relevant research literature. This seeks to pursue three main objectives: first, to assess the interest of researchers in political-economic issues when dealing with editorial cultures; second, to point out the differences between former communist countries and European democracies; third, to emphasise the main trends in recent investigations.

The next part of this chapter is centred on the empirical work constituted by the interviews. Here, the purpose was to examine what journalists say about economic constraints: the influence of the structures of ownership and market forces on their everyday practice, but also on their working conditions and on the way they cope with controversial issues.

The concluding section suggests a number of trends linked to the evolution of journalistic practices, as well as clues for developing editorial independence and promoting collective journalistic values arising from our interviews.

Some terminological issues

When talking about the *structures of ownership*, we refer here to the financial and legal status of media companies. Some are independent media, such as many papers: usually, the capital is supplied by their founders, non-profit associations or even groups of editors and readers (*Le Monde* in France), thus ensuring a majority holding the company; they draw their revenues from their subscriptions, sales of issues and advertising. Others are state-owned institutions, usually radio or television channels, whose budget may be entirely or partly covered by taxes or fees voted by governments; in the second case, extra revenues come from advertising, which means that many PSB stations or channels are in direct competition with private media. Some are private-owned profit-making companies and their capital is shared by private investors or shareholders (typically, with one having a majority holding) and they get their money from advertising and to a lesser extent from sales of programmes or by-products (Doyle, 2002).

Over the past 20 years, the structures of ownership have changed dramatically with new regulatory regimes, the digital revolution and the development of the Internet (Hesmondhalgh, 2002). Since the 1980s, the information sector has become a promising and profitable new market for a number of major national and international industrial groups. Often specialising in electricity or water supply, public buildings and works, telephone networks or civil and military aviation industries, big companies like Bertelsmann, Bouygues, Dassault, News International, Lagardère, and America Online massively invested in media as a way to diversify their activities and control complete areas in the field of publishing and journalistic activities. Many observers view this phenomenon of media concentration as a potential threat to pluralism (Mattelart, 2005).

The growing role of market forces has led to media concentration and economic globalisation. Based on a rationalisation of production processes, free flow of information, free markets and economies of scale, market forces lead to fierce competition, thus weakening the independence of journalists as well as their working conditions. Competition particularly affects those working in private media. In Eastern and Central European countries, market forces are all the more powerful since the transition towards capitalism and democracy has been accompanied by a widespread rejection of everything related to state regulation and control.

As for controversial issues that journalists now have to cope with, the range of sensitive topics goes far beyond traditional political interference and now includes self-censorship due to conflicts of interests with economic actors such as private media owners who have other industrial activities, advertisers or shareholders. However, when the interviewees mention controversial issues, they do not necessarily express a consensus on the matter. They sometimes refer to common national or international issues, like urban unrest, the European Constitution or the war in Iraq; they talk about ethics and even more specific realities like football matches, privacy, the uses of images, the Dutch royal family, corruption. In all cases, journalists claim a balanced, unbiased and respectful news coverage according to their journalistic codes of ethics.

Political-economic approach

Over the last 15 years, major changes have occurred in media landscapes making it all the more necessary to take into account political-economic approaches in order to understand newsmaking and journalistic practices.

The relevance of economic factors is evident in many recent developments in the organisation of printed media, radio networks and television channels. On the whole, the part played by states or governments is on the decline, especially in the field of regulation policies, while neo-liberal logics increasingly permeate every interstice of human activities. In this particular context, advertisers, private entrepreneurs and shareholders have become the main actors. Deregulation processes have been shaped by strong lobbying efforts by important international companies like Dentsu, Saatchi and Saatchi, Young and Rubicam, McCann Erikson, Walter Thompson or Publicis, whose aim was to develop world-wide networks in order to control the management of advertising spaces in the media. In this light, advertisers are not only major financial contributors, but they also shape the form and contents of media (Mattelart, 1991). Advertising being the main source of revenue, news media services must pursue audience-maximising alongside 'the additional factor of seeking to please and also not offend key advertisers' (Whitney et al., 2004: 406).

As for private groups, media are part of a global strategy developed to diversify their activities and make a profit. The novelty is that media and their contents are considered as mere short-term financial operations that participate in what observers call the 'speculative bubble', i.e. markets whose actors buy stocks or assets they usually sell as soon as they can expect substantial profit (Bouquillion, 2005).

Such tendencies considerably weaken journalistic newsmaking, which traditionally tends to rely on a steady professional environment capable of guaranteeing editorial independence and attractive working conditions. Owing to industrial mergers, and companies restructuring or dabbling in stocks and shares, many papers, magazines, radio stations and television channels change hands for reasons that have little to do with editorial logics. In the end, this system favours big companies and 'established news media are likely to be owned or controlled by large media corporations or wealthy individuals' (Whitney *et al.*, 2004: 406; see also Tunstall and Palmer, 1991).

Thus, political economy approaches address the influences on newsmaking related to media ownership and concentration, financial mechanisms, conflicts of interests between press freedom and economic pressures (from shareholders or advertisers) as well as more traditional forms of direct political intervention. They are also concerned with the threats to media pluralism and influences on journalistic autonomy related to weak levels of job security, cross-media linkages and contracts, and the absence of appropriate regulatory policies.

If we largely concentrate on the above-mentioned issues and influences on news, we can however note that the scope of contemporary political economy approaches also includes issues such as (i) the international organisation and influence of major news agencies, and (ii) the growth of public relations, sponsorship and related 'information subsidies' (besides advertising) as influences on journalism and newsmaking. For reasons of space, these two sets of issues are addressed elsewhere in this book (Chapters 4 and 8, especially).

Research in a political-economic approach

The media and journalism studies fields have been strongly influenced by the early research carried out in the United States in the mid-twentieth century. They are marked by the paradigms based in functionalist sociology or political science which pay little attention to the structural effects of economic factors on the organisation and production of media. This lack of economic perspective and the neglect of the political constraints hanging over the means of communication was pointed out by subsequent researchers who sought to analyse the complexity of the media system (Mattelart, 1994; Mattelart and Mattelart, 1998).

The emergence of a political economy of communication

The long history of political economy approaches to media and communication processes can be traced back to the nineteenth century (Hardt, 1979). In terms of the modern academic agenda, they took a major step forward with the emergence of a set of theoretical frameworks in the 1970s. Indeed, Miège and others emphasise that the 1970s were a crucial laboratory and starting point for new political-economic analyses of the communication services which grew rapidly over the following decades: audiovisual media, telecommunication networks and data processing (Miège, 2006: 105). These new techniques appeared after the 1968 protest movements, whose promoters paid special attention to cultural and information matters. In this context, many individual contributors were involved, but several key authors can be identified: Herbert Schiller (the first author to conceptualise the notion of *cultural imperialism*), Thomas Guback, Dallas Smythe, Graham Murdoch, Nicholas Garnham, and Armand Mattelart.

Unlike the ethno-centric assumptions of earlier media theorists, the new political economy school tended to favour an international perspective on media production, including the exchange of cultural goods and the flow of information. They addressed media and journalism not only in terms of national-level political and economic developments but also the evolving role of the media in international relations. They interrogated the meaning and limits of the cultural independence of many countries – especially the Third World – in light of the hegemony of multinational firms. They suggested that whether in the film industry, in television programming, in the flows of information driven by news agencies, or in telecommunication networks, the media landscape was strongly influenced by American rationales, interests and standards (Mattelart, 1991; 1994).

South American countries were also concerned with issues related to cultural independence. A whole generation of critical researchers questioned the theories and strategies of modernisation promoting a vertical vision of technological development (Antonio Pasquali, Hector Schmucler, Osvaldo Capriles, Luis Ramiro Beltrán; Armand and Michèle Mattelart from their experience with the Allende government). Contrary to that of Europe, the model of media development was closer to the commercial system prevailing in the United States. Therefore, they argued, what mattered was to link demands for social change and the democratisation of the means of communication. If Latin America produced so many founding studies, it is mainly because, at that time, the whole region accounted for two-thirds of all media resources available in the Third World (Mattelart, 1994, Mattelart and Mattelart, 1998).

Both in Europe and Latin America, many debates centred on the public control of audiovisual media and communication networks in order to protect national cultures from the hegemony of the American cultural industries. The potential social uses of electronic media were also addressed, including the possibilities for alternative forms of communication and the enhanced exercise of communication rights (Schiller, 1976; Mattelart, 1994).

Some of these academic themes and debates were echoed within UNESCO, where Third World representatives argued that media and journalism could not be driven solely by the initiatives of Western corporations or a *global market place*. They proposed a New World Information and Communication Order (NWICO) as a way to counterbalance the flows of information and cultural exchanges. In 1980, the MacBride Report suggested a number of strategies and measures to defend cultural policies and communication rights, but it faced strong opposition from the United States and Britain, whose representatives wanted to impose their *free flow of information* doctrine (Mattelart and Mattelart, 1998). Some of the recommendations directly concern journalism and its relation to economic factors:

> removal of obstacles and restrictions which derive from the concentration of media ownership, public or private, from commercial influence on the press and broadcasting, or from private and governmental advertising. [...] Effective legal measures should be designed to limit the process of concentration and monopolization [...] reduce the influence of advertising upon editorial and policy and broadcast programming.
>
> (MacBride Report, 1980/2004: part IV, arts 36–37)

These recommendations went totally unheeded.

Recent concerns due to political and technological changes

As far as our review is concerned, with the exception of Britain and France, there appears to be little research literature engaging with the influence of economic factors on editorial cultures and practices in most of the countries under study.

We observe that economic aspects of the media received relatively little attention from academic researchers until the end of the 1970s, as most media worked at national level and far from the upheavals of globalisation. Things changed from the 1980s down to the late 1990s, a shift linked to the 'cultural turn' in analyses of the media (Curran, 1990).

Indeed, research literature on economic factors comes later and is often linked to the political changes and technological advances which also affect the new media organisation: privatisation and creation of commercial channels constitute one of the major consequences of democratic transitions.

In the comparative study, there is obviously a clear-cut separation between former communist countries and European democracies when it comes to the speed of change. On the one hand, researchers point out a very quick shift from totally state-controlled media towards commercial or market-based systems of press freedom. Journalists had to cope with a new approach to newsmaking and question the professional codes of ethics. In just a few years, they passed from propaganda to information models and their newly gained independence was not necessarily easy to defend in the face of commercial interests and market forces. For instance, in Hungary, if journalists had a long-established experience of resisting political pressures, they appear to be unprepared when pressures come from publishing companies or major advertisers (Kovács *et al.*, 2006: 10). In Slovenia, the transition towards democracy brought radical changes such as privatisation of the media, liberalisation of the print media market, and little regulation in the field of broadcasting (Zagar and Zeljan, 2006b: 7). Very quickly, the interests of profit strengthen and journalists are urged to adjust to satisfy advertisers' demands (Zagar and Zeljan, 2006b: 7). The Serbian case is different and results from the political crisis following independence and particularly the beginning of Milosevic's regime in 1997: there was a fierce repression and most Serbian journalists and editors working for major media were dismissed, forbidden to write and replaced by liege men who could serve the regime's nationalist propaganda. Since 2000, when the democratic opposition in Serbia won the elections, political pressures have lessened.

On the other hand, European democracies went through a slower process of change, in three stages. First, in the late 1970s and early 1980s, most broadcasting monopolies were abandoned. Second, deregulation policies were adopted, leading to the creation of independent or private commercial media competing to extend their share of the advertising market. Third, in the 1990s, media concentration became a rule within and across countries with the expanding role of a limited number of big companies investing in media outlets, including News International and Sky (under Murdoch's control), Bertelsmann, Berlusconi, or Lagardère Médias (Mattelart, 2005).

Common trends affect all the countries studied, most of them related to the ever-increasing importance of economic logics in the organisation of media. It suggests that journalists have been under pressure because of the following kinds of development. First, heavy competition between and within media due to the expanding number of new media, channels and networks. Competition has been speeded up by the deregulation policies and to an increasing extent, the codes of entertainment took over from those of information (Hermans, in Guyot *et al.*, 2006: 11). This situation can lead to short-time thinking within media companies as well as bad editorial decisions. Besides, the editor's freedom is largely determined by media owners (Horgan, 2006: 16–20). The arrival of free newspapers like *Metro* has also tended to destabilise the independent press (ter Wal, 2006a: 8).

The second development has been the increasing role of advertisers and economic actors, thus leading to more commercial, profit-making and entertainment-oriented media. The main concern for editors, publishers and media owners is to avoid losing advertisers or displeasing owners. A study conducted in Hungary shows that journalists feel that they are less free to choose their topics while more of them report attempts from economic players to influence their writings (Vásárhelyi, 2000, in Kovács *et al.*, 2006: 1). However, any such influence only 'concerns the others', as Vásárhelyi observes. The interviewees reported that they never personally felt pressures, but if they had, they tended to say they were able to resist. The orientations and attitudes of journalists have changed as they became more aware of the commercial aspects of their work and integrated this dimension to their know-how (ter Wal and Valeriani, 2006: 14).

Third has been the relative decline of public broadcasting services or independent media facing competition with privately owned media. Some researchers point out that some public television channels or quality papers still manage to resist the economic pressures and market policies of their publishers (ter Wal,

2006a: 6). However, what is generally put forward is the lack of regulating bodies and policies, particularly in the broadcasting field, in order to ensure a fair balance between editorial independence and commercial interests (Zagar and Zeljan, 2006b: 7; Guyot *et al.*, 2006: 11).

Fourth, there has been media concentration: in many countries, large conglomerates have been laying their hands on major segments of the media sector for some decades (e.g. Garnham, 1990). For example, in Italy, big enterprises took control of large parts of the newspaper industry in the 1970s. Soon afterwards, the same phenomenon was observed in television where 90 per cent of the market was shared by two giants: the public RAI and Berlusconi's Fininvest (ter Wal and Valeriani, 2006: 13). In most countries, researchers observe the effect of extended globalisation on media organisation. This is the end of the era of 'captains of the press'. Now, the common rule is the diversification of industrial activities for companies viewing the development of digital media, multimedia and information technologies as a profitable market (Mattelart, 2005, in Guyot *et al.*, 2006). The newcomers may already be in the media business, but many are involved in activities that have little to do with media – such as banking, insurance, the public buildings and works sector or the arms industry.

In France, most media are now in the hands of five groups, four of them having international activities: Bouygues/TF1, Bertelsmann, Vivendi/Universal, Lagardère and Dassault (Brémond, in Mattelart, 2005). In the Netherlands, many foreign companies have become quite active in the media market (ter Wal, 2006a: 8). Now, multinational and multimedia firms play a major role in shaping the economy of media landscapes.

On the whole, the influence of ownership on journalistic culture and editorial content is a recurrent theme, particularly when dealing with newspapers. Even if the answers are necessarily complex, what is often argued is that media diversity supposes both diversity of title and diversity of ownership (Horgan, 2006: 21).

At the same time, we observe that political pressures have not totally disappeared. In many countries, the bonds between the political power and media are still strong, through, for example, the appointment of editors (ter Wal and Valeriani, 2006: 14) or when journalists have a sustained relationship with the establishment (Horgan, 2006: 22).

Newsworkers' views of the political-economic factors

Our research project's interviews serve to fill certain gaps of the literature review whilst this oral material also confirms the general trends observed in the previous section: the quick process of privatisation in Eastern countries, the fierce competition between and within media, the leading role of advertisers and the phenomenon of media concentration, all show how the economic organisation influences journalism, changes their working conditions and modifies the perception and journalistic treatment of controversial issues.

The influence of structures of ownership and market forces

Most interviewees agree on the growing influence of economic factors. But few countries associate the structures of ownership and market forces as one whole thing. Spain is one example where interviewees establish such a link and freely talk about it: 'They are companies looking for profit, they've got to survive, and we are workers', says a female radio editor. One television news editor observes that 'Means of communication are divisions of much bigger industrial conglomerates ... mercantilism increased with globalization' (Guyot *et al.*, 2006: 37). In Italy, the problems were amplified in the years when Berlusconi was prime minister, with the consequence that one person held the powerful roles of both head of the government and ultimate owner of the major private sector television networks. One female newspaper editor refers to this 'Italian scandal where it is completely evident that we live under a monopolistic roof (Berlusconi)' (ter Wal and Valeriani, 2006: 29).

However, the interviews suggest an overall impression that ownership has fewer implications for journalistic practices than market forces. When asked about the weight of structures of ownership, two points of view are generally expressed:

First, in very paradoxical ways, media professionals are usually reluctant to acknowledge direct intervention from owners in editorial matters. The question itself sometimes raises suspicion, as in France where a radio editor's first reaction was: 'But, this is a Marxist question'! The TF1 correspondent 'did not understand the question'; as for Radio Monte Carlo's chief editor, 'A journalist has a professional status in France which guarantees some kind of independence from his hierarchy management, he has the right to say ... I don't want to treat this subject this way, because it is against my values'. But he quickly acknowledges that 'A broadcaster, a radio, a TV, a paper, today in France, are also private companies which need to live, to survive, and market data naturally affect the way to work ... in choosing the subjects, we have some kind of marketing approach' (Guyot *et al.*, 2006: 20).

If they experience limitations in their work from employers/owners, journalists usually deny any pressure in front of the researcher, who is considered an 'outsider'; but these limitations do implicitly exist and 'are formulated in economic, organisational and technical terms' (Kovacs *et al.*, 2005: 21). One explanation for such reluctance undoubtedly lies in the occupational myth shared by most newsworkers – especially in Great Britain – that journalistic values and codes of ethics insulate them from outside influence, whether political or economic. This myth seems to be particularly strong in Great Britain (Preston, 2006a: 7), but when RMC's chief editor refers to his professional status, he also claims the independence and autonomy of the journalistic field. In the Netherlands, interviewees suggest that ownership 'does not influence professional standards. Thus is not an issue ... as independence and freedom of the press and of other media is held extremely high' (ter Wal, 2006a: 15).

When journalists do acknowledge the role of such influences, they usually point out that they were never directly confronted with such pressures themselves, rather these are issues of concern to other journalists or media institutions. In other words, the *influence affects the others*.

(Preston, 2006a: 42)

As Trevor Kavanagh of the *Sun* puts it: 'I can't answer for anyone else but it does not affect me at all. ... I know it must affect other people in the paper and elsewhere'. Indeed, the latter interviewee goes on to add: 'I know that in the past, Murdoch has actually taken on advertisers who threatened to withdraw their patronage' (Preston, 2006a: 43). For a senior Irish journalist working for the Independent Newspaper group, headed by Sir Anthony O'Reilly, the stakes are quite simple and the owner 'does not interfere as long as the bottom line is OK' (Horgan, 2006: 29).

The persons having more direct influence and power over the editorial line are the 'middle managers', as one Irish radio presenter calls them. Indeed, this interviewee, who 'has worked in media for a long number of years' suggests that: 'People outside the media have historically over-hyped the question of ownership. The people who, I think, exercise great control are the middle managers. They are the executives hired by the owners and they can put an enormous influence on what goes before the public' (Horgan, 2006: 29).

Second, there still is a cleavage between public service or independent media and privately owned groups in some of the European countries. The prevalent impression is that editorial freedom is easier to exert in public media, especially in the audiovisual sector. Pascal Verdeau, a permanent correspondent in Brussels for French public television channels, suggests that the pressures are very strong for 'the colleagues working in private companies. I deal with a particular owner, the State, which has slowly faded with the years' (Guyot *et al.*, 2006: 21).

This point of view confirmed by a reporter working for a private television company: 'Less freedom [as there is a] mobilisation of the hierarchy checking everything beforehand: "who are you going to meet?" and further down: the subject is viewed with potential requests for corrections' (Guyot *et al.*, 2006: 23).

However, a Czech editor working for the regional public television reports a difference between private media and public service television: in the first case, journalists have to face financial pressures, and in the other political pressures which appear difficult to personify, as 'They do not call us ... they can call the editor-in-chief ... it is filtered through but you can feel the pressure ... you suspect that the director ... the editor-in-chief was approached by someone who is on the Council of the Czech Television ... sometimes, one's reaction is self-censorship' (Cisarova, 2007a: 3).

In the Netherlands, professional practices are affected by economic limitations and, when competing with commercial channels, public television would suffer less from market forces than commercial channels. According to one correspondent based in Brussels:

I do notice a different role with the colleagues from commercial broadcasting. At most, they have to pay more attention to their budget or they are faced with not being able to do certain things because there is no money for it. But these are limitations in the amount of news supplied, not in the nature of it.

(ter Wal, 2006a: 15)

In Italy, some interviewees suggest that greater freedom of information can be found in 'alternative channels that are published on the Internet and/or local radios' (ter Wal and Valeriani, 2006: 28).

In Serbia, the distinction between state media and others is not very clearcut and does not mean much according to PSB standards. As the research report for Serbia puts it:

State television, for instance, has not yet been transformed into the public service. ... Ownership structures in many media are practically the same as in the time of Slobodan Milosevic. ... The State provides money to many media and this is why the state still controls the media.

(Zagar and Zeljan, 2006a: 17)

As for Slovenia, in spite of the privatisation law in the media sector, the state still has important shares in most major broadcasters, whether public or commercial (Zagar and Zeljan, 2006b: 10–11).

There is a consensus among interviewees around the effects of market forces. All media, particularly in the audiovisual sector, are marked by growing concerns about advertising costs and/or audience ratings (ter Wal, 2006a: 15).

For some respondents, PSB had to undergo a real 'cultural revolution', as Tim Marshall from BSkyB puts it, 'market forces have always played a dominant role [and] even the BBC has to chase ratings' (Preston, 2006a: 42). This point of view is shared by Haasbroek of NOS Journaal (public Dutch TV and radio) who notes:

that in reality, in public television audiences, figures play a big role too, just like in commercial television, and that advertising costs constitute also one third of the income of public television, so that they are to some extent commercial too.

(ter Wal, 2006a: 15)

In other words, the commercial pressures shape the news agendas as journalists are forced to be closer to the so-called audience demands. Therefore, information becomes more fragmented, with more consumer issues, entertainment and lifestyle news, a trend that can be observed in many countries (Guyot *et al.*, 2006: 36; Preston, 2006a: 42; ter Wal, 2006a: 16; Zagar and Zeljan, 2006b: 11). Bernardo Díaz Nosty sums up the situation that can be extrapolated from the Spanish case: 'In the last years, what increased in Spain is what we could define as a leisure/entertainment-oriented model' (cited in Guyot *et al.*, 2006: 36).

Journalists' working conditions

Before moving on to recent trends and changes in journalists' working conditions, we must flag a potential bias in the findings from our interviews. In our project, most of the interviewees comprised senior journalists and editors. Whilst this may introduce a certain bias in the interview findings, many of our respondents seem quite aware that their relatively high and steady professional position protects them from certain direct pressures experienced by more junior colleagues. Quite clearly, working conditions and other pressures are very different in the case of young journalists employed on short-term contracts.

All interviewees underline the increasing competition as one of the major consequences of the economic reorganisation of journalists' working conditions. Competition is the general rule, even for what was long considered as an independent quality press, like *Le Monde* in France or the *Irish Times* in Ireland (Horgan, 2006: 30). The proliferation of commercial television and the arrival of the Internet increased the level of competition between and within all traditional media. Thus, the journalist becomes more vulnerable (Guyot *et al.*, 2006: 35–37) as he or she is just one employee among many others working for a company struggling to defend its position on the market, produce a balanced budget and in many cases make profit.

As a consequence of competition and media concentration, the printed press faces drastic reductions in its revenues, especially those from advertising. But it also have to compete against other media that put less money into collecting the news. For a journalist working for *Le Monde*, the impoverishment of the press comes from the fact that the quality papers usually have a long-term and costly policy of maintaining permanent foreign correspondents, while private television channels tend to 'pump' from the news agencies or other media:

> I do not think it is fair to give the information you collect free of charge. ... In Germany, where TF1 had closed its office ... they would call us to know what was going on ... I told them it was out of the question, my paper has been investing for 4 years in me.
>
> (Guyot *et al.*, 2006: 22)

The deterioration of working conditions is manifest in the type of contracts being issued to newly recruited journalists. As one interviewee put it:

> We can note that papers gradually (become) impoverished and behind that situation, more and more young inexperienced journalists working on short-term contracts are given heavy issues to investigate and they haven't

necessarily got the nerve to resist the people in front of them; and this weakens the information we offer.

(cited in Guyot *et al.*, 2006: 22)

One Spanish researcher and former journalist noting the trend to employ inexperienced young journalists, is very pessimistic about the evolution of the job:

What happened is intensive proletarianisation, so that, in front of ethical codes, social responsibility and professionalism, what prevails is the working law; and in many cases, [what happened is] a decline because of practices like employment of grant holders or students for positions that have nothing to do with training as they are regular jobs.

(Guyot *et al.*, 2006: 34)

One case study focused on the employment of young French journalists shows that most of them are freelance workers (a situation they have not really chosen), who have to lobby potential editors or news desks in order to sell the reports they produced on their own budget and sometimes during their holiday; they end up with poor incomes which put them among the low-income socio-professional groups (Le Bohé, in Mattelart, 2005).

However in some cases, young journalists perceive working conditions as better and freer than in the past. In Hungary, 'the young generation talks about an ever increasing freedom in media, about improved working conditions' (Kovács *et al.*, 2006: 20). One possible interpretation is that, thanks to the democratic transition and also the development of new technologies, it would now be easier to work as a journalist, especially for people who, because of their age, did not have to cope with the straightjacket of state-controlled media. In a quite different context, the technological argument is also mentioned in the Netherlands where 'against (or in spite of) the forces of market, a new form of journalism is created' (ter Wal, 2006a: 17). However, this new form of journalism has little to do with an organised full-time job where you can make a living, as 'Journalism is no longer necessarily a paid profession' (ter Wal, 2006a: 17).

The interviewees reveal a cleavage between two positions. On the one hand, a majority of journalists who believe that only more regulation and legal frameworks can protect their profession against economic influence and competition with other media; on the other hand, a young generation who emphasise the potential of new professional standards (with more freedom, more professionalisation and more technologies). In both cases, the proposals are viewed as the best way to promote and protect editorial independence.

The final aspect of working conditions concerns the social relationships between journalists within the news desk. The combination of technological changes, competition and the need to produce information within very short time periods have contributed to a considerable recasting of the journalist's role, modus operandi and location within a certain socio-professional environment.

For example, one interviewee reports that: 'The culture of drinking and socialising has been replaced by one of sobriety. ... Now all the socialising is replaced by longer hours at the desk and PR circuit' (Preston, 2006a: 26). This point of view is confirmed in other ironical terms by a Spanish chief editor:

> In the old times, people would be in bars, in cafeterias, in the streets. We are becoming sensitive to cold, we are frozen. We do not sound out the streets. We don't know what the citizen thinks. We live in capsules.
>
> (Guyot *et al.*, 2006: 40)

Political-economic and controversial issues

When tackling sensitive or controversial issues, the tensions existing between journalistic values and economic logics clearly appear, challenging journalistic codes of ethics as well as editorial independence. Indeed, the critical point of view or the thorough analysis of facts and events are not easy to put into practice when heavy competition, lack of job security or short-time contracts drive media professionals to self-censorship, shallow investigation and infotainment.

Dealing with controversial issues: the terms of the debate

First of all, when questioned about sensitive or controversial issues, we observe that interviewees tend to identify a wide variety of subjects which can be classified into four categories: (i) topics related to national concerns such as violence during football matches, urban unrest, or bombings by the Basque ETA or Islamic radicals; (ii) international issues such as the referendum for the European constitution, the rise of religious fundamentalism, terrorism or the war in Iraq; (iii) business matters which are linked to conflicts of interests with advertisers, shareholders or owners; and (iv) coverage of celebrities, social gossip about royal families, sports or media stars, or of trivial events about ordinary people.

Second, many interviewees mention that most topics, if not all, are controversial (Guyot *et al.*, 2006: 23). Mediating controversial issues lends credibility to contemporary journalism (Zagar and Zeljan, 2006b: 11) and the journalists sometimes feed controversies. In their everyday confrontation with sensitive topics, interviewees strongly suggest that a set of basic professional rules should be merely applied: balanced treatment, respect for diverse views by the presentation of different opposing points of view, respect for truth, awareness of the audience in order not to offend people's sensitivity (Guyot *et al.*, 2006: 23, 39; Horgan, 2006: 32; Preston, 2006a: 43; Zagar and Zeljan, 2006b: 11).

An Italian journalist sums up the ideal configuration:

> We seek to give as many viewpoints as possible. For example, when yesterday the Royal Institute said that the Iraq war has increased the potential for

terrorism (e.g. favouring recruitment), the indignation of Islam towards the West, we have given this report. But we have also sought comments that somehow could allow people to understand this Royal Institute report which the British government and prime minister Blair have denied.

(ter Wal and Valeriani, 2006: 28)

As previously noted, newsworkers can draw on media routines as well as occupational rules and procedures to validate their news frames and stories, or they can refer to the internal organisational guidelines produced by some of the larger media (Guyot *et al.*, 2006: 39). However, professional ethics often appear as little more than a pious hope against the constraints journalists have to cope with. Many acknowledge that ethical rules are constantly challenged by the shift towards stardom, sensationalism and infotainment; an Irish journalist is clear about it:

The heroes ... or the icons of modern journalism are the people who take very partisan view of issues, whether from a left or right-wing perspective. The old concepts of impartiality, objectivity (and) balanced reporting are in decline and sometimes openly derided.

(Horgan, 2006: 31)

A variety of pressures

In practical terms, it appears that three kinds of factors interact in a constant tension when dealing with controversial issues:

First, we observe ideological pressures: this was the case during the war in Iraq when the general trend, after the shock caused to public opinion by the 9/11 terrorist plane crashes, was to privilege one side of the story; says an Italian journalist: 'We can say that the global press, but even the Italian one, has taken sides in favour of the war and this was in name of the fact that Saddam Hussein had to be eliminated' (ter Wal and Valeriani, 2006: 30). A British journalist spoke of the 'immense pressure to fall down on one side of the argument or the other', although he was grateful that broadcasters were legally prohibited from doing so (Preston, 2006a: 43).

Second, we find pressures from economic players in the case of conflicts of interests with advertisers, shareholders or owners. It is never good to take unnecessary risks, as pointed out by a French journalist:

The press is in such a bad financial state that papers lose money ... We can see it with Libération, for example ... The chief editor says that when an article talks about a shareholder, [he] must take a close look at it. The drastic separation of the editorial aspect and the financial/advertising dimension tends to blur. If you write a violent article against Dassault or

Lagardère, they can take off their advertising budget, and everything depends on advertising.

(Guyot *et al.*, 2006: 21)

Third, there is the issue of journalists as members of an elite. The interview materials and research materials suggest that this may be more or less a French speciality. They tend to emphasise the collusion between a minority of well known journalists, the political establishment and business circles. Journalists were quite prejudiced when they promoted the European Constitution and lost part of their credibility. One of the editors of France's *Le Monde Diplomatique* speaks about 'the general indignation of the population', adding that:

> [media professionals] cannot be totally disconnected from what the majority of people think ... They got it wrong with the referendum as all the media, almost all of them, in a quite scandalous way, were favourable to the Yes and disparaged the No. Yet 56 percent of the people said No. This is a slap in the face for the media. They haven't drawn any consequence out of it.
>
> (Guyot *et al.*, 2006: 30)

The issues surrounding journalistic ethical standards related to the use of images were raised in at least two different contexts: on the one hand, urban unrest, terrorism and warfare; on the other, interference within people's private sphere. Regarding the first aspect, taking the example of suburban unrest in 2005, France 2 television noticed that the main problem was to find the right treatment between 'too much or too little information' with a recent change towards what he calls: 'The ethics of responsibility ... a collective decision "not to broadcast information about the number of burnt cars to avoid drifting off towards overbid from the young who were burning vehicles"' (Guyot *et al.*, 2006: 23).

Irish journalists share some similar concerns when they decide not to show everything, questioning 'the role of broadcasters in assessing visual material which could have been generated as part of terrorist propaganda, and other questions of an editorial nature such as the use of embedded journalists' (Horgan, 2006: 31). In Great Britain, journalists point out the responsibility to publish or not photographs of demonstrations that allow the police to identify protestors, or explicit pictures of dismembered bodies from war zones (Preston, 2006a: 44).

Journalists are found to practise self-censorship in several respects. As far as privacy is concerned, most journalists view in a very negative way the general trend to get into people's private life, should they be known or not. An Irish journalist mentions the case of the death of the MP Liam Lawlor in a car crash in Moscow and the salacious report made by a number of Sunday papers (Horgan, 2006: 31). The quest for sensationalism is very common, with the interviews pointing to many examples of growing media intrusion in people's privacy posing questions about the violation of several basic human rights:

examples range from David Beckham's private life (Preston, 2006a: 43) to the Dutch royal family, diplomats or ordinary folks (Kovács *et al.*, 2006: 22).

The ways in which controversial issues are dealt with may help shed light on the balance of powers inside media, says a French journalist:

> It precisely depends on the 'weight' of journalists in their company. When the professional code of ethics, particularly the respect for truth – prevails over all other economic considerations, people's right of information is respected. When commercial or private interests are dominant, the journalist can only choose between resignation or self-censorship.
>
> (Guyot *et al.*, 2006: 24)

Implications for the practice and study of journalism

The analysis of the literature review and interviews with media professionals allow us to identify certain general trends which are important in understanding the changes in editorial cultures and the prevailing pressures on journalists' daily practices. At this stage, let us give a brief summary of these main trends.

How is it to work as a journalist?

Many journalists acknowledge new forms of censorship, at least when talking about their colleagues, even if they are reluctant to talk about their own personal experiences. Censorship takes more subtle ways than before, not only in former communist countries that were used to more direct and immediate pressure from their governments.

Today, journalists face a mixture of growing economic pressures as well as older and newer forms of political attempts at influencing the news agenda. Within media organisations, the direct agency of influence is often assumed by the 'middle managers' who act as buffers between the owners and the journalists. The relevant influences may also arise from the friendly and sustained relationships between media owners or top executives and politicians. In any case, it seems that journalists now tend to face more subtle or implicit nudges rather than explicit instructions to change the editorial line or modify some of the content of news coverage.

For well established journalists in national media, the relevant pressures – whether they come from owners, advertisers or politicians or combinations of these actors linked by common interests – comprise an open secret. The result often takes the form of self-censorship amongst media professionals who interiorise political, economic, and market-based constraints. However, through its unions and professional bodies, the occupation must continue to defend editorial independence and above all media pluralism.

Indeed, the most pressing challenges journalists have to cope with concern the security of their jobs and professional autonomy as well as the protection of press freedom in the face of media concentration and commercialisation trends. Usually, company mergers and media restructuring lead to drastic cost reductions affecting staff working conditions. The first consequence is the increase of short-term, cross-media contracts. This major change does not seem to affect the new generation of journalists who take it for granted that the job is permanently modified by IC technologies, thus pushing them to find other sources of revenue. This generation gap illustrates how journalistic cultures built through an adhesion to collective values (for example the editorial responsibility shared by the members of a news desk) are dissolving in favour of more individualistic approach: in this respect, the freelance journalist may become a new professional archetype.

However, interviews reveal that most journalists are not satisfied by the present situation and believe legal measures should be taken to limit the trends towards media concentration, advertising and commercialisation processes. Two directions are privileged. On the one hand, a need for regulation policies from national and international authorities in order to provide a firmer legal framework to guarantee editorial and financial independence. On the other hand, the provision of professional training to all journalists so they can better resist economic and political pressures. These claims reflect a certain crisis of identity experienced by most journalists. Many feel they have lost their legitimacy because their ability to make the news according to the professional standards of journalism is threatened by the growing sway of market forces.

Political economy as a research prospect for journalism studies

Obviously, political-economic factors play an important role in journalistic cultures. Many interviewees indicate that they have integrated this dimension; they are aware that the capitalistic organisation of media shapes their practices and the forms of professional discretion or leeway left to them.

In this particular context, political-economic explanatory approaches can highlight the dynamics of 'advanced capitalism' in reshaping the environment in which newsmaking takes place. Special attention must be paid to assess media pluralism, but also to take into account the strategies journalists display in order to cope with the consequences of concentration and monopolisation on editorial freedom. This comparative survey helps to identify and categorise the major trends or evolutions in journalistic practices in European countries.

One last point concerns the education and training of journalists. The curricula offered in many journalism schools do not include courses dedicated to these political-economic factors, or to changes brought by the internationalisation of cultural industries – and above all to the ways media professionals may deal with them. Unfortunately, the reference to the ideals of the profession does not have much sense when most journalists work in globalised media subject to subtle if pervasive commercial influences. The theoretical and empirical contributions of political economy research can help future journalists to engage with new challenges to building a more democratic social and political order.

Chapter 7

'The cultural air'

Ideology, discourse and power

'The cultural air we breathe': key themes

We now move on to consider the final, and broadest, of our five explanatory perspectives concerning the influences on news and journalism, one which we labelled earlier 'the cultural air we breathe'. Borrowed from British cultural theorist Richard Hoggart, this pithy phrase embraces those influences on news-making related to 'the whole ideological atmosphere of our society' which in turn tells us how 'some things can be said and others had best not be said … ' (Glasgow Media Group, 1976: x; cited in Eldridge, 1995: 8). As noted, the image of 'the cultural air we breathe' evokes the total or surrounding atmosphere of prevailing ideas, ideologies and discourses which permeate news content, its language, forms and 'feel' in a given societal context. Furthermore, it embraces matters that are both spoken in the everyday discourses of a particular culture as well as relevant factors that remain unspoken and subject to forms of self-censorship or other discursive silences.

This perspective also connects with the concept of *structure of feeling* which Raymond Williams defined as 'the culture of a period … the particular living result of all the elements in the general organization', where a period's arts and their 'characteristic approaches, and tones in argument', are of major importance (Williams, 1961: 64–65). The 'structure of feeling' is not shared in the same way by all individuals in any community, as it is shaped by special interests, including those of class (Eldridge and Eldridge, 1994: 79–80). Yet, it has 'a very deep and very wide possession, in all actual communities, precisely because it is on it that communication depends', even though it is not learned in any formal way (Williams, 1961: 65). In this sense, news now constitutes one important dimension of the wider culture or 'arts' of a particular period and community.

In some respects, this broad explanatory perspective on news culture has a long history. It was shared by many pioneering and early academic efforts to conceptualise the influences on news and journalism in a rounded or holistic manner but which were sidelined by the emphasis on micro- or meso-level theorising favoured by US-based academic studies in the mid-twentieth century.

For example, some of the pioneering US theorists of journalism and its role and responsibilities in relation to the public were well attuned to holistic analyses embracing cultural power and ideological factors, as well as the inter-linkages between individuals and the broader social setting in which they are situated (e.g. Park, 1940; Dewey, 1927). It has long been recognised that just as 'there is something reciprocal in the relations of the press to the public', the news 'cannot be studied or fairly judged' apart from its environment because like all institutions, it is 'caught in the complex of our actual state of civilization' (Ogden, 1912: 322).

In reflexive mode, we might note that academic fields engaged in studies of news culture (i.e. not merely their objects of study) have been influenced by 'the cultural air we breathe' – including, in this case, the context of the post-war social democratic settlement and its attendant political culture. This may help explain why, in Britain and France, the early post-war decades witnessed two distinctly innovative approaches to the analysis of media and popular culture – as exemplified in the work of Raymond Williams and Roland Barthes, respectively. These were developed quite separately and independently – indeed undertaken with a degree of isolation that seems quite remarkable when viewed in retrospect today, only some 40 to 50 years later (Mattelart, 2007). Yet these early post-war French and British approaches to media culture shared several important features which distanced them both from the general thrust of work then underway in the USA. We may identify three such distinctive features, and these also inform many of the subsequent studies of concern in this chapter: (a) an explicit or direct concern with questions of power and its unequal distribution across different class groups or sub-cultures; (b) a concern to relate studies of the media to the macro (overall) processes or structures of the social and cultural formation – in contrast to the micro- or meso-level concepts favoured by the dominant strands of US media research of the time; (c) an orientation to the study of collectivities (social and cultural groups) rather than individual-level analytic categories. For example, Williams in Britain and Barthes in France both emphasised how the subtle operations of communication must be understood in terms of power relations and the role of (more or less) shared cultures, codes or communities in shaping the meanings and interpretation of media content or texts.

Some seminal studies: 'the cultural air'

Encoding/decoding news: Hall and the Birmingham School

The encoding/decoding model (or sometimes called the 'reception model') comprises one of the most influential challenges to the 'transmission model' and its associated 'strong effects' theories of the mass media which had dominated the field from the late 1940s to the 1970s. Stuart Hall and his colleagues at Birmingham University's Centre for Contemporary Cultural Studies were the most prominent proponents of the encoding/decoding model. Their work provides some key exemplars of the distinctive features of the explanatory per-spectives highlighted in this chapter. The early formulations of this model were animated by the critical spirit that informed many of the young researchers then entering this expanding academic field in the 1970s, even if this aspect of the model largely 'withered away' during the 1980s.

The encoding/decoding idea emphasises that media texts or messages are open and 'polysemic' (possessing multiple potential meanings) and that these are interpreted in accordance with the particular context and the culture of recei-vers. This model expressly challenged the key tenets and methodologies of empirical social scientific audience research and humanistic studies of media content on the grounds that they failed to take due account of the role or 'power' of the audience in giving meaning to media messages (McQuail, 2000). The origins of the reception model lie more in the domain of cultural studies than in the social sciences, and it may be seen as strongly linked to the rise of 'reception analysis' (ibid.). It emphasises that the key role of readers or viewers in the meaning-making processes associated with mediated communication, draw-ing attention to the *interpretation* of the messages conveyed by media texts, not merely their *authoring or design*.

Stuart Hall (1980) is widely credited with articulating the most influential account of the encoding/decoding model. However, we must note that rather similar ideas were developed and refined in detailed reception and audience stu-dies by a number of other British researchers (e.g. Morley, 1980; Silverstone and Hirsch, 1992; Silverstone, 2005). Whilst broadly following the British cultural studies path pioneered by Raymond Williams and others, Hall's approach is also informed by several prior theoretical strands, including continental theorists such as Barthes and Gramsci. First, Hall argues that communicators such as journal-ists and media institutions tend to encode messages for situational, ideological or institutional reasons and so media texts or messages are 'encoded' with a 'pre-ferred reading'. Second, the receivers (or media audiences, readers or viewers) may not necessarily accept, 'read' or 'decode' the message as intended by the sender or source (the encoded 'preferred reading'). Rather, Hall suggests, audi-ences can and do 'resist' or subvert the originator's intended meaning or its ideological influences by adopting alternative or even oppositional readings. Such decoding processes will vary according to the receivers' situated context, experience, outlook or culture. In essence, Hall is arguing that audiences read between the lines of mediated messages, imposing their own interpretation, or even reversing the intended meaning or direction of the message as encoded by the sender. Thus the eventual and primary meaning derived from any news item or other media text is that imposed by the reader and this will vary in line with different 'interpretative communities'. In some formulations, Hall's encoding/decoding model also goes on to suggest that the reader's decoding may involve 'dominant', 'negotiated' or 'oppositional' readings of the text.

Hall's now-famous encoding/decoding model clearly places a lot of emphasis on the capacity of the active audience to negotiate the meaning of the text, especially when contrasted with prior media theories emphasising 'strong effects'. However, in relation to the subsequent trajectory of reception and audience analyses, it should be noted that Hall did not seek to (re-)propose any absolute 'death of the author' nor any totalising understanding of the audience's autonomy and capacities for 'resistant' readings. Indeed much like Barthes, Hall continued to pursue a critical, if subtle, interest in the operations of ideology and in the institutional bases of power and their capacities to shape the 'primary definitions' of news and other media texts. The same, however, cannot be said of many of those other scholars favouring the 'reception approach' who have appropriated elements of Hall's concepts and approach for subsequent research on audiences and news or other media genres.

There have been many challenges to the concepts and argument as advanced by Hall *et al.* (1978), including those from liberal pluralists. The latter in particular, have accused Hall (1978) of overemphasising the capacity of the news media to structure public debate in ways consistent with the interests of the powerful in society, and of neglecting what some note as the absence of any singular interest amongst these elites (McQuail, 2000; Allan, 2004). Some subsequent studies have not only criticised aspects of Hall's work whilst endorsing other elements, but they have also set out to refine the methods and approach. For example, in *Reporting Crime*, Schlesinger and Tumber (1994) tend to accept the argument that journalists' practices typically end up privileging and promoting the views of authoritative sources; but, when it comes to the study of crime news, they also advance several important points of criticism of the approach, methods and conclusions of Hall *et al.* (1978).

'Bad News': The Glasgow Media Group

The early studies of the research group known as the Glasgow Media Group (GMC), have often been regarded as 'pathbreaking' in several respects (Whitney *et al.*, 2004: 400). The group's early studies (1976, 1980, 1982) drew on cultural and critical studies traditions to examine television news culture in Britain, but their work and findings have many resonances with the institutional studies examined earlier (in Chapter 4). These studies also enjoyed a relatively high public profile in Britain, although some media professionals and news organisations were very critical of the work and its findings (Eldridge, 2000: 115).

The Glasgow Media Group took television news culture and newsmaking as their object of study, building on the critical studies tradition to interrogate the 'common sense' view that television news is a neutral product. The neutral conception of news was 'held to be an illusion', but in order to demonstrate that the Glasgow group set out to examine 'how television news was structured and organized and to unpack some, at least, of (its) constituents' (Eldridge, 2000: 114). The group's main research method was that of content analysis, but this was complemented by interviewing and participant observation techniques. The GMG research team undertook a pioneering, large-scale academic analysis of television news by video recording and analysing all news bulletins over five months, rather than samples. The group's quantitative analysis addressed 'the selection of news stories, their ordering and frequency', but it also addressed qualitative aspects of the narrative organisation of stories and visual representations, paying particular attention to news coverage of industrial relations and the economic affairs (Eldridge, 2000: 115).

The GMG research pointed to many significant similarities in the news bulletins of the two national broadcasters, BBC and ITN, suggesting that news culture was the product of a shared code of television news production. For example, it pointed to essential similarities with respect to the frequency and ordering of news items, the selection of stories, the language of news, the use of sources and the related news values. Second, by identifying a shared code of television news production, the Glasgow group found it possible to examine how the code was utilised and the types of encodings adopted in the production of television news messages. The research revealed how these routines and shared practices underpin newsmakers' decisions and judgements concerning 'what is to be included and how it is to be covered' and so they offer one particular path towards 'the study of agenda-setting, gatekeeping and news values' (Eldridge, 2000: 115).

Multiple dimensions: culture and journalism

Despite the diversity of 'cultural' perspectives on news, reviews of the literature emphasise how they present very distinct angles on the 'construction' of news compared to those of institutional and organisational studies (e.g. Schudson, 2000). Where the latter tend to emphasise 'interactional determinants' of news in the relations between people, 'the cultural view finds symbolic determinants of news in the relations between "facts" and symbols', according to Michael Schudson (2000: 189). In this light, newsworthy events are not to be treated simply as happenings in the world, rather they are viewed as the product of the *relation* between a given culture (or 'symbolic system') and the selection of certain happenings. Thus, such accounts of news are deemed to be particularly helpful in explaining how journalism may resonate with cultural tendencies or moods in particular times or societies. These include the role and features of stereotypes or other kinds of generalised images in news media, not least those related to ethnic or racial groups. For example, Hartmann and Husband's pioneering analysis of media coverage of racial conflict in Britain noted how the local cultural traditions had many elements that were derogatory of blacks and other foreigners, especially those from former colonial countries. This study reveals how in their given setting, the British news media tended to 'operate within the culture' and so were constrained or inclined to use pre-existing 'cultural symbols' some of which date from Britain's role as the homeland of a major imperial system (Hartmann and Husband, 1973: 274; cited in Schudson, 2000: 190).

But whilst 'cultural givens', such as racial stereotypes might well reflect long-term tendencies, culture must also be viewed as dynamic, evolving and open to change. Cultural analyses have also been helpful in revealing how crime stories, especially unusual or sensational events, have long been a prominent feature of popular media and mediated news (Williams, 1961/1965). Yet, what passes as crime news is subject to change, fashions and trends, with certain types of events receiving much more attention than others at various times even within the same (national) news culture. At the same time, studies indicate how the media in many countries tend to over-report violent crimes relative to their actual occurrence. Tendencies towards sensationalism and over-reporting of crime are manifest not only in the popular press but also to some extent in the mid-market and quality press (Schlesinger and Tumber, 1994). Such considerations suggest that there are limits to the sole reliance on broad-sweep cultural explanations. They also point to the potential benefits of explanatory accounts combining insights from both 'general cultural' and more specific, or empirically grounded, social-organisational approaches to newsmaking (Schudson, 2000).

Research linked to the notion of 'the cultural air we breathe' may be divided into a number of dimensions. According to Michael Schudson, the concept has 'both a form and content' and it also involves a specific 'occupational cultural air' linked to journalism's 'cultural routines' (2000: 192). By 'content', Schudson refers to the substantive, if taken-for-granted, values of a certain cultural setting which have been addressed in many studies (e.g. Gans, 1979). This dimension comprises those 'unquestioned and generally unnoticed background assumptions' through which news is gathered and within which it is framed by journalists in any given socio-cultural setting (Schudson, 2000: 192). For example, Gans' (1979) study of the USA case indicates how the substantive 'content' elements include ethnocentrism, altruistic democracy, responsible capitalism, small-town pastoralism, individualism, and moderatism. These content elements 'fit conventional notions of ideology' or 'the common sense of a hegemonic system', even if Gans refers to them as 'para-ideology' (Schudson, 2000: 192). Second, the 'form' dimension of the cultural air we breathe operates at a 'more subtle level' according to Schudson. The 'form' aspect refers to 'assumptions about narrative, story-telling, human interest' and the conventions of visual and linguistic presentation in news production. Although these forms and conventions might change over time or between different media platforms, many studies reveal them to be culturally shaped (ibid.: 193). Furthermore, newsworkers may also be seen to 'breathe a specifically journalistic, occupational cultural air' in addition to that which they share with fellow citizens. Indeed, Schudson identifies a number of specific aspects of a 'cultural air' peculiar to the journalism profession (ibid.: 193).

Variations on a 'cultural' air

Culture: 'one of the most complicated words'

If this fifth explanatory perspective (or layer of influences) on newsmaking tends to be centred around three key words 'culture', 'power' and 'ideology' (alongside hegemony, or discourse), it is worth noting that each of these three terms is heavily freighted with multiple meanings. Indeed, even the core word 'culture' itself constitutes 'one of the most complicated words' in the English language as it is used for important concepts in several distinct, if not incompatible traditions of thought (Williams, 1976/1988: 87). One result is that we find a great many published works contending for attention as 'cultural' studies of news and journalism (Golding and Murdock, 2000) in addition to those 'British' studies where 'cultural milieu serves as the overarching determinant of content' (Whitney *et al.*, 2004: 400).

This large portfolio of research includes several sub-strands. One comprises North American studies drawing on the narrative theory tradition (e.g. Darnton, 1975) which emphasise that news stories 'are just that – stories' so that journalism's 'facts' and its story telling are seen as mutually constituted (Whitney *et al.*, 2004: 400). Although a new story may require facts for its validity or existence, 'the facts demand a story for theirs' because those facts 'attain relevance only when the writer knows what to make of them', usually by selecting from a culturally given repertoire (ibid.). Another, neighbouring, strand of cultural research draws on the notion of news as *ritual* or *myth* to address the ways in which journalists seek to make sense of particular kinds of occurrences (e.g. Elliott, 1972; Carey, 1989).

Framing, culture and news selection

The cultural approaches addressing the narrative or ritual aspects of news have clear overlaps with some institutional approaches to news frames or framing as well as the seminal work of Galtung and Ruge on news values, as noted in Chapter 4. Some institutional studies approach the selection and making of news as a dual process of inclusion and exclusion, focusing on certain 'principles of organization' or 'frames' (Goffman, 1974). These principles of organisation or 'frames' are deemed to impose order on the multiple happenings of the social world and thus serve to render them into a series of meaningful events (Tuchman, 1978; McQuail, 2000; Allan, 2004). In this sense, news frames 'facilitate the ordering of the world in conjunction with hierarchical rules of inclusion and exclusion' (Allan, 2004: 59).

Gitlin (1980) extended the ethno-methodological notion of 'frame' to address how the daily routines of journalism strive to naturalise the social world in accordance with certain discursive conventions. He argued that news frames make the world beyond direct experience seem natural and given as they involve 'principles of selection, emphasis and presentation' which comprise 'little tacit theories about what exists, what happens and what matters' (Gitlin, 1980: 6). Gitlin's approach suggests that once a particular frame has been selected for a news story, its principles of selection and rejection tend to ensure that only certain kinds of information will appear in the news account – those which are deemed to be legitimate or appropriate within the conventions of newsworthiness (Gitlin,

1980; Allan, 2004). In later writings, Gitlin has challenged the idea of 'national culture' arguing that it needs to be decomposed and specified because it comprises 'an amalgam, an overlap, and many times a self-contradictory force field of forces and tendencies' which have a history (Gitlin, 2004: 310). He proposes that media studies need a more sophisticated 'social psychology' within which 'cognition, emotion, and calculation all play their parts' (Gitlin, 2004: 310).

Another concept linking news to broader patterns of cultural and social power is that of 'a hierarchy of credibility' which was advanced by H. S. Becker (1967: 241) to argue that in a system of ranked groups, most participants will assume that members of the highest group are best placed to define 'the way things really are'. In sum, Becker's concept suggests that 'credibility and the right to be heard are differentially distributed through the ranks of the system' (cited in Allan, 2004: 63). This idea was employed in some of the seminal work on labelling theory applied to studies of media and sub-cultures of deviance (Cohen and Young, 1973). The basic idea was further developed by others, including Fishman, in his (1980) *Manufacturing the News*. The core concept was adapted and elaborated by Hallin (1986, 1994) to explore how the dictates and operations of 'objective' reporting tend to ratify a normative order of 'credible' sources, especially whenever challenges to the status quo are involved. Hallin proposes that the journalist's world can be seen as divided into three spheres or regions, which may be imagined as three concentric circles: (i) the sphere of consensus; (ii) the sphere of legitimate controversy; and (iii) the sphere of deviance. Each of these three spheres tends to be governed by different standards of reporting (Shoemaker and Reese, 1996; McQuail, 2000; Allan, 2004).

Overlaps with political economy and other influences

As noted earlier, the founding figures in the British cultural studies tradition placed power at the centre of their analyses of media production, content or texts and their reception. Thus, this school has been concerned with whether and how the symbolic content and meanings in the news media, may be linked to the broader patterns of power, including those related to socio-economic and cultural hierarchies.

In viewing the forms and patterns of communication as lying at the centre of the fabric of society, Raymond Williams observed that it was impossible to discuss communication or culture in society without addressing the issues of power. Williams noted that 'there is the power of established institutions and there is increasingly the power of money' with the latter imposing certain patterns of communication that are becoming more influential in society as a whole (Williams, 1958/1989; cited in Eldridge and Eldridge, 1994: 99). At the same time, Williams argued that all forms and patterns of communication are human constructions, and so are subject to both critique and the possibilities of change (ibid.). Despite Williams' emphasis on the growing role of economic factors in modern cultural formations, these linkages have been neglected in many subsequent cultural studies approaches to newsmaking processes (Golding and Murdock, 2000). The so-called 'cultural turn' in media studies during the 1980s and 1990s was often marked by a striking neglect of material factors. But the fashion for such 'new revisionism' (Curran, 1990) has now declined and we have seen a distinct growth of attention to economic and material aspects of media production in more recent years (e.g. Hesmondhalgh, 2002).

We find considerable overlaps between the concepts and concerns of the political economic perspective and those informing cultural and ideological analyses of newsmaking, as noted in prior reviews of the literature (e.g. Shoemaker and Reese, 1996; Golding and Murdock, 2000; Whitney *et al.*, 2004: 400). For example, Golding and Murdock (2000: 71) note how the *critical* strands of both political economy and cultural studies approaches to media research tend to favour a holistic approach that is attentive to the interplay between the symbolic and material dimensions of public communication and the unequal distribution of such resources; furthermore, both draw on 'a theoretically informed understanding of the social order in which communication and cultural phenomena are being studied'. Gitlin argues that in late modern society, it is difficult to draw clear boundaries between political economy and (broadly defined) cultural influences on newsmaking: 'call culture political economy and it may sound rather "harder" than if you call it culture, but it remains a complex of human values and practices' (Gitlin, 2004: 309).

These overlaps are exemplified in the well known 'propaganda model' of news advanced by Chomsky and Herman. In *Manufacturing Consent*, Herman and Chomsky (1988: xii) combine concepts from political economy as well as linguistic, semiotic and other cultural studies fields to identify the forces deemed to cause the news media in the USA to play a propaganda role, including 'the processes by which they mobilize bias'. However, as noted in Chapter 4, such work is excessively functional in the view of some contemporary cultural theorists (e.g. Schudson, 2000).

From ideology to discourse to CDA

Ideology, hegemony and news culture

We have seen that the concept of the 'cultural air we breathe' has been closely linked to that of ideology and often includes the idea that some news stories may remain untold. The latter type of analysis is usually based on critical theories of *ideology* which view power in society as highly concentrated or unequally distributed amongst social and other interests. Some examine how unequal power relations in society may be expressed through the typical operations of media if they serve to systematically reproduce certain sets of ideas and values, thereby helping to reproduce mass consent to the established social order. For some, the news media may contribute to the process of *hegemony*, which concerns the maintenance of domination 'through means other than violence or direct state control' (Barnhurst, 2005: 241) and/or 'its acceptance as normal reality or "commonsense" by those subordinated to it' (Williams, 1976/1988: 145; see also Gitlin, 1980; Glasgow Media Group, 1976). Clearly, such views run counter to the dominant liberal and neo-liberal theories based on various pluralist models whereby power is seen as widely distributed in modern capitalist societies, or at least balanced by its circulation amongst competing institutions and interests, avoiding any significant patterns of concentration.

Much like Raymond Williams, Stuart Hall emphasised the concepts of ideology and hegemony in much of his earlier research on news and media culture. But these concepts have generally fallen out of fashion from the 1980s and been largely replaced by 'discourse'. These shifts were due in large part to the general influence of the so-called 'cultural turn' and 'new revisionism' since the 1980s as well as the influence of French poststructuralist and postmodernist ideas in British media studies (Curran, 2000). With the swing back to more material concerns in recent years, both concepts have been the subject of renewed interest (e.g. Allan, 2004; Barnhurst, 2005; Johnson, 2007). For example, Johnson (2007: 96) argues that Gramsci's notion of hegemony and related ideas provide a rich legacy of concepts for understanding contemporary political and cultural shifts, including 'the global reach of power and communication' as well as 'the role of neo-liberal intellectuals and of a deepened individualism in everyday life'.

In similar vein, Barnhurst (2005) provides an insightful application of the concept of ideology in relation to studies of news and journalism by drawing on research in neighbouring fields. He suggests that since the nineteenth century, ideology has had two principal meanings, 'both of them under attack' (Barnhurst, 2005: 241). Drawing on Eagleton's list of the six ways that 'meaning sustains domination' Barnhurst indicates how ideological analysis can help to explain certain apparent contradictions in recent research on journalism and news forms (Barnhurst, 2005: 241). More specifically, Barnhurst shows how ideological analysis helps in understanding the contradictions between findings from his empirical studies of news forms and culture in the USA and many taken-for-granted assumptions or professional myths shared by journalists.

From ideology to discourse?

Some of the seminal institutional studies of newsmaking (considered in Chapter 4) also engage with ideological and cultural issues. This is evident, for example, in Gans (1979) and Tuchman's (1978) analyses of the core or implicit values underpinning journalism in the USA, and in Galtung and Ruge's (1965) pioneering work on news values. Many recent sociological and cultural studies of journalism and news culture tend to invoke discourse rather than ideology. They also tend to emphasise that news stories are less about 'reflecting' the reality of an event, and rather more about providing a codified definition of what should count as the reality of the event. However, whether they invoke 'ideology' or 'discourse', sociological approaches tend to treat newsmaking as a structured or patterned institutional process – rather than implying or ascribing any conscious bias on the part of the individual newsworkers situated in such institutional settings.

CDA studies: critical discourse analysis

In its formative stages, the communication studies field in Europe borrowed a lot from prior scholarship in neighbouring fields such as linguistics. This tradition has continued in more recent years especially through a 'friendly invasion' of some new concepts and theorists originating in linguistics and expressed in the form of critical discourse analysis. One major influence on critical discourse analysis (CDA) as a vibrant and growing approach to media comprises the work of Norman Fairclough (Fairclough, 1989; 1995; Chouliaraki and Fairclough, 1999). However, Fairclough's work has connections to a wider group of European CDA theorists who share some common orientations and concerns (Wodak *et al.*, 1999: 7–12; Erjavec, 2005a; 2005b).

Fairclough applied the CDA approach to the study of the news and other media genres, and his studies include an analysis of the long-established BBC Radio 4 programme *Today*. The latter is broadcast early on weekday mornings and is generally regarded as the single most influential radio news programme in Britain as its audience includes many 'opinion leaders'. Fairclough's (1998) analysis of the *Today* programme demonstrates how, in their interactions with studio guests and other interviewees, the interviewers play a crucial role in re-articulating different discourses together. Fairclough identifies the construction or presence of a 'lifeworld discourse', that is the presenters' rendition of the 'discourse of ordinary people in ordinary life'. Fairclough adds that, despite appearances to the contrary, the voices of ordinary people on the *Today* programme are much more 'ventriloquized' than they are 'directly heard'. (Fairclough, 1998; Allan, 2004).

Another influential exponent of the CDA approach is Ruth Wodak. For example, Wodak's (1996) *Disorders of Discourse* presents a case study that focuses on news, its language and how it is understood by different social groups. Although the dominant theories of democracy assume a well informed citizenry, in practice it appears that the levels of understanding news (one of the main resources for informed citizenship) are relatively low and unevenly distributed across different social groups (Wodak, 1996; Fairclough, 1999). Whilst the CDA approach is a relative newcomer in the news and media studies context, it is possible to identify some concerns or elements in common with prior cultural approaches to newsmaking and other forms of media production. One of the core features of CDA is that it 'centres on authentic everyday communication' in institutional, media, political or other locations rather than on sample sentences or sample texts constructed in linguists' minds (Wodak *et al.*, 1999: 8). Some proponents position CDA as committed to 'an emancipatory, socially critical approach', which 'allies itself with those who suffer political and social injustice' and as aiming to intervene discursively in given social and political practices (ibid.).

This relatively new research strand seems to fit well with concepts and spirit of some of the seminal 'cultural' studies examined above and it appears to be winning support from a growing cluster of new scholars. For example, Erjavec's (2004) study of 'hybrid promotional news discourse' provides an interesting example of the potential of the CDA approach. It demonstrates how Fairclough's basic approach may be expanded to enable the combination of textual analysis with an analysis of discourse processes in the study of news content production and interpretation. Erjavec applies this methodology to identify and analyse new forms of 'promotional news' reporting linked to advertising and public relations interests and to address novel elements of promotional practice which are drawn upon within journalism.

Mediatisation, 'media logics' and 'dumbing-down'

Mediatisation: PR, promotional politics and news media

The term 'mediatisation' has been invoked to describe certain important changes in the features and conduct of formal political processes compared to earlier periods of modern liberal democracy. Essentially it refers to the growing role of the media in the very conduct or performance of formal 'politics' alongside the professionalisation of the processes, practitioners and practices of politics and policy formation, including the growing role of public relations specialists. These are seen to have led both the erosion of the potential and actuality of grass-roots participation in formal political parties or processes, as well as a decline of politicians' accountability to political party members or other citizen groups.

Compared to earlier stages of modern electoral democracies, the media are deemed to be replacing political parties (with their local branches and annual policy-making conferences, etc.) as the major institutions where political issues are defined, debated or monitored, and where politicians are deemed to be held accountable. The mediatisation concept suggests that 'the media seem to be increasingly an autonomous force, independent of political parties' even if in a broader view of public life, it remains the case that 'news institutions do not define politics any more than political structures fully determine the news: there is ongoing interaction' (Schudson, 2000: 175). Yet for many, the mediatisation of politics is intimately bound up with the contemporary 'crisis' of political participation, as marked by declining membership and citizen participation in political parties and the marginalisation if not elimination of open policy debates at annual party conferences in favour of tightly managed presentations and promotion of policies decided by a small core of party leaders (Sampson, 1996; Blumler and Kavanagh, 1999; Curran et al., 2005).

We suggest that the processes now referred to as mediatisation appear to have emerged first in the USA during the early decades of the twentieth century, according to the (much-neglected) work of Robert Park. He was one of the first to note the significance of the emergence of the 'public relations counselor', as 'a certain class of publicity man is now called' (Park, 1927:, 809). When the US government, 'in order to maintain the national morale' set up a press bureau, 'it created a new type of political institution' which has enabled every president 'to speak, more or, less directly, to the public'; one key effect has been 'to increase enormously the President's prestige and to enable him to maintain an ascendancy over Congress that he formerly never possessed' (ibid.). Thus, whilst the process of mediatisation is not exactly new, many contemporary studies suggest that it has accelerated in more recent decades. Gianpietro Mazzoleni defines these developments as a 'revolution' in political communication, as its core location shifts from parties to the media (Mazzoleni, 1995).

News, 'media logics' and 'entertainment formats'

The term of 'media logic' has been invoked by researchers such as Altheide and Snow (1979) to describe the widespread tendency of media producers to seek out and mobilise certain conventions, grammars and codes that are deemed to increase audience attention and satisfaction. The 'media logic' idea draws attention to the deeply-patterned and pervasive role of pre-existing definitions or expectations with respect to any given type of content as well as key features of its mode of presentation, media grammar or look and feel (McQuail, 2000; Altheide, 2004).

For Altheide, the concepts of 'media logic' and 'entertainment format' are used to address how mass media and popular cultural content and social forms 'influence journalism culture and political communication' (2004: 293). This applies especially to the USA where research shows 'very clearly that news and politics are immersed in the entertainment format' and where this emphasis has 'changed the organization as well as the working assumptions and culture of journalists and audiences' (ibid.). As a consequence, the 'infotainment news perspective' holds that, for practical reasons, 'any event can be summarily covered and presented as a narrative account with a beginning, middle, and end'. As a result, Altheide claims, audiences 'now find it perfectly sensible to "cover the world in 60 seconds," to watch the war "live," or to see major social events cast as music videos' (2004: 294).

Altheide (2004: 294) argues that the two concepts of 'media logic' and 'entertainment formats' are helpful 'in clarifying some important changes that have occurred between news and politics'. For Altheide, *media logic* refers to 'the assumptions and processes for constructing messages within a particular medium', including the features of 'rhythm, grammar, and format' (2004: 294). The notion of (entertainment) 'format' comprises one feature of media logic, but it is singularly important because it refers to the rules or 'codes' for defining, selecting, organising, presenting, and recognising information 'as one thing rather than another' (Altheide, 2004: 294). For Altheide, such codes help us recognise and define some programme as 'the evening news' and not as a 'situation comedy' or a 'parody of news' (2004: 294). Media logic embraces 'the rationale, emphasis, and orientation' promoted by media production, processes, and messages and it 'tends to be evocative, encapsulated, highly thematic, familiar to audiences, and easy to use' (ibid.).

Media logic is seen to have 'transformed journalistic culture', as even changes in the way in which journalists conduct interviews pose significant consequences for political communication (Altheide, 2004: 294). The prevailing criteria for newsworthy stories, especially among TV journalists, are appropriated by news sources and other newsmakers as well. As journalists and news sources increasingly share the understandings of 'media logic and formats' for what comprises a good story and a good interview, 'the occupational and perspective lines that had separated them became blurred' (Altheide, 2004: 294). The resultant new form of journalism has been defined as *postjournalism* in some studies (e.g. Altheide and Snow, 1979).

The perceived 'postjournalism turn' fundamentally challenges 'the autonomy and relevance of professional journalism's training, ethics, and truth claims' (Altheide, 2004: 295). Altheide argues that such political communication did not grow out of an independent journalism profession 'but, rather, reflects the growing network of media culture promoting products, information, and cultural consensus' (2004: 295).

As regards news or informational content, media logic is seen to privilege immediacy, including dramatic illustrative film or photos, fast tempo and short 'sound bites' (Hallin, 1992), as well as 'personally attractive presenters and relaxed formats' such as the so-called 'happy news' format (McQuail, 2000: 296). Furthermore, the 'bias' of media logic is systematic and deeply embedded in media-organisational working arrangements and forward planning. For example, researchers such as Hallin (1992) have demonstrated clear correlations in US news coverage of elections between 'horse-race coverage' and 'soundbite news', and 'the more the former, the shorter the latter' (McQuail, 2000: 297).

'Dumbing down'? Tabloidisation, celebrity culture and news

Clearly the issues posed for news culture and journalism by the concepts of media logic and entertainment formats have overlaps with the large literature on 'dumbing-down', tabloidisation and celebrity culture. As the research literature focused on the latter is larger, longer-established and better known, it will not be addressed in detail here, not merely for reasons of space, but because most of the substantive issues have been covered under other concepts or headings.

However we would flag two brief observations or clarifications at this point. Whilst we share some of the critics' concerns about deteriorating news values and standards in the media of public communication, like others (e.g. Turner, 1999) we propose that the term 'tabloidisation' is too imprecise and laden with multiple values. Thus, alternative and more nuanced, concepts and analytical categories seem to be better equipped to fully address the trends and fundamental issues at stake. Second, we must note that in the homelands of the now 'dominant' or 'hegemonic' Anglo-US model of journalism, expressions of concern and criticism, on the part of both professional journalists and academic researchers have been much amplified in recent years. One key concern here is that 'serious journalism' is now on the retreat and the types of news values or standards with which it has been associated in earlier periods of modernity, are being dramatically recast in the present media landscape. We find, for example, many expressions of concern that news is moving away from foreign affairs towards domestic concerns, from politics towards human-interest stories; from issues to people. Furthermore, the expressions of concern about declining journalistic standards and new values 'strike an equally powerful resonance in other national contexts' (Allan, 2004: 196).

Here we note that these concerns and arguments have not been confined to the rather specialist domains of media studies literature. In recent years they have also achieved some prominence in the wider media and the public sphere, including forums and debates in which journalists have themselves engaged. Indeed one notable feature of recent developments in Britain is the extent to which many news media professionals have themselves engaged proactively and reflexively in these debates. These include distinctive contributions from media professionals which move beyond mere defensive modes of engagement with such issues and which seek to identify the fundamental points of concern, their origins or causes (e.g. Lloyd, 2004; Rusbridger, 2005).

Cultural 'embeddedness' of journalism: national/local

Whilst many sociological studies of news and journalism have noted how journalists tend to subscribe to the core values of their national political culture, this point is even further underlined by the cultural perspective. Indeed, some early researchers on news (e.g. Park, 1940) have observed the dense and complex ways in which 'journalism is a craft of place; it works by the light of local knowledge' (Carey, 2007: 4). These highlight how, in many important respects, newsmaking tends to be deeply embedded in particular local cultures or national social formations as well as specific temporal contexts. In many respects, what journalists 'know and how they know it ... what stories interest journalists and the form that interest takes, is pretty much governed by the here and now' as Carey put it (ibid.). Furthermore, 'this localism, even ethnocentrism', can be rendered in various ways as the 'we' at its centre can mean members of a congregation, those of a common race, gender, ethnicity, 'but most often, it refers to "we fellow citizens" of a country, state, or region' (ibid.). In sum, we note here that news, as a specific form of knowledge or story telling, is highly attuned to the prevailing ideas, experiences, customs or even certain shared 'feelings' in specific communities and time periods.

Not only 'truth': amongst the casualties of war

It has long been recognised, both within the modern journalism profession and without, that 'truth' has always been one of the first casualties of war. Indeed, alongside truth, we might add many of the other key values and standards of modern journalism such as objectivity, balance, and checking sources. If the origins of the now dominant Anglo-US model of journalism can be traced back to the decades surrounding the turn of the last century, then this was accompanied by an implicit assumption or acceptance that war (like colonialism and imperialism) was to be treated as a major exception when it comes to application of professional values and ethical codes. For it was precisely in those decades that the dark arts of spin related to modern 'information warfare' and propaganda techniques were first institutionalised by specialist military and political strategists (Taylor, 1997). It was also in those decades that the emerging Anglo-US model of journalism was embedded in a culture of extreme nationalism linked to the legitimation, if not active advocacy, of colonial adventures and imperial domination of other nations.

In some respects, we may understand the unwritten and unspoken 'war exception' clauses within the codes of modern journalism as a particular or unusually heightened expression of the national 'embeddedness' of news cultures. After all, the two major wars of the twentieth century were largely organised and performed as 'total system' wars whereby the resources of all the nation's industrial sectors were to be mobilised and harnessed to defeat the enemy, and so journalists and news media might be seen as simply contributing their roles and resources. But such functional analyses do not sit comfortably with a cultural or ethical perspective on either war or journalism. As regards the former, the old questions of just or legitimate versus unjust wars remains a vital question, but one now to be framed in the norms of international law (Habermas, 2006). For the latter, the acute issues of journalists' ethical positions when it comes to the coverage of the different categories of war remains something of a neglected black box in the relevant literature on professional codes and values. Yet, these issues have been bubbling away underneath the business-as-usual news media coverage of the invasion and war in Iraq undertaken by the USA and its partners in the 'coalition of the willing' since 2003.

The debates surrounding the morality as well as the legitimacy (under international law) of the invasion and war in Iraq have provoked many strong passions and some compelling attempts to address these larger issues by writers on both sides of the Atlantic (e.g. Levy *et al.*, 2005). That war also led to massive demonstrations on the streets of major cities in Europe, the USA and elsewhere, but without any direct 'public opinion' effect on military policy or journalistic discourse. It has, however, yielded studies of how the new media framed and covered these manifestations of opposition (e.g. Luther and Miller, 2005). There have also been several analyses of how this war was framed and 'marketed' to the citizens of the USA and the wider world (e.g. Thrall, 2007). Several recent studies describe how the news media in the USA tend to operate a hand-in-glove relationship with the White House, abandoning independence in favour of supporting the official line in times of war and international crisis – such as the invasion of Iraq and its lead-up (Bennett *et al.*, 2007; Friel and Falk, 2007).

Friel and Falk (2007) provide a detailed analysis of the *New York Times* coverage of the lead up to the USA-led invasion and war in Iraq in 2003 and its aftermath in light of a long-run account of the newspaper's treatment of US foreign policy over the past half-century. This case study is instructive because the *New York Times* (*NYT*) occupies such an 'exalted place in the political and moral imagination of influential Americans and others', often treated as the most authoritative source of information and guidance on issues of public policy. The newspaper has acquired a special status as the newspaper of record in the USA and it is regarded as 'a trusted media source that supposedly is dedicated to truthfulness and objectivity, regardless of political consequences' (ibid.: 2). The authors describe how the *NYT* fails to live up to the high standards attendant to its special status when it comes to wars or other military adventures undertaken by the US government and when it comes to foreign news coverage in times of heightened crisis – precisely the times when independent thinking and analysis is most required. Friel and Falk (ibid.: 15) examine how the *NYT* editorial pages failed to fully consider the legality of the invasion of Iraq although it had 'an obligation, as the most influential newspaper in the United States, to publish its opinion about the legal status of the invasion'. They describe how the newspaper's editorial page 'made no discernible effort' to hold the Bush administration's threats and use of force against Iraq accountable to any law, unlike the coverage in many overseas media (Friel and Falk, 2007: 17).

Friel and Falk's study also finds that the *NYT's* Iraq coverage in this regard was 'not unusual' because 'ignoring international law when it applies to US foreign policy is a fifty-year-old practice at the *Times* editorial page' since the latter has rarely acknowledged US violations of the UN Charter since its founding in the 1940s (2007: 17). They argue that any threat and use of force in violation of international law by the USA 'is a fact of enormous global significance' that is reported as such by much of the world's news media even if US news media ignore such violations of international law (ibid.: 16). This gives rise to 'an imbalance of knowledge' between the United States and the rest of the world which makes it relatively easy for national political leaders to manipulate US public opinion against foreign critics whilst 'also increasing the supply of anti-American terrorists for reasons that escape public comprehension in the United States' (Friel and Falk, 2007: 17).

Institutionalism-II: Bourdieu, Hallin and 'new institutionalism'

Finally we turn to another category of news and journalism research which we might dub as a second category of institutionalist studies (or institutionalism-II). These studies tend to examine newsmaking in the context of the broader set of institutions in modern society and so they share elements of the more holistic perspective favoured by both political economy and the cultural studies work considered earlier. Yet, they also differ from many of the studies addressed in Chapter 4 which tend to place a primary focus on media and those neighbouring institutions most directly or explicitly involved in shaping news production.

Hirsch's seminal study (1972) involved a 'depoliticized exploration' of what the Frankfurt School had earlier characterised as the 'culture industry' or the industrialisation of culture (Hirsch, 2000: 356). In this and later work, Hirsch seems to bear a rather weak or strained relationship to the kinds of meso-level theorising in media studies favoured by the earlier US work of Merton and Lazersfeld (Frenzen, Hirsch and Zerillo, 1994; Hirsch, 1997: 1707). In later work, Hirsch engages with contemporary debates concerning the direction of institutional theories in general (e.g. Hirsch, 1997) and this also links to more recent neo-institutional approaches to newsmaking and political communication (Benson, 2004; Sparrow, 2006).

Examples of the kind of work in mind here comprise several contributions by Daniel Hallin (e.g. 2000; 2005; Hallin and Mancini, 2004). Hallin (2000) provides an insightful account of the many changes in institutional processes and organisational strategies over the past 20 years which have tended to narrow the presumed separations between the business and editorial aspects of commercial news media. This account concurs with trends noted in consideration of recent empirical studies (in Chapters 4 and 5), suggesting that such shifts are eroding the space or potential for journalism that is independent of business norms or other economic pressures. Reviewing the important shifts in the organisational structures and strategies of news media in the USA since the 1980s, Hallin (2000: 221) suggests that the prior model of journalism is increasingly giving way to concepts such as 'total newspapering'. He also suggests that news organisations have been increasingly subject to the same profit-maximising logics prevailing in other business sectors with managerial strategies or 'policy' promoting the idea that 'circulation, sales and editorial efforts must be integrated, all directed towards the project of marketing' to audiences defined as consumers (ibid.). More broadly, when it comes to the selection of editors and other editorial management staff, newspapers and other news organisations now place much greater emphasis than before on business and marketing skills, and marketing research plays an increasing role in shaping the strategic direction of editorial policies. Key management decisions and policies are laid down at corporate meetings where few, if any, staff 'with a reporter's mentality' are present (Hallin, 2000: 220). Although there are variations in the extent and intensity of such shifts across media organisations, Hallin points to increasing tensions between 'the cultures of journalism and marketing' and these are manifest in a news agenda moving away 'from traditional public affairs' towards lifestyle features and 'news you can use' (ibid.: 221).

In a subsequent work, Hallin (2005) further explores the key theoretical and systemic issues impinging on journalism's autonomy from both political and economic factors. This is achieved by analytic reviews of 'differentiation' theories of the media, Bourdieu's field theory and Habermas' colonisation concepts as well as debates over de-differentiation trends. Such work provides an interesting contribution in terms of linking some of the classical sociological concepts to the recent growth of interest in Pierre Bourdieu's more culturally nuanced work on the autonomy and specificities of the journalistic field (e.g. Allan, 2004; Benson and Neveu, 2005; Benson, 2006; Kaplan, 2006). Benson (2006), Kaplan (2006) and others have recently sought to embrace Bourdieu's field theory and to link it to the 'new institutionalism' approaches to journalism advanced by Sparrow (2006) and others in the USA. According to Benson (2006), Bourdieu's field theory and the 'new institutionalism' comprise complementary approaches which may be combined to offer new insights on journalism and newsmaking. Benson (2006: 188) argues that both these approaches call for a new unit of analysis for journalism studies: 'between the individual news organization and the society as a whole, the "mezzo-level" interorganizational and professional environment of the field/institution'. Sparrow's (2006: 146) 'new institutionalism theory of news' is rooted in the open-systems approach developed in organisational theory. It argues that news media develop routines and 'practices-institutions' in response to three kinds of uncertainty: whether or how they will make a profit, establish their legitimacy, and find timely information. In turn, these routines and practices become taken-for-granted assumptions or guidelines for producing news 'that span across news organizations to compose an institutional regime of news'. Sparrow (ibid.) argues that the resulting regime serves to 'constrain' journalists working within major mainstream media organisations 'to produce extraordinarily homogeneous kinds of news'. For Kaplan, the new institutionalism helps to highlight how, since the turn of the last century, the transformations in journalism's mission 'have been reflected and refracted by more overarching shifts' in the political system, especially in the US case (Kaplan, 2006: 174).

Concluding comments

In reviewing the broad spectrum of cultural perspectives we note that some highlight how newsmaking is deeply embedded in particular cultures or national social formations as well as specific temporal contexts (Carey, 2007). The question of whether and how this is now changing in light of the much cited tendencies towards 'globalisation' – and especially in the context of the intensified processes of trans-nationalisation in the EU region of the world – will be addressed in Chapter 9. But before that, in Chapter 8 we turn our attention to audiences and issues concerning their changing roles, characteristics and status in relation to news culture.

A key relation

Journalists and their publics

Monika Metykova

A key relation: audiences and publics

The public: 'the god term of journalism'?

This chapter focuses on key issues concerning the relations between journalists and their readers/audiences and how these have been changing over the past two decades. It must be noted, however, that throughout this book, audiences are understood as a crucial consideration or factor for most if not all layers of influences on journalism practices and news cultures. For as noted earlier, the audience – at least in the sense of the public – is nothing less than 'the god term of journalism ... the term without which nothing counts' (Carey, 2007: 12).

The chapter opens with a discussion of different conceptualisations of audiences and sources of audience change. It then moves on to outline understandings of audiences as active participants in the mediated communication process. The middle sections of the chapter discuss the impact of new consumer cultures as well as technological changes on the relationship between journalists and their audiences. Similarly, trans-national migration and the increased importance of multiculturalism have played an important role in the changing nature of audiences and media practices, and these are discussed in the final part of the chapter.

The chapter presents empirical findings from our interviews with European journalists and is further informed by roundtable discussions with media professionals, politicians and media users/consumers (including non-governmental organisations) about the preliminary results of the research.

Audiences through the lens of media organisations

'Audience' is a term used in communication research from its early days, however, the meanings associated with it can vary significantly. Audience is an abstract and debateable term that does not denote an identifiable social collectivity. At the most elementary level media audience implies an aggregate of the readers, viewers or listeners of different media or their contents. Media audiences are characterised by a certain duality; in simple terms, audiences are at the same time at the root of media contents and a response to them. The media audience has been studied for a variety of purposes and within a range of frameworks. A basic distinction can be made among structural, behavioural and socio-cultural approaches. Structural approaches aim to describe the composition of the audience, behavioural ones target the effects of media messages on individual behaviour, while socio-cultural approaches concentrate on meanings of media content as well as processes of media use in social and cultural contexts. The following parts of this section deal with characteristics of audiences that are key for media organisations as commercial players.

When approaching the media audience from a market point of view, it has a dual significance for media organisations: on the one hand the audience is an aggregate of potential consumers of a media product and on the other hand it is in itself a product, 'media firms produce content, then either give this content away or sell it in order to attract audiences. Media companies then sell audiences to advertisers who are seeking the attention of potential consumers of their products or services' (Napoli, 2003: 2). The majority of media companies operate on both markets (content and audiences), while their performance on the audience market is to a large degree determined by the media organisation's success in attracting an audience's attention on the content market. Moreover, advertisers are likely to be interested in certain demographic groups who then become the target of increasing amounts of media content.

In this respect it is important to remember that advertisers consider particular segments of the audience most valuable. They attempt to place their advertisements within such contents whose audiences include the most likely consumers of their products. Usually the presumptions made by advertisers about purchasing habits involve demographic factors, such as age, gender, and income. 'Younger audience members (e.g., those aged 18 to 49) generally are more highly valued than older audience members (e.g., those older than 50)' (Napoli, 2003: 104). The attractiveness of a particular gender for advertisers is highly dependent on the advertised product; however, women are often more valued by advertisers as they make the majority of decisions on household products. As a rule advertisers prefer audiences with higher incomes. Research in this vein suggests that audiences and products and the measurement of such products are of key importance in securing financial profits.

For many decades media management, marketing and advertising interests had been investing heavily in finding out about their audiences' routines and tastes. Yet, up till the 1980s, it appears that the routines of journalists and editors engaged in newsmaking were rarely informed by the findings of audience or market research undertaken by management in media organisations (Gans, 1972; Shoemaker and Reese, 1996). But this has changed in recent decades, as noted in earlier chapters. Changes in organisational processes and strategies over the past 20 years have tended to narrow the presumed separations between the business and editorial aspects of commercial news media. News organisations have been increasingly marked by managerial strategies or 'policy' promoting the idea that all staff, including those in editorial and journalistic departments, 'must be integrated, all directed towards the project of marketing' to audiences defined as consumers (Hallin, 2000: 221).

Role of audiences as 'active' participants

In terms of academic media research, the understanding of audiences as active participants in mediated communication has been gaining strength since the 1980s. By this time research on media audiences had become increasingly concerned with the possible and actual uses of media by an audience conceptualised as 'active'. It was the so-called uses and gratifications tradition that opened up research into 'what people do with the media' as opposed to previous research which was concerned with 'what media do to the people' (for more on the history of audience research see Morley, 1992). In essence, reception studies are concerned with the attribution and construction of meanings derived from the media by the receivers (media audiences); reception analysis involves the 'comparative textual analysis of media discourses, whose results are interpreted with emphatic reference to context, both the historical as well as cultural setting and the "context" of other media contents' (Jensen and Jankowski, 1991: 139).

David Morley's *Nationwide Audience* (1980) is understood as the most influential piece of research in the emergence of reception studies in Britain. Stuart Hall's encoding/decoding model was of key importance for Morley's study when in 1976 and 1977 he conducted research to explore the relationship between the interpretation of the *Nationwide* programme and the socio-cultural background of the viewers, analysing the link between codes used in the media message and the interpretative codes of various socio-cultural groups. The new type of qualitative research into the reception of media texts produced several significant works in the 1980s (among these we find, for example, Seiter *et al.*, 1989; Morley, 1980). Early studies in this tradition were mainly concerned with factual genres, in particular news; however, within reception studies in this period we also find research that shifted from ideology in the political sense to questions of pleasure, mainly under the influence of feminist film studies. This shift enabled the exploration of women in the role of active and selective readers/viewers/listeners, a celebration of pleasures linked to femininity as well as an uncovering of voices subjected to the power of ideology and discourse (e.g. Ang's work on the reception of *Dallas* published in 1985, Hobson's on *Crossroads* published in 1982, Radway's work on the reading of romance novels published in 1984, Modleski's work on fantasies for women published in 1982).

In the 1990s new audience research within British media studies can be characterised by a widening agenda. Apart from a concern with the reception of media texts within a variety of contexts and by individuals and collectivities with a variety of socio-cultural backgrounds, studies are also characterised by an increased interest in the use of media (including new media – the Internet and digital media) within the context of everyday life (e.g. Silverstone and Hirsch, 1992; Moores, 1996). Other more recent strands within audience research explore links between citizenship and media (media as part of the public sphere). The 1990s have also witnessed an increase in comparative audience studies, for example, Livingstone (1998).

Changing audiences

Changes in audiences are largely due to the co-evolution of changes in both communication technologies and societal structures and processes. In historical terms, the research literature suggests three important stages in which the nature of audiences changed: the emergence of a reading public (following the invention of print), the commercialisation of forms of public communication (formation of media industries) and spread of electronic media (and the subsequent fragmentation of audiences). The following sections of the chapter discuss some factors that played a role in the changing relationship between journalists and their audiences in the last two decades.

Implications of recent technological changes

In recent years we have witnessed a surge of research focused on the impact of new technologies on journalism. Pavlik (2000), for example, argues that there are at least four broad areas in which new technologies influence journalism: journalists' work, news content, structure and/or organisation of the newsroom, and the relationship between media, journalists and their audiences/publics. Pavlik argues that journalistic work resembles a dialogue between the press and the public in particular in the case of news organisations committed to publishing online:

> In these cases in particular, audience members have joined in significant numbers in online discussions with reporters and editors to debate and discuss coverage of important events. E-mail has become a vital and instantaneous link between readers and reporters, often shaping reporters' knowledge and attitudes as much as an initial report may have influenced the public.
>
> (Pavlik, 2000: 235).

The research literature suggests that there has been a distinct shift towards media practices and formats which permit or encourage certain forms of audience participation or modes of 'interaction' in both new and old media (e.g. vox pop segments in print and broadcast media; phone-in segments in broadcast programmes; or the encouragement of email responses from audiences). A Dutch study notes that due to the growing use of Internet by audiences, 'according to more than half of the journalists [surveyed] offering an inter-pretation, and not just handing out facts, becomes an increasingly essential function of journalism' (Pleijter *et al.*, 2002: 29 as quoted in ter Wal, 2006a). The rise of 'reality' television has brought about a 'new' participatory relationship between viewer and screen (see e.g. Holmes, 2004). It is uncertain, however, as to whether these changes amount to much more than a technological updating of more traditional forms of interaction, e.g. in the case of print media of 'letters to the editor'. Very few newspapers, for example, have established a readers' ombudsman position with an active (as opposed to token) role and status. It also needs to be borne in mind that new technologies lead to an increase in everyday news sharing (as opposed to professional news); this involves informal private news such as stories about what happened at work (see Gans 2007).

Although findings presented in the literature do not clearly support a thesis about audiences' increased interactive use of journalism, in particular in relation to news (see e.g. Hujanen and Pietikainen, 2004), it is doubtless that in the last decades opportunities for the public to interact with content providers and to create contents have increased significantly. Internet users can engage directly with content on websites of various media (e.g comment on articles), they can also use blogs, chat fora as well as personal websites to publish their own con-tents. There are different types of online sites which work with user-generated content; some have no editorial function, for example YouTube, Wikipedia and Wikinews, while in other cases the agenda can be set by an editor, for example, an online newspaper providing space for a discussion on its content. It is not unusual for a mainstream medium to develop strategies of incorporating user-generated contents in its services, for example when audience members submit their own images and videos.

In addition, the consumption of online media contents provides the audiences with more options than the consumption of traditional media contents. Websites offer easy access to stories of interest as they are equipped with search options as well as topical categories, thus audiences are able to create more personalised information environments (see Geens *et al.*, 2007). It has been argued that such environments shut audiences off from larger currents of public information in society, thus further fragmenting news audiences. Schoenbach *et al.* (2005) empirically tested the hypothesis according to which print media are more effective in widening their readers' awareness of public topics, issues and events than online media. The results of the representative survey of almost 1,000 respondents show that both types of media contribute to widening the audience agenda; however, in the case of online newspapers this effect applies only to the most educated section of society.

Clearly, recent years have witnessed a huge surge of research interest in new types of journalism – participatory, online journalism as well as so-called wiki-journalism. Some researchers claim that these developments are leading to the blurring of the distinction between media content producers and media content consumers, at least in some contexts. Indeed, some enthusiasts even proclaim a certain 'death of the audience', suggesting that the rise of new media platforms and ease of access to new media forms such as blogs and blogging mean nothing less than the impending disappearance of 'the people formerly known as the audience' (Rosen, 2006). Yet for others, such rumours of the demise of the audience are somewhat premature. They remain sceptical that any significant shifts in audience status or roles are emerging relative to those of well established media operators, or well funded news sources and agenda setters such as advertising, public relations or other business and commercial interests.

Growth of infotainment, dumbing-down and celebrity culture

Media research conducted in various European countries has documented tabloidisation – 'a trend characterized by emphasis on both private life and "soft" news coverage' (Sparks, 2000; cited in Uribe and Gunter, 2004: 388), as well as less space devoted to information (Rooney, 2000) and less attention to 'hard' and foreign news (Winston, 2002), increased visuals and decreased text (Djupsund and Carlson, 1998) and an increasing personalisation in the coverage (Sparks, 2000). In other words there is less 'hard' news and information content and increasingly more emphasis on entertainment and sports content; related terms used to describe this trend include dumbing down and infotainment.

The usual reason cited for these trends is the expanding number and variety of media, especially in the broadcasting sector, and consequent increased competition for audiences. However, more complex views regarding this trend have also been expressed. Buonanno (1999) argues that the trend of popularisation in Italian print journalism had started in the mid-1980s and intensified in the 1990s, and is the outcome of a number of circumstances: the growth of advertising investments and opening to market logics; new social groups, in particular women and youth, among the readership; an extension in the geographical coverage of news as well as more varied types of news; the increasing importance and autonomy of news media in the society and a boom in local news and newspapers. At the beginning of the 1990s this process was further strengthened by the appearance of new models and formats of current affairs programming on television (ibid.).

It is not surprising that media organisations have made use of digital technologies in their competition for audiences. Klinenberg and Fayer (2005), for example, argue that digital technologies have allowed media corporations to take the principles of target marketing to new levels, making specialised media products for niche groups of consumers. Some newspapers are applying digital production technologies to print more specialised editions of newspapers, engaging in target marketing, with most of the targets being affluent audiences (ibid.: 58).

A different tendency which supports the overall tabloidisation trend has been highlighted by British and Dutch researchers who express growing concerns about the highly incestuous or 'intertextual' character of journalistic discourse and editorial cultures (Preston, 2006a; ter Wal, 2006a). This leads to an increasing prevalence of journalism making references to journalism, and is linked to the personalisation of news values and the growth of celebrity culture within journalism itself.

In some cases increased competition is related directly to audience demographics and results in deteriorating editorial quality. Aldridge (2003) demonstrates this in the case of local and regional titles in the United Kingdom. These papers are in a difficult position when competing for audiences, as commuters' use of local papers leads them to be less local (Aldridge, 2003: 492) and young people are not targeted in local papers (ibid.: 493). The papers, as Aldridge shows in the case of predatory paedophiles and asylum seekers, then manipulate public fears to create news and gain readers.

New relations between audiences and news culture

Up to now, we have addressed some of the audience issues and trends discussed in the prior research literature. We now turn to our own project's findings to consider how journalists from 11 European countries view the unfolding changes.

New technologies

A greater degree of feedback from readers and viewers and improved communication lines were most frequently mentioned in connection with the impact of new technologies. However, the view that print media are not interactive enough was also voiced by our interviewees. Inevitably, blogs and the existence of 'lay journalists' came up in our interviews; in general this development is seen as a positive one – journalists have an increased pool of information at their disposal – yet, as one of our journalists says, blogs can become very disruptive as they lead to huge amounts of news. Journalists also acknowledge that more attention is paid to audiences through focus groups and other forms of market research.

'Disconnected' from the public

When asked about changes in relationships with their audiences a number of our interviewees pointed out that trust and respect for the journalistic profession has been on the decline. Journalists from former communist countries suggested that media professionals value their audiences more but at the same time the audiences trust the journalists less, even less than they did under communist rule. The reasons for the distrust that interviewees identified included factual mistakes in reporting, but also misunderstanding of the public's views at key moments, for example, during the French vote on the European constitution.

The sense of 'disconnectedness' from the public was perhaps most notable in the case of Dutch journalists (ter Wal, 2006a). All Dutch interviewees mentioned the rise of the populist politician Pym Fortyun in the spring of 2002 as a key event that has changed Dutch editorial culture and relationships with readers/ viewers. In the words of one of our Dutch interviewees:

> The reader is now as displaced and emancipated as the voter. The voter no longer lets his party or pillar tell him what he should think. You could say the reader has also become more emancipated. He can get his information from anywhere. He no longer lets you tell him what to think.
>
> (ter Wal, 2006a)

The situation resulted in various attempts made by Dutch journalists to 'reconnect' with the society, for example, by increasing the number of regional correspondents, covering more varied topics, and also assuming a less politically correct approach to asylum issues.

The sense of 'disconnection' from the public as a result of major socio-political changes is also expressed by journalists from former communist countries. These countries have undergone major changes since the fall of communism in the late 1980s and early 1990s which have, naturally, affected media as well. In less than two decades public service broadcasting as well as commercial media were established. In some cases post-communist governments interfered significantly in the independence of media. For example, in the case of the Slovak Republic after the fall of communism and the break-up of Czechoslovakia, a nationalist government led by Prime Minister Vladimír Mečiar gained control of public service broadcasting and interfered in the allocation of licences for commercial broadcasting. These and other practices (e.g. only selected journalists could attend government press conferences) polarised not only media professionals but the public at large. The government fell in 1998, yet some of the journalists we interviewed still perceive the impact that this polarisation had on their relations with the public.

Slovak as well as Czech journalists argued that the degree of trust in their relationship with audiences is, paradoxically, worse than in communist Czechoslovakia. A Slovak interviewee expressed the view that:

> today there is more scepticism about what appears in the papers, on television … the relationship between media and readers has paradoxically worsened, media enjoy less trust than under communism which is weird … today they are not taken seriously … they are understood more as entertainment.
>
> (Cisarova, 2007b)

Adjusting to audience 'demands'

The scepticism and questioning related to content that our interviewees referred to can be related to general populist trends in media such as tabloidisation and dumbing down. Journalists themselves acknowledge the shift in news selection which supposedly results from attempts to engage with audience demands and everyday interests, through light news topics such as lifestyle or health. As a consequence foreign news appears to have lost some of its news value. Journalists feel that their choice of topics is limited and at the same time, in the words of an Italian print journalist, 'we now worry more about talking to a reader also culturally less prepared, to extend the market but also the comprehension. There is the invasion in newspapers of so-called infographics which also aims to explain better to the reader what we are talking about' (ter Wal and Valeriani, 2006).

Some journalists point out that print media face specific problems when attracting audiences as they are competing with television and the Internet in terms of coverage.

> The main issue is that we talk to audiences about issues or events they already have taken from television, so that we must try to go beyond – finding new themes and doing backgrounds or in-depth articles on the themes covered by television.
>
> (Italian journalist quoted in ter Wal and Valeriani, 2006)

Some journalists commented on the supposedly increased power of audiences to influence media content. A French print journalist observed on the issue: 'the reader is not the one who tells us what to write. The reader can tell us which issues are interesting, but about what we put in the paper, for example the death penalty, we don't give a damn whether the reader is for or against. We are against' (Guyot *et al.*, 2006). Audience pressure is also perceived in public service media; a Czech journalist working for public service radio explains that the listener is the boss. 'Not to a tabloid extent but we are here for him and he is paying us' (Cisarova, 2007a).

As the quotations above suggest, our interviewees identified market pressures as potentially having a major impact on their relationship with audiences. Commercialisation has meant that a greater effort is made to gauge the interests and opinions of the media consumers and to tailor news content to appeal to them, as well as making it more accessible. Interviewees noted that this was happening across the board but particularly in relation to certain demographic groups: for example, a British interviewee noted that his paper attempted to 'attract younger readers, and in order to do that, we are running stories that we might have rejected a number of weeks ago. ... Similarly, if I can have a story that will appeal particularly to women we'll go for that' (Preston, 2006a). An Irish interviewee illustrated the importance of the Joint National Media Research figures in determining the content of newspapers, in terms of gauging the socio-economic and age makeup of the readership.

> There is a sense that in general, and in Ireland in particular, society (and therefore the reader) has become more middle class. This has tended to

produce forms of journalism that are more consumer-driven – by that and by lifestyle issues.

(Horgan, 2006)

Covering controversies

The coverage of sensitive or controversial issues raises a number of questions related mainly to ethical principles and professional values. This section is devoted particularly to cases in which journalists' decision about whether and how to cover a controversial topic is related to their concerns not only about credibility and professional standing but their audiences' reactions.

A Spanish interviewee summed up the manner in which he and his colleagues deal with controversial issues in the following way: 'We play safely. ... We take few risks in our job ... because we may offend the reader's sensitivity' (Guyot *et al.*, 2006). This leads us to the question of self-censorship for the public good. Such cases were noted by our interviewees, particularly, by the French editors who had the recent experience of reporting on the suburban riots in Paris and elsewhere in October and November 2005. In this case, as one of our French interviewees noted, there was 'a collective decision not to broadcast information about the number of burnt cars to avoid drifting off towards overbid from the young who were burning vehicles' (ibid.).

British journalists referred to issues of privacy. One of them, for instance, spoke of how the BBC had not run a story about David Beckham's private life, because there were no ramifications for the public interest (Preston, 2006a). A Hungarian journalist acknowledged that he would be willing to jeopardise someone's privacy in case this was in the public interest (Kovács *et al.*, 2005).

New multicultural publics and diversifying audiences

One of the major changes in the research on editorial cultures over the recent past is the increasing attention to the growth of trans-national migration, both within the European Union area and from beyond. In an increasing number of countries, this phenomenon, together with a new sensitivity to the increasingly multicultural character of European social formations, is now viewed as a major challenge for both the study and practice of journalism. Indeed, in several countries, the issues of multiculturalism and their implications for research on editorial culture and practices, comprise one of the significant changes in the research agenda, to mention some of the themes explored: internationalisation of European broadcasting, the production and consumption of diasporic media, broadcasting for minorities and its role in the public sphere (see e.g. Negrine and Papathanassopoulos, 1990; Chalaby, 2002; Georgiou, 2005).

In general terms increasing migration has been reflected in media and communications research in various European countries since the 1980s with a great increase in studies on the nature, production and consumption of media contents about and for minorities and migrants since the 1990s. In the Netherlands media coverage of migration has been studied since the 1980s (see van Dijk, 1991). The more visible presence of such research often goes hand-in-hand with an increased visibility of migrant populations in European media. For example, in Italy migrants have featured in the media since the 1980s; however, coverage increased in 1991 with the arrival of refugees from neighbouring Albania following the disruption of the regime of Enver Hoxa (ter Wal and Valeriani, 2006). In comparison, in the case of the Republic of Ireland, traditionally a migrant-producing country, migration trends have changed significantly by the mid-1990s. While in 1988 Ireland produced 60,000 emigrants and received 19,000 immigrants, in 1998 the number of emigrants was down to 22,000 but the number of immigrants was 43,000. Although these numbers were small by European standards they created an immediate negative response in the Irish media (Horgan, 2006).

In what follows we briefly consider some of the key issues and trends in the media coverage of migration and minorities, in terms of content as well as production processes. Attention is also paid to the consumption of minority and migration-related content by audiences.

Coverage of migration

As noted, a growing share of recent European media research has concentrated on the analysis of media coverage of migration. These studies use qualitative and quantitative methods of content analysis, and their most frequent finding is that media coverage of migration tends to be biased, in some cases outright racist. For example, van Dijk's pivotal study (1991) presents a content and discourse analysis of coverage of ethnic minorities in seven national Dutch dailies from August 1985 to January 1986. His main conclusion is that the various elements of coverage, from headlines, topics and subjects, to quotes, argumentation, style and rhetoric contributed to the negative portrayal of minorities and to the separation of in-group and out-groups, or, in the theoretical framework adopted in this study, to the 'reproduction of racism' (ter Wal, 2006c).

Research in other European countries arrived at similar conclusions. For example, Slovenian researchers paid significant attention to changing coverage of trans-border issues after the break-up of Yugoslavia:

> After 1991, field research shows a tendency of radically diminishing any forms of trans-border contact both in terms of their dynamics and structure. ... What has been a 'no border' before 1991 has become a rigid divide between two post-socialist nation states. ... In this respect, we claim that the case of the Slovenian-Croatian border transformed from the most open to the most closed border.
>
> (Zavratnik Zimic, 2001: 67–68, as quoted in Zagar, 2006)

A study of a Slovenian daily tabloid (*Slovenske novice*) between January and May 2001 found that the xenophobic, conservative and intolerant discourse typical of the daily strengthened at times of illegal immigration crises, and four 'streams' of discourse were identified: (1) illegal immigration presents a severe threat to the nation and the state, (2) criminalisation of immigrants, (3) defensive discourse claiming that Slovenes do not suffer from xenophobia, (4) militant discourse against illegal immigrants (Kuhar, 2001; Zagar, 2006).

Research on Italian media coverage of migration found that in general issues related to cultural and religious diversity were not given salient attention in the media (Panarese, 2005). Rather, media concentrated most often on events in the sphere of deviance and crime. The second most frequently covered topic involved arrivals of migrants in large numbers, e.g. Albanians in 1991 and other migrants arriving by boat on the shores of Italy (ter Wal, 2006c). According to Panarese (2005) the third most frequent topic associated with migration in Italian media is terrorism. It is important to note that this topic occurred not only frequently but was also used lexically in association with immigration while the events covered in the article were not related to terrorism (ibid.).

Changing personnel, contents and audiences

The increased attention that media pay to migrants and minorities (including socially excluded groups) has had an impact on the changing composition of newsrooms as well as media contents.

Research in European countries suggests that media organisations target minorities and migrants as a specific audience and in some cases they have been hiring media professionals with skills and backgrounds that would enable the production of content for these audiences. For example, the Irish public service broadcaster RTÉ creates new regular television programmes, and it also recruits and trains ethnic minority reporters. Some media, such as the *Irish Times*, created specialist correspondent positions to deal with issues of ethnicity and racism (Horgan, 2006). However, despite such initiatives minorities as well as women tend to be under-represented in European media organisations. Deuze (2002) conducted a survey among journalists in the United Kingdom and found a poor level of minority representation (1 per cent) in the profession (ibid.: 138). Women were also underrepresented (25 per cent), and in fact the United Kingdom had the lowest percentage of female participation in the profession of all the countries surveyed (ibid.: 136). In the Netherlands Ramdjan (2002) used interviews with journalists and visits to newsrooms of different media to explore the role of ethnic minority staff members. The report concludes that Dutch editorial culture is not open and accessible for ethnic minorities; they face a high threshold, while newsrooms are ethnically homogeneous, have a rather invisible editorial hierarchy and lack mechanisms to promote new talents. Another Dutch study explored how reporters of minority background were hired to work on a news programme (the *Journaal*) mainly in the coverage of Islam under the presumption that such reporters can more easily establish a dialogue with representatives of the Muslim community (Fleury, 2006; ter Wal, 2006c).

The increased importance of multicultural programmes is also reflected in the growing number of studies devoted to such programming. Leurdijk (2006) explores the conceptualisations of multicultural programming by commissioning editors and programme makers working for public service broadcasters in Austria, Belgium, Germany, the Netherlands, Great Britain, Finland, Ireland and Sweden between 2001 and 2003. The author argues that although the debate on multicultural programming has not been satisfactorily resolved (e.g. its nature, forms, goals, etc.), European public service broadcasters enact policies to produce separate multicultural programming (in the countries under study there are various legal obligations and measures in this respect). At the time of the research and in the case of the concerned public service broadcasters, all multi-cultural programming was aimed at minority as well as majority audiences. The editors and programme-makers from the various countries shared a range of problems, among them that of explaining particular experiences and cultural practices to mainstream audiences. In the countries under research the editors also used similar formulas to help make various issues attractive for mainstream audiences; these include portraying remarkable individuals, focusing on everyday lives, and on 'universals' (such as death, birth, love). There are also formats which have cross-cultural appeal, these include music programmes (or pro-grammes based on urban youth culture), comedy and 'interventionist doc-umentaries' (these deal with questions of cultural and ethnic identities in innovative ways).

Similar approaches and concerns were also identified by Cottle (2000) in research into the production of ethnic minority television programming in Britain, and that of the BBC as well as independent (commercial and commu-nity-based) producers. He argues that ethnic minority television producers are marginalised at the BBC and they adopt the stance of BBC professionalism – 'a disinterested programme-making stance that disengages from the surrounding field of "race" and minority ethnicity and which seeks to avoid community backlash and corporate censure by avoiding "difficult" issues' (ibid.: 116). Cottle deals specifically with 'the burden of representation' – black film makers are faced with so few opportunities to make programmes that once they have the chance they feel the need to 'represent' black interests and viewpoints and counter dominant mainstream images, which is artistically constraining. Independent (commercial and community-based) producers face similar issues as those at the BBC; in addition to those, however, there are also questions of structural disadvantages (scale, funding and location).

In terms of contents read, viewed and listened to by minority and migrant groups, these are not necessarily generated or broadcast in the migrants' or minority's country of residence. The global flow of media products and contents combined with technological developments make media contents of various geographical 'origin' easily accessible. A number of studies deal with the ways in which diasporic audiences use and appropriate media contents. Gillespie (1995) explored how television and video are being used to recreate cultural traditions within the South Asian diaspora, and how they are also catalysing cultural change in the local community of Southall. Georgiou (2005) maps diasporic media cultures across European Union member states, Aksoy and Robins (2003) deal with the development of Turkish trans-national television across European spaces.

The early 1980s witnessed the creation of pan-European television channels such as MTV, Eurosport and the news channel Euronews. In the 1990s, however, these channels began to localise their pan-European contents. Chalaby (2002) identifies four types of localisation: local advertising, dubbing, local programming and local opt-out. The localisation strategies can be seen as evidence of persisting significant differences between European national cultures.

Another research topic concerns minority language media, mainly television and radio. Campaigns for the establishment of minority language television broadcasting in European countries emerged in the 1970s. Hourigan (2001) argues that the impetus for indigenous minority language television broadcasting is stronger in the case of communities which are ethnic as well as linguistic minorities. Other factors that play a role include the political status of the indigenous language, territorial concentration, the political culture of the state and the level of integration between the central state and regions, and also the symbolic status of the language. It is also important to note here that in some cases we find a conflict between minority language rights and market forces.

In some European countries broadcasting in minority languages is the responsibility of public service broadcasters. The way this responsibility is defined and translated into actual practices varies. For example, Hungarian public service television has regular programmes in minority languages which deal with events, traditions and lifestyles within these communities. A public service television channel broadcasting in the Irish language is available in the Republic of Ireland, with the public service broadcaster having an obligation to produce 365 hours of Irish-language programming for this channel annually. In many cases the foundation of minority media has been assisted by a turn in thinking about minority languages at the supra-national European level, that is at the European Union and the Council of Europe with initiatives such as the European Council's European Charter for Regional or Minority Languages, as these make the maintenance of linguistic diversity a key part of cultural policies and minority rights.

Research findings on coverage of migration

Our interviews with journalists did not make specific reference to the coverage of issues related to migration or multiculturalism. When talking about audiences, in general our interviewees did not single out minorities or migrants as a specific audience. Rather, in terms of the audience that the media address our interviewees acknowledged that stress has been on the national audience as the primary one without specifically taking into account minorities or migrants.

Dutch journalists mentioned changes in the coverage of issues related to migration. A Dutch interviewee working for *Volkskrant* cites lesser political correctness in the coverage about migrants. 'Neighbourhood conflicts about disturbances caused by Moroccan youth are now published front page and with a special reporter doing a series of articles. That would have been impossible in the 1980s' (ter Wal, 2006a). The change, he argues, brings journalists closer to the public.

Journalists, management and the new challenges

This chapter has considered how the relationships between journalists and their audiences underwent significant changes during the last two decades. These arise from a combination of socio-economic, cultural and technological changes, some of which have been discussed in this chapter. When exploring the ways in which journalists and audiences interact it is important to bear in mind that the increased presence of the market point of view and intensified competition tend to promote a view of the audiences as a product which is sold to advertisers. In some cases, as literature and empirical research suggests, the increased pressure to compete for specific demographic groups of readers, viewers or listeners and profit-oriented approaches result in low-quality news production and the journalists' alienation from audiences or the public at large. The development of new communication technologies which promote interactivity in the relations between audiences and journalists has not necessarily provided a remedy. It appears that more successful attempts involve increased high-quality coverage of local and regional news.

In terms of larger social changes related to audience composition, this chapter has also addressed aspects of the increasing presence of migrants and minorities in European countries. In general coverage related to migrants and minorities tends to be heavily biased and members of minority groups and migrants are under-represented in the journalistic profession. A number of media organisations have adopted strategies that aim to increase the number of staff of minority origin yet it appears that in some cases this 'magic formula' does not work very well. For one reason the presence of a journalist of a minority origin does not necessarily in itself mean improved relations with and access to a given community. Indeed, in some cases, it might be counter-productive as such journalists might feel increased pressure to represent these minorities in a more positive light to balance the negative coverage. It appears that for the majority of European media (apart from minority language ones) the national audience remains the primary one, thus coverage of minority or migrant-related issues needs to be interesting and accessible for a majority audience.

Chapter 9

'Where's Europe?'

Emergent post-national news cultures

Media space and the deepening integration in the EU

Focus and scope of this chapter

For more than five decades now, the member states of what we now know as the European Union (EU) have been engaged in a process of deepening economic and political (and more recently, military) integration. But has this process of increasing integration been accompanied by a converging or common news culture and journalism within the 27 member countries that now comprise the EU area? This chapter examines whether or how there are any traces of an emergent or common 'European' journalism culture today and whether there are any patterns to the way in which 'European' topics or issues are covered by the news media. In addressing these questions, the chapter draws on our original multi-country research, including in-depth interviews with almost 100 journalists and reviews of national research literature in 11 countries. It is further informed by a series of seminar and roundtable discussions with media professionals, politicians and non-governmental organisations centred on the preliminary results of the research. But first, we move on to consider why and how the issues surrounding 'European' level news cultures and an emergent supra-national public sphere matter.

The EU integration project: a case of 'intensified globalisation'

The issues of whether and how there is an emergent common public sphere or shared news culture in the EU area are a matter of particular importance to 495 million people – considered as citizens and not merely consumers – residing in its 27 member states. But the key questions and issues at stake are also of much wider interest in an era of increasingly dense and intensified forms of 'globalisation', internationalisation or transnationalisation. Indeed, the EU context provides a fruitful site or case study to examine the implications of 'globalisation' – the spatial dimensions of socio-economic and political change – and especially the implications for journalism culture and newsmaking practices. There are a number of reasons why this is so.

First, in many respects it is fruitful to view the overall project of increasing EU economic and political integration as a particular case of intensified internationalisation at the level of one major world-region. Indeed, the EU is often hailed as the most ambitious project of multinational economic integration and governance in the modern world (e.g. Schlesinger, 1999; Preston and Kerr, 2001). Of course, tendencies towards the spatial expansion of economic exchanges and interdependencies as well as political and social relations are not exactly new, at least in Europe. They have been a particularly prominent or core feature modernity as it has evolved over the past two to three hundred years. However, since the 1980s, political, economic, and social researchers in many countries have been emphasising the heightened role and importance of globalisation processes. It is widely believed that trans-national relations and exchanges are tending to transcend or undermine the role of the national or territorial state system that framed earlier stages of modernity. The roots of such space-time compression are usually deemed to arise from a combination of economic, political and technological forces, including media related factors (Preston and Kerr, 2001). One policy aspect of these processes is the role of the World Trade Organization in establishing new regulatory regimes for the internationalisation of ownership and trade in services sectors which were previously organised largely on a national basis, and/or often provided by state-owned rather than private corporations. Another aspect is the formation of new kinds of regional trading systems, or 'common markets', such as NAFTA and its equivalents in Asia and Latin America. But the forms and degrees of trans-national integration in the EU area are much more ambitious and intensive than those in other world-regions.

As noted, the member states of what we now know as the European Union (EU) have been engaged in an intensive process of deepening economic and political (and, more recently, military) integration. This began with relatively modest efforts at the coordination of economic planning for the coal and steel industries of six countries in the early postwar decades. Since then, the number of member states has grown from six to the current 27 whilst the forms of economic and policy integration have deepened and expanded significantly. The latter have deepened to embrace more intensive forms of coordination and have widened beyond extractive and manufacturing industries to include all kinds of services. For example, from the late 1980s, the EU area has not only introduced a single market for television and telecommunication services, but it has also established a common overarching framework for policies and regulations related to television and other electronic communication services.

One highly symbolic aspect of these ambitious forms and intensified levels of trans-national integration has been the abolition of national currencies when euro notes and coins were introduced in the 12 euro-area countries in 2002. But even more far reaching and contentious have been the moves towards deeper levels of political coordination and integration in more recent years – and consequent crises when citizens rejected such moves. The political leaders in EU countries established a Convention on the Future of Europe which completed its work on the draft European constitution and an intergovernmental conference responsible for drawing up the constitutional treaty started its work in October 2003. In October 2004, the European Constitution was adopted by national political leaders meeting at the European Council in Rome, but subject to ratification by member states. In subsequent referendums, the citizens of France and of the Netherlands voted to reject the proposed constitution in 2005. This brought the ratification process in other countries to an abrupt stop, not least because the citizens of France and the Netherlands had been amongst the most proactive supporters of the EU integration project from its earliest days.

Some two years later, the political and administrative leadership set about devising a new 'reform package', and in October 2007 they agreed a Reform Treaty. Amongst other things, this 'reform package' proposes the creation of a new post of President of the European Council (the EU's highest body). According to the European Commission, the aim of the Reform Treaty is 'to make the 27-nation Union more efficient and more democratic' so that the 'EU will be better able to meet our expectations on issues like climate change and energy security, cross-border crime and immigration'; furthermore it will allow 'Europe to speak with one voice through a High Representative for Foreign Affairs and Security Policy' whilst 'the European Parliament will have greater powers and national parliaments also get a bigger say in EU policymaking' (http://ec.europa.eu/snapshot2007/reform/reform_en.htm).

The Reform Treaty of 2007 has to be ratified by each of the 27 EU countries before it can come into effect. But one important feature of the proposed new 'reform package' is that it can be ratified by parliaments in most countries (apart from Ireland) since it is defined as a treaty rather than a constitution. For some critics, however, the proposed Reform Treaty is little more than a born-again version of the European constitution that was grounded after its rejection by voters in France and the Netherlands in 2005. Whether the EU's political and administrative leadership succeed in their aims to continue the process of deepening integration by having the treaty ratified and in force before June 2009 remains to be seen (at time of this writing). But the very existence of such 'constitutional' debates indicates how far the EU has moved way beyond the original 'common market' project over the past 50 years to embrace much more ambitious forms and intensified levels of trans-national integration.

Thus we can treat the issues surrounding an emergent public sphere in the EU area (or indeed the issues of a 'democratic deficit') as leading exemplars of the challenges posed by deepening space-time compression or 'globalisation'. Indeed, they may be taken as prefigurative of trends that appear to be unfolding in other regions of the world. This is especially the case because mediated communication (including news media) are often seen as central to the processes of 'globalisation' and presumed to be key drivers of the deepening internationalisation of political and cultural relations (Preston and Kerr, 2001).

'Democratic deficits' at the EU level

Second, the EU case study is instructive since it clearly involves much more than the intensified 'globalisation' of so-called private sector economic issues at a world-region level. Alongside the deepening transnationalisation of finance and industrial capital, production and trade leading to integrated or single 'markets' within the EU area for most sectors, there has also been a significant shift of political and regulatory authority from the national to EU-level institutions (even if not taxation). As the reach and scope of EU-level institutions has grown, so the key processes of decision-making related to the design, implementation and monitoring aspects of an increasing array of public policies and regulatory activities now takes place in Brussels rather than in national capitals. Yet, the systems and processes of political debate and public communication have failed to keep pace with such economic, financial and regulatory developments. In sum, such recent developments in the EU area yield an additional spatial layer to the contemporary menu of 'democratic deficits' and related challenges for those concerned with a renewal of the public sphere.

The concept of the public sphere lies at the core of much contemporary debate on the so-called 'democratic deficit' in the EU region, including discussions of the role and scope of the news media in engaging with the operations and transparency of EU-level institutions and their accountability to citizens or the public. This is particularly evident in the recent academic research focused on the actual or potential role of political communication, including news media, to address the perceived deficits in citizens, engagement with EU affairs and/or the accountability and transparency of EU-level institutions. It is also evident in the European Commission's (2006) 'White Paper on European Communication Policy' which frequently invokes the concept of public sphere and which also acknowledges significant shortcomings and failings with respect to the construction of any emergent or embryonic European public sphere.

The roots of the 'democratic deficits' in the EU area cannot be defined solely or primarily in spatial terms, especially for researchers working with a public sphere perspective (Splichal, 1999; 2006). Even the European Commission (2006) has acknowledged that the public and citizenry in the EU area are not only alienated from 'Brussels' but that this reflects a wider disenchantment with contemporary politics more generally. At the same time it is now acknowledged – by the European Commission (2006) as well as academic researchers – that there are specific layers of information and/or communication 'deficits' when it comes to citizens' engagement with EU-level politics and the crucial issues of public support for the project of deepening integration (Kaitatzi-Whitlock, 2008). This was manifested most dramatically when the citizens of France and the Netherlands voted to reject the proposed European Constitution in 2005, but it is also evident in the declining levels of public support for the EU project as indicated in Eurobarometer and other opinion surveys (Kaitatzi-Whitlock, 2008).

We may also note that the recent growth of research focused on 'European' dimensions of the news media and political communication has been concerned with much more than the spatial shift of standard measures from national to EU-level registers (or simply empirical issues). It has stimulated renewed debate on the appropriate conceptualisations of the 'public' (sphere, opinion, or publicness) and the precise forms or sources of the democratic deficits and social exclusions at stake. These debates also extend to methodological issues concerning how best to operationalise or measure the key concepts. Issues in the debate include whether or how contemporary research may draw on the prior work of seminal European and US-based theorists (e.g. Kant, Tarde, Lippmann, Dewey, Luhmann) as well as the tricky question of whether the deficits in democracy are to be understood as the consequence or the source of deficits in the form and operations of public communication.

In *The Postnational Constellation*, Habermas (2001) addressed the issues posed by the tensions between the nation state and its associated systems of public communication on the one hand, and the increasing salience of EU-level developments on the other. Habermas suggests that just as the modern state was transformed into a national state by the symbolic construction of 'the people', it is also now possible to imagine a project for new cohesive political unions and cultural identities at the continental level. He identified a number of major conditions to render this possible. Here Habermas (2001) identified two priorities: one was the renewal of the social Europe agenda to impose strong redistributional obligations to offset the growing sway of capitalist and market forces; the second was the generation of new collective identities transcending the boundaries and limits of nationhood (see also Kaitatzi-Whitlock, 2008).

Whether or not citizens favour the current reform package or the model of deepening EU integration, it remains the case that the political, policy and regulatory processes taking place in 'Brussels' or EU-level institutions now have a major impact on social and economic affairs (Schlesinger, 1999; Preston, 2005). Thus, the forms and extent of any emergent European public sphere along with the contours and operations of the prevailing system of public communication have become increasingly central issues – for citizens as much as for media researchers.

EU integration: a counter to 'hegemonic unilateralism'?

Third, we observe that the recent debates on the European Union integration project and related debates on the salience of supra-national public spheres have taken on a heightened charge and sense of urgency in more recent years as a direct result of international geopolitical and military developments. The invasion and war in Iraq, led by the USA and its 'coalition of the willing' in March 2003 prompted the largest mass demonstrations seen in European capitals since the end of World War II. It also led to major tensions and debates amongst political and intellectual circles in the EU area. The effects of the US-led coalition's 'impetuous break with international law' were amplified by the subsequent efforts of certain US-based political spokespersons and state agencies to create divisions between 'new' Europe and the 'old' – indeed, the chain of movements served to 'ignite a debate over the future of the international order' in Europe as elsewhere in the world (Habermas and Derrida, 2003/2005: 5).

These developments prompted various intellectuals, including Jürgen Habermas, Jacques Derrida and Umberto Eco, to take on untypical roles as public intellectuals. Habermas and Derrida urged more rapid moves towards 'strengthened cooperation' amongst the core countries of the EU as steps towards 'a common foreign policy, a common security policy' that would be an independent power and counterbalance to 'the hegemonic unilateralism of the USA' in working with international institutions in a 'complex global society' (Habermas and Derrida, 2003/2005: 5–6). If the large mass demonstrations against the Iraq war in various European capitals was taken as evidence that 'the power of emotions has brought European citizens jointly to their feet', the two philosophers recognised that their proposal raises tricky questions of 'European identity'. In essence, the authors argue that their proposal 'presupposes a feeling of common political belonging', not least as the population of the member states 'must so to speak "build up" their national identities, and add to them a European dimension' (ibid.: 6–7).

Prior research on trans/post-national news media

Our cross-national research project commenced with a review of the prior academic research literature in the 11 countries under study. One key aim was to identify and examine those prior studies concerned with the manner and extent to which journalists deal with EU-related news and current affairs topics and related European themes, as well as issues surrounding the potential emergence of a common European news culture or post-national public sphere. Another was to examine how the prior research addresses those factors or influences shaping the coverage of EU-related news and the forms or extent of any emergent European public sphere.

Relative paucity of research on 'European' media issues

In one important respect at least, the 'coverage' of European-related topics in the academic research literature focused on news and journalism cultures appears to be rather similar to the coverage in its object of study. Just as in the news media, the coverage of 'European' themes and EU-related research topics have comprised only a small, indeed marginal, portion of the total output of the media and journalism studies field in the 11 countries studied. But the number of relevant academic studies has grown significantly since the early years of the present decade, partly prompted by the increased funding incentives for such work within the EU's research programme.

Little by way of an emergent 'European' public sphere

We observed in earlier chapters how modern journalism and newsmaking practices tend to be strongly embedded or framed around national cultures. This insight is particularly pertinent when understanding the extent and forms of media coverage of European or EU-related or new topics. Indeed, even when it comes to explicitly European themes, such as elections to the European Parliament, we find that the framing and content of news coverage varies significantly by country (Preston, 1999). In the case of such a 'common' and shared European-wide event, the agenda of key issues tends to be appropriated or framed and treated in very different ways in line with the orientations of the news media and political culture of the various member states (e.g. Preston, 1999).

The research reviewed in our 11 national reports suggests that there is little by way of an emergent 'common' European media space or editorial culture. The general finding is that news and current affairs genres remain strongly orientated around national frames or epistemic communities. Even when the phenomenon being addressed is a 'common' European or EU-related topic, this is treated and addressed in very specific ways in each national setting. The most popular forms of 'common' European coverage seem to lie in the realm of entertainment and sport, but these tend to be occasional or event-specific rather than routine in character (for example, the good old Eurovision Song Contest; in sports, the European Championships).

Whilst there has been an increase in the transnational ownership structures and pan-EU policy and regulatory frameworks related to the media, this has not been replicated at the level of media content production or editorial cultures. There has been a growth in the cross-border application of certain programming formats originating in Europe (e.g. *Big Brother*) and in the co-production of films and television programming. But these 'universal' formats tend to be highly localised in the way they are adapted and attuned to local cultural codes and conventions. The single most important source of non-national programming in the television sector in most EU countries remains the US-based audiovisual industry.

In essence, media cultures remain largely stamped by the stubborn resilience of 'banal nationalism' as even EU issues are still largely viewed and treated via 'national prism'. Of course, these findings are 'no surprise' when considered in light of the accumulated body of research in the media studies field on the making of news. But they also reflect the 'long revolution' involved in the construction of the 'modern' social and cultural media-space framed around the system of territorial (nation) states and what James Carey and others referred to as the cultural 'embeddedness' of journalism and newsmaking.

How EU news issues are addressed in national news media

Our reviews of the prior research in media and journalism fields in the 11 countries found that European themes or EU-related topics accounted for only a small minority of total studies. These included several relevant and empirically grounded studies of the manner in which journalists and the media deal with EU news and current affairs information.

For example, our review of the French literature describes approximately eight such studies, noting that they represent a small portion of the relevant national literature on newsmaking and news cultures (Guyot *et al.*, 2006). One study examined journalists accredited to the European Union and compared EU news coverage in French and British papers. This study's findings suggest that the two journalistic cultures tend to treat European topics in rather different ways. It noted that coverage of European topics tends to appear in the home-news column in the case of the British press, whilst the French newspapers present them in the international columns. The same study also found that British correspondents tend to adopt a political point of view while French papers privilege a more technical, professional and expert tone. The latter finding prompted the author to underline the role of expertise and expert speech within different journalistic cultures (Guyot *et al.*, 2006).

Other relevant French studies examining the production routines related to European information have highlighted the role of national cultural prisms in the presentation of events to the public, including elections to the European Parliament, the 1999 European Summit, the mad cow crisis and the Kosovo warfare. Some studies have addressed the importance of the national interpretative framework for journalists in their presentation of EU news to their audiences. They highlight how the selection of events by journalists essentially takes place within a national perspective as the public is deemed to be more receptive to information when it is presented from a national point of view. These assumptions underpin the culture and practices of the journalists, comprising key elements of newsmaking routines and values or implicit 'professional' codes of practice (Guyot *et al.*, 2006).

The drift of these studies suggests that the notion of an emergent common European editorial culture or public sphere is difficult to defend. They tend to emphasise how the national 'prism' (or point of view) comprises a necessary and inevitable condition to secure a better reception of European issues (ibid.). The French research also matches the findings of several other studies reported in the project's review of the research literature in other national settings (e.g. Britain, Ireland, the Netherlands). Indeed, such findings resonate closely with prior research on the role of media routines in framing newsmaking and with culturalist theories of news and journalism examined in earlier chapters.

EU policy impacts on European media landscapes and culture

One of the most common 'European' or EU-related themes revealed by our research project's literature reviews concerns the role of supra-national policy, regulatory and economic changes affecting the media environment and/or their implications for media content and editorial cultures. For example, some French studies have addressed European audiovisual policies with respect to the protection of cultural and linguistic diversity and the hegemony of the English language (Guyot *et al.*, 2006). British researchers have also undertaken many studies of the role of EU policies and their implications for the direction of news and other media cultures (Preston, 2006a; 2006b).

Several of these studies have identified tensions between various strands of EU communication and media policies and questioned their coherence with respect to the creation of a stronger EU media sector or the construction of a common European media space. For example, some have examined how the growing array of commercial and cable or satellite television channels (promoted by recent EU-level and national policy changes) has led to an expanded demand for programming or 'content'. However, the biggest supplier and beneficiary has been the US audiovisual sector rather than the EU industries as the policies presumed or promised (Preston, 2006a; 2006b).

Still elusive? A shared 'European' news culture

We now summarise some of the main findings from our in-depth interviews with senior journalists concerning the patterns and ways in which 'European' topics are addressed in the media. We are particularly concerned with responses and discussions surrounding the question of whether there is a distinctive 'European' journalistic culture or set of practices reflecting an emergent sense of common identity or purpose, however tentative or embryonic.

Are there common 'European' news cultures or practice(s)?

The vast majority of the journalists we interviewed clearly indicated that they did not subscribe to the notion of a common, or increasingly shared, European journalistic culture. Our respondents tended to emphasise that newsmaking and journalism practices throughout Europe are still highly attuned to national cultural codes and conventions, or orientated towards specific instutional norms and settings. If our interviewees identified any emergent or common trend, this pointed to a tendential or potential convergence towards the Anglo-US model of journalism.

Not surprisingly, perhaps, journalists based in the newest member states of the EU tended to experience and express the strongest sense of major shifts and change in newsmaking culture and journalism. For instance, many of the Slovenian journalists interviewed noted the difference between European journalism and that of the USA. Nevertheless, they also suggested that there was no commonality between (for example) the writing styles or story ideas that would dominate individual states. Similarly most of the Hungarian editors interviewed were unable to define any common European journalistic culture, believing national characteristics to be more important. However, many made reflexive references to differences between American and European journalism, although they could not give specific examples of this. A number of French journalists also made the distinction between European and American styles. Overall, however, our findings suggest that 'there is no European journalism ... there is journalism on Europe' as Bernard Cassen of *Le Monde Diplomatique* succinctly put it (Guyot *et al.*, 2006).

Although our respondents tended to emphasise the continuing lack of any common or pan-European journalistic culture, it is notable that some of these journalists did identify similarities between certain countries within Europe. For instance, some Spanish journalists observed certain similarities between the media in Spain and in France. Some Irish informants identified increasing similarities between the Irish press and British tabloids, and not in a positive sense. However, this is not surprising when one considers the common language and relatively high media penetration of British press and television in Ireland.

British journalists were the most clearcut in their rejection of the notion of a common journalistic culture. Many of the British journalists pointed to the media specifically in France and Germany (no other countries were cited) as examples of profoundly different styles. Both were seen as less vigorous, more reserved or 'boring', and much less likely to deal with controversial stories than were the British media. For instance, one interviewee, working in British television, suggested that the French media had refrained from covering the Paris riots of 2005 in 'a way which would be inconceivable' in Britain.

Some other informants spoke of the 'Brussels bubble', with 'a collective of people working in the different countries but who belong to the same structure', and who think of themselves 'in a more European manner', and so in this sense, there may be a certain 'European journalistic culture'. But this view was rejected by another Spanish editor, who argued, 'it is too early to talk about a European journalistic culture, because there are still many things, for instance in Spain, which divide us from our neighbours' (Guyot *et al.*, 2006). One Irish interviewee noted that the opportunity of working in Brussels had made Irish journalists less inclined to look to London for career advancement. Yet, even if this opens up new career horizons, this was not reflected in a common style of writing. This interviewee argued that 'there is a major problem in that Irish journalists by and large don't understand Europe' and so it is quite difficult to sell European stories to the Irish media (Horgan, 2006).

Only for elites? Aspects of an emergent European public sphere

The prior research suggests that the strongest or most creditable evidence for an emergent 'common' or shared news culture across the core EU area takes a highly restrictive and elitist form. The relevant candidate comprises a single newspaper, the London-based *Financial Times*, which is now printed in 22 major cities worldwide, of which seven are in the EU area, including Brussels. Our interviews indicate that the *Financial Times* enjoys a high profile amongst top-level EU political leaders and officials. They also indicate that this elite medium is accorded a privileged position by these same politicians and officials when it comes to the release of information related to EU developments. Clearly, the *Financial Times* uses twenty-first century technology for its timely printing in multiple cities and for online delivery of its news directed at the financial, industrial and political elites of Europe and beyond. Yet its status and role as the pre-eminent medium catering to the common or transnational news needs of elites has many echoes with much earlier forms of organised news production and distribution linking the economic and political elites of the major European cities, as outlined in Chapter 2.

How journalists address 'European' and EU issues

We now consider the main findings from our interviews concerning the patterns and ways in which 'European' topics are addressed in the news media. We also consider whether or how such coverage differs by specific kinds of media, etc.

Key features of how 'European' issues are addressed

Amongst the editors interviewed in our research, the common view was that European issues and EU-related topics comprised an extremely difficult area for news media. In most cases, our informants tended to portray EU-related issues as alien or highly problematic with respect to the conventional yardsticks of news values and newsworthiness. They suggested coverage of EU affairs frequently presented them with the problem of trying to make 'complex', bureaucratic or highly political issues interesting and relevant for a largely uninterested public.

Most of our informants did not perceive particular patterns in the coverage of European issues, rather they emphasised that most such news stories were dealt with on the basis of their newsworthiness. Certain major EU events, particularly summits, or strategic developments, such as enlargement, could be almost guaranteed coverage. In such cases, however, the level of coverage depended on the degree of national interest a state had on the particular issue at stake. Thus, while questions related to the enlargement of the EU potentially affected all member states, it was considered obvious or natural that such issues would receive greater coverage in countries such as Serbia than in the UK or Spain.

Most of the editors interviewed in our research tended to emphasise that the selection of European stories was usually based on whether or not they had direct national relevance. Nevertheless, even when newsworthiness and national relevance had informed the selection of European stories, many of our informants indicated that such news items presented very particular challenges with respect to engaging their audiences. Indeed our informants repeatedly underlined what they perceived as the lack of interest amongst their readers or audiences for matters 'European'. As an editor from one Irish newspaper put it, the very mention of Europe 'caused people's eyes to glaze over' (Horgan, 2006). Readers were only interested in EU issues which directly affect them in a very immediate way (such as the introduction of the Euro), although not necessarily in a profound way, as the furore over the abolition of duty-free shopping on internal EU travel showed some years ago.

Specific challenges for TV news routines and codes

Coverage of Europe was regarded as a particularly difficult area by some of the broadcast journalists, including those in France. As an informant from France 3 explained, 'the issues are complicated and television is not the appropriate medium to deal with that', not least because stories which lack images, 'we don't treat'. Similarly, an interviewee based in TF1 argued, 'television is a totally unsuitable tool to the knowledge of European institutions,' indicating that major efforts to deal with some of the technical aspects of the Constitution during the French referendum had failed to make any impact on the public. France 3 tried to 'deal with current affairs and present debates', but TF1 offered only 'the minimum' in this area (Guyot et al., 2006).

Several interviewees report how broadcast media have tried to get around these difficulties by moving away from a focus on Brussels and the institutions towards people-centred stories of EU issues to better reflect the situation closer to the ground.

These interviewees suggest a tendency for coverage of EU and European issues to move away from the more abstract treatment of legislation or political debates towards a more personalised approach. Indeed, they also suggest a belief that viewers and readers are more likely to be interested when a comparative approach is taken towards EU-related subjects. As one French interviewee explained, if 'we are going to talk about the minimum wage, should it be raised or not, we'll have a French debate on that particular issue, but we are going to see how the British do, the German, the Spanish – not necessarily taking the twenty five countries, but three or four that are significant' (Guyot et al., 2006).

There is also the question of what European issues are considered newsworthy. As one Spanish informant observed, 'Europe sells in the media when there is a crisis [...] we know Europe through clichés' (ibid.). This is largely because it is useless to provide in-depth analyses as people (journalists and viewers) find it hard to make the effort to understand the complex matters at issue. This viewpoint was also shared by editors in the Netherlands, who noted that the issues associated with coverage of Brussels are either stereotypical (on economic affairs) or negative (political conflicts, democratic deficit, subsidiarity, rejection of the Constitution).

Special roles and responsibilities of public service media?

Our interviews draw attention to certain observable differences between the public service broadcasting remit of the BBC, for instance, and the more commercially driven ITN. Having considered his channel's treatment of European issues, ITN's Robin Elias concluded, saying:

Our lives are busier now. News viewing figures are massively in decline as well as newspapers ... We need to make sure that we're of interest, and relevant to a diverse and often a non-white population, otherwise there's a danger that they will see the news as not relevant to them.

(Preston, 2006a)

The relevant research literature suggests that the role of public service broadcasting (PSB) has been one of the most distinctive features of the media landscapes in almost all European countries since the early or mid-twentieth century. PSB has been frequently characterised as framed around a specific editorial culture and attendant journalistic ethos ('to educate, inform and entertain' as the BBC's first director-general defined it) combined with a commitment to a diversity of both programming content and universal service with respect to the national audience.

The scope of relevant national and EU-level policies as well as the definitions and formats deemed to express the specific news values and media culture of PSB have changed significantly in recent decades. These have evolved in line with shifts in policies and socio-cultural norms as well as the competitive and inter-textual relations prevailing between PSB and the increasing range of commercial broadcast services. The general result has been that the relative roles of PSB services have declined significantly in most EU countries compared to the situation some 10–20 years ago.

Some of the literature reviewed in the national reports indicates that one major source for such developments have been policy changes at both the national and EU levels (e.g. Preston, 2006a; 2006b). At the same time, the increasing role and power of commercial broadcasting services, allied to public policies favouring such competition, has led to a certain convergence in the programming content, schedules and formats of PSB services and their competitors.

Yet as the British national report indicates, the public service broadcaster is deemed (by government-appointed inquiries) to have a special responsibility for the provision of 'European' news and current affairs coverage – including the 'education' of the public with respect to such affairs (Preston, 2006a). The research materials generated by our project suggest that such policy strategies may be extremely limited in their impacts or even counter-productive. Given the overall policy pressures and increasing economic pressures framing the operations of PSB services, their potential role in this regard is highly limited. Indeed, the research considered here suggests that such policy strategies may even be counter-productive given the competitive and inter-textual relations prevailing between PSB and the increasing range of commercial broadcast services (e.g. Preston, 2006a; 2006b).

Clearly, the issues surrounding PSB should be looked at also from an audience perspective. In some countries PSB has declined to a tiny fraction of the total television viewing audience, especially those where there has been a distinct failure to ensure its institutional insulation from direct government influence (e.g. Greece). In other countries, such as Britain and Ireland, PSB shares of broadcasting audiences have remained relatively high. At the very least, this suggests there is a need for some fundamental research in this area, especially to examine the scope and potential for maintaining a future role for PSB as a prominent feature and distinct domain of journalistic culture in European countries.

Paradoxically, it may well be that PSB, although formerly criticised for its uniformity and even, in certain cultures, an unwillingness to explore controversial issues because of apprehension about the role of governments and regulators, may now be poised for a new role. It offers one of the best, and in some countries perhaps the only, basis for enhanced media diversity in a world where most commercial media are tending to serve up the same 'product'.

Variations in 'European' news coverage across countries

The review of the French research literature suggested one interesting aspect of journalistic practice not revealed by the interviews with practitioners. When the work and practices of French and British-accredited correspondents in Brussels are compared, two very different journalistic approaches are observed: European issues are dealt with in a political way by British journalists while French correspondents favour a more technical and expert point of view.

The Netherlands report makes the point that the media seem to 'wish to translate Europe for their audiences' but at the same time they risk being part of an elite discourse 'when defending Europe as an important dimension' of news or treating it in positive terms. This became an issue of particular concern to the media in the Netherlands following the swing in support towards Pim Fortuyn, but one which was highlighted once again by the defeat of the European constitution by the Dutch electorate in 2005.

Effectively, the press in the Netherlands had tended to follow a generally pro-European course. When it came to coverage of the referendum on the proposed European constitution, this tendency merely added to the sense that the media were part of a European elite which was far removed from the citizens who felt they were not being listened to. In light of this, some of the journalists interviewed in our research tended to highlight an interest in returning to issues that were most pertinent to the domestic situation. The relevant issues posed here included the democratic deficit, the distance between politics and citizens that is felt in the Netherlands, and a felt need for journalism to be closer to citizens. This orientation was deemed important given the (then recent) events where the Dutch media appeared to have failed to fully engage with their audiences: the rise of Pim Fortuyn, and the rejection of the European constitution. Somewhat similar concerns are reflected by the points made by several French journalists concerning the national media's rather restrictive treatment of the varying issues and viewpoints related to the referendum on the European constitution.

Our interviews underline how the situation is very different in Britain where the print media have for long been strongly divided over the question of Europe. The centre-left or liberal press (the *Guardian* and the *Independent*) tend to be either favourable or neutral to the EU, alongside the *Financial Times*. But the majority of the print media tends to take a strongly Eurosceptic approach and so several of the British interviewees were taken from the Eurosceptic side of this divide. This is particularly apparent in the case of the *Sun*, a populist newspaper known for many years for its brash, arguably xenophobic, coverage of Europe. However, according to its political editor, this has changed in recent years. 'With the introduction of cheap air travel, *Sun* readers have come to love Europe, but the European Union remains something which is remote and none of them likes it'. He observed that the *Sun* receives a huge response from its readers on the question of Europe. The paper has a feature called 'You, the Jury', and if it's on an issue like the European constitution or the single currency 'we get tens – hundreds – of thousands of calls saying how much they are against it'. This same informant observed that other British newspapers, such as the *Daily Mail* and the *Daily Telegraph* are also anti-EU, 'but the proportion of their readers who are anti-EU would be nowhere near as high as ours'. He added that 'probably three quarters of our readers are very sceptical'. Similarly, Sean Ryan who works for another News International title, the *Sunday Times* explained, 'Certainly, our European coverage is affected by the way Europe is seen from Britain. It doesn't often get into the top ten read stories, even during the British presidency of the EU' (Preston, 2006a).

Resources and coverage of 'European' news topics

As noted in Chapter 4, resources have a major influence on newsmaking, but it is difficult to discern any single trend in terms of the levels of resources allocated to European coverage. In the case of British media, the trend may be towards declining resources according to those interviewed. This is in part because of the view that there are fewer pressing issues being decided in Brussels at the moment compared with earlier years. For instance, as Sean Ryan of the *Sunday Times* noted, 'we have what would be called a Eurosceptic view on the European currency and on some of the prospective moves towards a federal Europe'. The latter issue was deemed live and pressing until the rejection of the European constitution in the French and Dutch referenda so that 'now the heat has gone out of that debate'. The paper used to have a staff member in Brussels 'but we don't have one there now' as the paper's resource managers do not see the need to have a full-time staffer in Brussels 'now that the debate is no longer as pressing as it was when it seemed that we might be going into the single currency'.

But if there is a perception that Brussels is less important at present compared to the recent past, this may also be related to wider shifts in foreign coverage in recent times. As one editor from a middle-market newspaper observed, 'A lot of the papers have scaled back their bureaux. I don't think there are any permanent foreign staff on our paper now'. This informant's paper has two stringers in the USA and one in Australia, 'but no full time bureaux – quite different from ten or fifteen years ago'. This informant also reported that in recent years, the *Daily Telegraph* announced plans to 'slash the budget of its foreign desk by £250,000 a year, and there was a big campaign against it'. He also stated that the British media are now 'really very parochial' and although his paper used to have bureaux in Delhi and in Beijing, 'there was virtually nothing in the paper from these sources'.

This account of declining resources for European or foreign news more generally does not reflect the situation across the whole spectrum of British media. One other interviewee indicated that the *Independent* was trying to 'beef up' its coverage of Europe and make it more of a selling point, while the BBC had recently appointed a European editor to improve their coverage. The *Independent* is generally favourable to the EU. As a public service broadcaster, the BBC is perhaps best described as Euro-neutral although, as noted earlier, recent government reports have given it a special brief for informing the public on EU-related affairs.

Perhaps the difference in approach between the two sections of the British media is that the Eurosceptic media are only interested in printing bad news, so when it feels there is little at stake, it prints nothing. Pro-European media or PSB media tend to perceive a greater obligation to report on EU-related topics generally and allocate their resources accordingly. Somewhat similar divides between media organisations in terms of resource allocations for coverage of EU-related news apply also in other countries. The project's interviews with informants in the Netherlands suggest that the commercial station RTL Nieuws has no correspondent in Brussels, whilst the public news broadcaster NOS Journaal had recently increased staff numbers in its Brussels desk by two 'because coverage about Europe is gaining importance'.

Why so few traces of an emergent 'European' news?

In sum, although European-centred studies comprise a relatively small share of the national research on journalism and news cultures (in the 11 countries), the majority of these studies tend to emphasise that EU issues are still largely viewed via a specifically national media culture – or via the 'national prism'. Overall our research points to certain convergences between the professed ideals governing editorial cultures and journalistic practices in the 11 EU countries surveyed. We have also noted some other similarities across newsmaking cultures related to the pressures arising from increasing commercialisation and competition between media.

A comparative reading of the national research literature reveals a generally 'common' tendency towards both a quantitative increase in media outlets and, paradoxically, a failure to witness a parallel increase in the diversity or quality of information available to citizens in EU member states, especially as regards news and current affairs genres. The role, scope and power of the media seem to be increasing in every country surveyed. Even if the media are playing an increasingly important role in the performance of formal politics, we also find an increasing orientation of media content and journalistic practices towards entertainment, personalities and sports-related genres.

At the same time, the national literature reviews and interviews point to a general tendency for increased commercial and competitive pressures to result in the diminution of foreign news and current affairs coverage in the media. One aspect of that comprises pressures affecting coverage of European or EU-related news and current affairs matters. These are news events or subjects that, by their very nature tend to be unfamiliar, often long-drawn and thus 'complex': they are not readily or easily presentable according to the prevailing conventions and (national) cultural frames of news values or norms. Besides, when EU-related matters are covered by national media, they tend to be treated and represented very distinctively (via the 'national prism') in accordance with the specific codes, norms and conventions of the editorial culture in each national media setting.

These findings suggest that, despite the much-vaunted 'globalisation' impacts or potentials of new ICTs, there is no quick tech-fix or other easy route towards creating a common informational or editorial product across national/cultural boundaries. Nor is there any quick tech-fix to the deep-seated embeddedness or ethnocentrism of journalism cultures. This means that any enhancements of the technical capacities to deliver 'European' editorial or news culture or 'product' across different national cultures, will only succeed if that product's content style and presentation are consonant with those of the culture in which its anticipated audiences reside. At the same time, alongside the growth of migration across EU countries there have emerged new initiatives targeting diasporic or multicultural news cultures. These indicate some of the new potentials for innovative, diversified or hybrid news services.

In all countries covered by the research teams, we find a striking convergence of findings concerning the absence of any shared "European" dimension to journalistic cultures. In this regard, the French case may be treated as typical of the findings for most countries:

> There is no European journalism as such but journalists addressing European issues from different media, different socio-political and cultural backgrounds, using different languages. ... Most interviewees point out that a European journalistic culture is a mere utopia. There cannot be common references as professional practices are marked by national traditions or systems of interpretation.
>
> (Guyot *et al.*, 2006)

Such findings are echoed in the national reports of our project's research in other countries, for example, the Netherlands. Here, both the literature review and interview stages converge around the finding that 'European issues are predominantly reported from a domestic perspective, with a focus on domestic actors or concerns' (ter Wal, 2006b). The importance of the 'national prism' in the selection and packaging of any EU/Europe-related news items was confirmed by the interviewees, who claimed this was the condition for making news about Europe newsworthy and for tailoring the news to their audiences. As in other countries, several interviewees also emphasised the need to translate or link European issues to the question of how decision-making in Brussels affects ordinary citizens in their daily lives – hinting at economic or quality of life influences, consumer-oriented interests attributed to audiences (ter Wal, 2006b).

Industrial routines and organisational factors rather than bias?

We have seen that European and EU-related news and current affairs topics tend to play relatively minor and sporadic roles in the overall content of the mass media. This trend is not necessarily the consequence of any deliberate or conscious anti-EU or anti-European bias on the part of newsworkers, although it may be so in some cases. Rather, to a great extent, these findings can be explained by the 'normal' operation of media routines, newsmaking, organisational procedures and professional roles and norms that generally guide the selection and presentation of news (as discussed in Chapters 3 through 7). By definition, 'European' or EU-related political and policy issues are somewhat distant, if not alien to the distinctive national political conventions, cultural codes and rituals that have enframed newsmaking processes in the modern era.

But here, we may also note that the British case poses some interesting questions or ironies as to the meaning of such 'national' news frames and cultural values (or prisms) in light of the trans-national tendencies evident in the early twenty-first century. Take the case of the British newspapers that are most robust in invoking 'national' cultural values and traditions in their anti-EU discourses. Both happen to be effectively owned and controlled by a powerful multinational (multi-) media mogul. The key policies of these defenders of British 'national' cultural values and traditions are ultimately controlled by someone who traded his Australian citizenship for US citizenship some years back in order to better meet eligibility ('nationality') criteria for ownership of television services in the USA.

Chapter 10

New times, new news paradigms?

Introduction

This book began by observing how the field of journalism and newsmaking appears to be in a *state of flux* or deep-seated change at the start of the twenty-first century. We also noted contested views as to whether the 'modern' Anglo-US model of journalism was becoming *the* universal standard or whether various forms of crisis were evident in this 'news paradigm' (Høyer and Pöttker, 2005). In order to examine the forms and extent of the unfolding changes (and continuities) in contemporary journalism, we identified five major explanatory perspectives within the relevant research literature. We also argued that each of these perspectives should be seen as complementary, alongside its associated sets of concepts and factors deemed to be major influences on newsmaking. The heart of this book, Chapters 3 through 7, was framed around each of these explanatory approaches in turn. We identified some seminal studies, key concepts and influencing factors highlighted by each of the five explanatory perspectives, together with findings from relevant empirical research. The analysis drew on seminal studies, and recent research published by others as well as findings from our own multi-country project.

This final chapter will provide a summary recap of key trends and findings concerning the contours of change in mediated newsmaking in the contemporary 'network society' or 'knowledge economy' setting. It will provide an overall sketch of major shifts and the ensuing challenges for the journalism profession and the prevailing news paradigm. It explores whether or how the predominant 'modern' model of professional journalism and newsmaking, which emerged in the early decades of the twentieth century, is now facing significant challenges and changes. Is the prevailing model of professional journalism, together with the associated conceptions of the relative autonomy of journalists, being challenged by an emerging new 'news paradigm' in the context of a neo-liberal knowledge or information society? It also considers some of the requisite innovations and changes if journalism is to renew itself in keeping with its own self-understanding of its distinctive professional role, its values and norms and its orientation to the public.

This involves a rather tricky, hazardous and somewhat more speculative agenda compared to that of the preceding chapters. First, it is always much more difficult to discern or analyse the contours of historically significant change (or continuity) in any field in real-time terms, compared to the retrospective view afforded by the passage of time. Significant shifts to any new paradigms involve a complex process of social learning across many institutional and organisational domains, and the more persistent features may take some time to emerge and become embedded (Preston, 2001). Second, this agenda takes us into the intellectual terrain of historical or epochal change which is radically distant from the forms of knowledge or discourse that characterise our present object of study, the field of journalism and newsmaking. As noted earlier, journalism and journalists tend to breathe, live by and propagate present-time, here-and-now forms of knowledge (Carey, 2007). One consequence is that they tend to privilege the novel and the new whilst operating from a truncated or absent sense of long-run, historical perspectives on any field, including those related to its own practices. Another is that practitioners and researchers in this field frequently proclaim a sense of dramatic changes unfolding in news practices or the immediate environment of the newsroom, often linked to various 'effects' of the Internet (for example, graphic, headline-grabbing but erroneous claims of the demise of the category formerly known as the media audience). Our agenda is made even more tricky by prevailing fashions for technology-centred (or determinist) perspectives, in contemporary studies of journalism and media, as noted in Chapter 2 (Curran, 2002: 135; Carey, 2005). This is manifest in failures to consider the myriad ways in which the presumed 'effects' of new ICTs are not intrinsic or fixed, but negotiated or mediated by the interplay of institutional, managerial, organisational, and professional power – both in the newsroom and in the wider or socio-political settings in which new technologies and journalism are situated.

Recap: explanatory perspectives and news influences

First, let's recap on our story so far. For brevity, we can reframe our five explanatory perspectives or clusters of influencing factors in the relevant research literature into a more simplified three-fold typology (as indicated in Figure 10.1).

We commenced our substantive analysis of the explanatory perspectives and influences on newsmaking and journalism in Chapter 3 with studies focused on the individual characteristics and professional values or norms of journalists. In Chapters 4 and 5, we were concerned with those institutional, organisational and occupational factors most directly involved in the day-to-day operations of making the news, both within newsrooms and in those neighbouring institutions with which they are most actively engaged. However, we also recognised that this does not exhaust the relevant range of 'institutional' influences or modes of explaining the making of news. Studies of journalism and newsmaking must also be attentive to influences and factors operating outside as well as within newsrooms, as Gans (1979), Schudson (2000) and others have recognised. We must

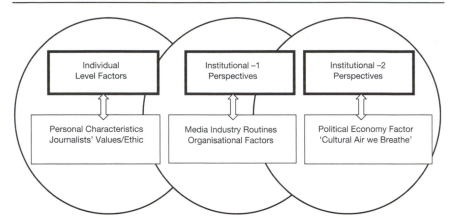

Figure 10.1 Simplified typology of five explanatory views of news influences

also consider the wider institutional-level environment in which journalism is situated, one which yields important if indirect, subtle and often taken-for-granted influences on newsmaking. For convenience here, we label these 'institutional-2'-level explanatory perspectives. Key aspects of these influences were addressed in Chapters 6 and 7 under the headings of political economy and the 'cultural air we breathe'.

Individual-level factors and professional values

As regards the individual characteristics of journalists, they continue to be highly educated relative to the general population, even as the latter's level of formal educational qualifications increases in line with what some define as a shift to a knowledge-based economy. Over time, an increasing number of journalists possess one, if not two, university degrees, often in disciplines other than journalism or media studies. If, a century ago, journalism was deemed not to be a fit occupation for 'young gentlemen', it has now become a much sought-after career choice for well educated young men and women. This shift in the perceived status of journalism may be partly to do with the changing social role of the media and the rise of celebrity culture, as the material conditions for new entrants (e.g. income and employment contracts) are often rather precarious (IFJ and ILO, 2006). Whilst freelance and part-time working has long been a feature of the journalism profession, especially for new entrants, the evidence suggests that this is increasing. The same applies to turnover in the profession, with an increasing tendency to leave after several years, often to take up work in public relations or related fields (IFJ and ILO, 2006; Nygren, 2007).

Recent studies of individual journalists suggest that their definitions of professional values and norms remain fairly constant, both over time and across cultures. Our own project's interviews with journalists in 11 countries found that they tended to profess a strikingly similar set of professional values. We also reviewed other research indicating a general convergence in the formal codes of ethics for journalists in European countries. Whilst working journalists seem to differ on the practical relevance of formal codes of ethics, they form a crucial component of the accumulated body of occupational norms and values. The latter are deemed to underpin the distinctive professional roles and autonomy of modern journalism vis-à-vis the influence or power of industry routines, news sources, organisational or managerial pressures, media ownership and regulatory factors, or indeed, that of broader political, economic or ideological forces.

The research literature and our own studies signal a general trend away from 'hard' news and information content in favour of an increasing emphasis on news-lite, consumerist, entertainment or sports-related content. There is a distinct, if long-standing, trend towards personalisation, life-style, consumerist and infotainment, in news and current affairs coverage (dumbing-down). The main reason cited for such trends is the expanding role of business values and financial criteria or pressures, including greater numbers of commercially driven media especially in the broadcasting sector. One of the other major trends concerns the highly self-referential or incestuous character of journalistic discourse and news cultures, indicating an increasing trend towards cross-media 'intertextuality' (e.g. Preston, 2006a; ter Wal 2006a). This is manifest, for example, in a growing tendency for journalists to interview other journalists, journalism to be concerned about journalism, trends linked to the personalisation of news values and the growth of celebrity culture within journalism itself.

The relevant roots or causes of these shifts are economic as much as technological, and they also include (national and EU) public policy shifts favouring the growth of private multi-channel television and radio services relative to public service media.

Surveys indicate that journalists' professional values have been under increasing pressures in recent times, not least from business and economic influences related to corporate profit-seeking, the increasing role of advertising revenue and numbers of outlets. Whilst such economic pressures and financial motives may be long established, for many practitioners and researchers they are growing in importance. The balance between these forces and the norms of professional journalism has changed significantly in recent times. This shift arises as news media become increasingly orientated towards 'making a business of information', subject to short-term financial disciplines and goals, and new organisational systems enhance managerial control. Our own study of European journalists, like other recent surveys, indicates a widespread view that industrial, commercial and managerial logics alongside 'financial forces are getting stronger' and journalistic norms or professional factors are becoming relatively weaker in shaping news media practices and routines (Nygren, 2007: 8). Rather similar trends, pointing to the erosion of the distinct spaces and role of professional norms are evident in academic institutions and other knowledge production sectors (Preston, 2001).

Key trends in media routines and organisational factors

Turning towards the issues of news industry routines, institutional patterns and organisational factors, we have identified multiple shifts and innovations which yield further pressures on the autonomy or potential influence of professional norms and values. We have described how many of these shifts have been enabled but not determined by technological innovations. The techno-economic features of new ICTs have helped to reduce the start-up costs required for new entrants in both television as well as Internet-based sectors. Policy and regulatory changes, at national and EU levels, have been equally important in facilitating the proliferation of media outlets. But the growth of media outlets has not been accompanied by any parallel increase in the numbers of professional journalists engaging in the practices of deliberative journalism orientated to the public. Rather, we have observed a growing trend in news industry routines orientated towards output or throughput, channelling the same news content across different platforms. This has been paralleled by a general tendency towards speed-up in news production practices and schedules and a concomitant diminution in the human, time or other resources available to check and interrogate information from sources. These shifts in industry routines reduce the capacity of journalists to undertake original research or perform the other time-intensive tasks related to investigative journalism in line with the tenets of the modern model of journalism.

We have observed many significant shifts in the forms and roles of organisational factors operating as 'powerful contexts' and influences on newsmaking. For example, new ICTs have not only enabled *product innovations* in the form of new news services, but they have also been appropriated by media corporations as the basis for multiple *process innovations*. In many cases, organisational innovations (management-led change strategies) involve not merely significant modifications to working practices and news production routines. They also serve to restructure the formal and informal power structures and processes of control within news organisations. The empirical evidence reported in Chapters 4 and 5 suggest that the general drift of such managerial and process innovations has been to erode the prior boundaries between the space of professional norms and practices and that of the business and commercial aspects of news organisations. Such changes weaken the already vulnerable role of professional norms and values and so diminish the relative autonomy of journalism. The power of commercial interests, managerial and ownership norms over those of professional journalist is further amplified by the growing tendency of news media organisations to employ journalistic staff on precarious (temporary or part-time) contracts. At the same time, managerial strategies tend to nurture and promote a small minority as star journalists or celebrities who are very well paid for their role as flagship personalities in promoting the appeal of the brand.

The successive generations of organisational and process innovations introduced by management since the 1980s seems to yield a fundamental shift in the lived culture (structure of feeling) as well as in the more visible aspects of work-ing practices in news media. The seminal studies of news organisations empha-sised the highly informal character of control structures and processes, often based around tacit knowledge and unwritten house rules as well as peer group or team working, with many journalists viewing their craft as more allied to literary rather than industrial work. The profession's *modus operandi* was highly (indeed, infamously) social in character and the informal social exchanges between members also served as important sources of information and informal power to counter the privileged position of management and owners. The various orga-nisational innovations introduced by management in recent decades have greatly contributed to the erosion of the time and space (and often, the locational) fac-tors which enabled such informal social networking. The post-Fordist managerial innovations in the larger news organisations tend to frame or situate rank-and-file news workers as interchangeable members of production teams. Whilst emphasising multi-skilling and convergent or integrated news production, they tend to reduce the status and play of tacit knowledge via greater reliance on formats and templates. In chaining journalists to their desks, screens and machines, they not only reduce interpersonal interactions with news sources. Time pressures also reduce the opportunities for informal exchanges and socia-bility amongst professional journalists themselves, further eroding the scope for collective sharing of knowledge essential to professional autonomy and control.

Broader political-economic, cultural and ideological trends

The research reported earlier points to certain common trends including the pervasive pressures of increasing commercialisation and competition between media. Our own studies suggest that the media are increasing their role, scope, reach and power within every country surveyed. Yet, we observe an increasing orientation of journalistic practices and content towards news-lite, entertain-ment, personalities and sports-related genres. At the same time, the media are playing an increasingly important role in the very definitions and performance of formal politics, as the concept of mediatisation indicates. This occurs as prior forms of popular participation in 'democratic' political processes and institutions continue to decline in the older-established liberal democracies, not least those with strong social democratic traditions.

Recent trends include increasing media commercialisation and competition, and this is accompanied by growing pressures on public service broadcasting. Some of the pressures on PSB arise from EU and national policy changes, whilst the latter in turn are influenced by demands from commercial media operators and advertising interests. Despite the relatively minor changes in the numbers of professional journalists, we observe a significant growth in the numbers and influence of public relations specialists and related promotional functions. As the same time, we observe major leakages of experienced staff and tactic knowledge from the newsmaking sector orientated to the public. In large part, this results from the increasing numbers of relatively secure and well paid jobs in the public relations and other promotional media services for staff with journalistic experience. The changing roles and status of professional journalism orientated to the public relative to the growing arrays of promotional news services orientated to the views, politics and values of partial or private interests pose major implications for the political public sphere. It also underlines the growing role and influence of information subsidies linked to powerful interests and sources possessing the financial resources to employ promotional specialists, lobbyists and related functions. Such trends are compounded by pressures towards speed-up and increased throughput of news content experienced by journalists operating in news media formally orientated towards the public.

Despite the widespread trend towards a quantitative increase in media outlets, the research indicates a general absence of parallel increases in the diversity of information available to citizens in EU member states, especially as regards news and current affairs genres. The literature reviews and interviews research all point to a general tendency whereby increased commercial and competitive pressures combine to diminish the extent and diversity of foreign news and current affairs coverage. This is an important if somewhat ironic finding in an era so frequently characterised as one of deepening 'globalisation' as well as Europeanisation. Examples noted by our research include reductions in recent years in the numbers of permanent foreign correspondents employed by two major national media organisations in Britain, despite some of these posts being long-established (Preston, 2006a).

EU-related news and current affairs matters comprise one area of non-national news where such commercial pressures affect the quality and extent of news coverage. Our interviewees suggest that important EU-level political issues tend to be 'complex' or 'difficult' subjects for news or current affairs coverage and that they are not readily embraced or easily presented according to the prevailing newsmaking conventions, practices and codes, which remain nationally embedded. When EU-related matters are covered by national media, they tend to be heavily filtered through the 'national prism' – treated and represented in line with the specific codes, norms and conventions of distinct news cultures and traditions within each national setting. As the EU becomes an increasingly important arena for political decision-making, such challenges must be addressed in a sustained fashion if news media are to meet their traditional orientation towards (or presumed role in) serving the public interest. This requires a serious commitment, not least in terms of additional resources engaged in the effort to educate and inform the public in line with such developments. As yet, there is little indication that commercial news media are willing to make the necessary commitments to this end.

The relevant research suggests that European and EU-related news and current affairs topics tend to play relatively minor and sporadic roles in the overall content of the mass media. This trend is not necessarily the consequence of deliberate anti-European or anti-EU bias (although that may feature in some cases). Rather, to a great extent, it merely reflects the usual operations of news selection processes, routine industrial practices and more general shifts in news values or journalistic practices, including:

- The long-established pattern whereby national news and current affairs topics have always had a privileged status relative to the seemingly 'foreign';
- The declining role of 'hard' news in favour of softer and more celebrity-focused news;
- The related shift towards more entertainment, sports and lifestyle-orientated media content;
- A consequent squeeze on 'foreign' news and current affairs reports (other than sports, travel and tourism issues).

Paradigm shift? News in the 'knowledge economy'

Institutional innovations and new socio-technical paradigms

Is the predominant 'modern' model of professional journalism (or news paradigm), which first emerged in the early decades of the twentieth century, now facing a veritable paradigm shift to some new form or mode of journalism?

Here we draw on the long-waves perspective and the idea of socio-technical paradigms introduced in Chapter 2. The approach here is informed by empirically grounded studies of major new technology systems, especially those historically rare systems with a 'potential' for pervasive applications and disruptive roles. In the case of the current wave of digital ICTs, this approach suggests significant potentials and incentives for various kinds of product and process innovations, especially in information-intensive services and functions, such as those in the media sector. But this socio-technical systems approach also insists that the extent and forms of any innovations associated with the application of new ICTs are not driven by any intrinsic, universal, or linear technical logics. Rather, they are co-produced by the interaction between technical, institutional, organisational, social and political (or policy) innovations, including those related to professional norms and practices. Even from a purely instrumental (performance or productivity-enhancing) perspective, the forms and extent of changes must be understood as dependent on the interplay between technical and an array of corresponding institutional, managerial, policy, etc., innovations. As noted, any shifts to new paradigms involve a complex process of *social learning* across institutional and organisational domains and so the more persistent features may take some time to emerge and become embedded. Sometimes the source of crucial innovations may be external to the system and driven by lifeworld needs, for example pressures exerted by social movements (Preston, 2001).

Applying this socio-technical system perspective to the news media services and journalism field implies that we must be attentive to shifts and changes in terms of all five of the explanatory schema and domains of influence on news as discussed in earlier chapters. This clearly embraces various micro-level and 'subtle social shifts' (Carey, 2005: 443) occurring in industrial routines or in professional norms and practices within newsrooms and their immediate institutional and organisational settings. But it also implies attention to emergent trends and shifts in the wider institutional, cultural and ideological settings (institutional-2) which have implications on the future modes of journalism and newsmaking. Several key aspects of the latter were addressed in Chapters 6 and 7 under the headings of political economy and the 'cultural air we breathe'.

Neo-liberalism and shifts in key steering mechanisms

The broadest institutional or 'steering mechanisms' of the modern social system comprise money (markets, economy, finance) and administrative or state power and both can be treated as alternate macro languages coordinating economic and political transactions (Habermas, 1989: 183).

Recent decades have witnessed significant shifts in the respective roles and forms of these broad institutional domains (Habermas, 1989: 183; Bausch, 1997: 321). The general shift from the Keynesian, welfare-state regulatory regime to neo-liberalism has wrought significant changes in the contours of societal development and in the distribution of material wealth and income, as well as power, since the early 1980s. Whilst its own discourses and practices prefer to frame such developments in terms of 'deregulation' or liberalisation, from this systems perspective neo-liberalism comprises another mode of regulation (or re-regulation). For sure these discourses and practices have privileged and promoted private sector interests, market-based processes and logics, individualised and consumer identities and roles over those of citizenship or the public. But in place of any fundamental 'rolling back of the state' we see a selective hollowing-out of certain state-based administrative and distributional roles accompanied by major extensions in other domains, not least those related to the enhancement of rights and privileges attaching to intellectual and other forms of property.

The neo-liberal turn has also seen a significant centralisation of power and control within the state administrative systems, in part facilitated (but not determined) by new ICT-enabled bureaucratic monitoring and other managerial innovations. This has been accompanied by similar shifts in the conduct of formal political processes deemed to regulate such systems, in part expressed in the processes of mediatisation and professionalisation of politics (Sampson, 2005). Other features of the neo-liberal turn include a propensity to import the values, norms and practices of the private-sector, market economy into public sector services. Notwithstanding the rhetorics of 'rolling back' of state engagement in specific industrial sectors, neo-liberal policy practices and discourses have also involved an array of initiatives directed at promoting the adoption and use of new ICT-based systems and networks. These include various 'information society' or 'knowledge economy' policy campaigns and strategies, since the early 1980s. They also include positioning all forms of knowledge production as 'a

new frontier' for exploitation by capitalist market forces, signalling a fundamental shift towards the deepening commodification, in line with 'making a
business of information' (Preston, 2001).

Re-marketisation and autonomy of 'new professions'

The macro-level institutional shifts briefly summarised above pose significant, if
often neglected, implications for the substantive characteristics of the 'knowledge
economy' or 'network society' in which journalism and newsmaking are embedded today. Since its first emergence in the mid-twentieth century, the idea of an
'information' or 'knowledge' society has always been closely bound up with the
question of changing class structures and power relations within the heartlands
of industrial capitalism (e.g. Mills, 1956; Bell, 1973). As Bell's influential account
makes clear, these debates have been especially centred on the expanding roles
and features of the so-called 'new professions', most of which first emerged
around the turn of the twentieth century – and amongst which we here count
journalism.

Bell and most other conventional 'information' or 'knowledge' society theorists
emphasise the autonomy or freedom and power of knowledge workers based in
the new professions, even if some, such as Mills, took a contrary view (Preston,
2001). In essence, they creatively appropriated and translated one old master
myth dating from the Enlightenment era (i.e. that knowledge = power) to the
analysis of diverse sets of 'new professions' that were growing relatively rapidly
from the early twentieth century. The focus falls primarily on certain professionals engaged in the production of technical, scientific, managerial and instrumental knowledge forms, with universities (and sometimes, high-tech firms)
identified as the leading or typical institutional expressions of this emerging new
order. These theories of the relative autonomy of the new professions were based
on the diminishing role of market forces and the rising role of public services and
state-based planning which typified the Keynesian regulatory regime from the
1940s to the late 1970s. Here the mixed economy implies a significant de-
marketisation of system incentives and logics, opening up new spaces where
alternative professional norms and vocational values have greater sway, including those orientated towards public service or civic improvement. The autonomy
of professionals to set their own agendas, plot and plan their particular knowledge productions flourishes as the power and influence previously attaching to
capitalist property rights and market forces is seen to diminish. Insum, the perceived autonomy and power of specialist knowledge workers is not only linked to
their specialist expertise and functional roles but also depends on a specific
configuration of macro-institutional conditions.

To the extent that the perceived autonomy of the twentieth century's 'new
professions' depended on such macro-level institutional norms, practices and
conditions, then it has been severely diminished since the 1980s by the features
of the neo-liberal turn summarised above. The latter involves a significant

process of re-marketisation, the expanding the sway of capitalism's utilitarian and instrumental logics, its competitive ethos and its rational-bureaucratic logics, reaching even into knowledge domains, public services and non-profit institutions previously distanced from such pressures. The process of extended marketisation, commercial and bureaucratic logics applies especially to the fields of knowledge production, as we have noted above. This is clear in the case of universities and other educational institutions, often deemed the archetypal institutional base for autonomous knowledge production. Here the neo-liberal turn has greatly diminished professional autonomy in goal-setting and daily practices in recent decades, largely in favour of a distinct re-orientation towards private sector industrial values and interests, or those set by governmental agencies, not to mention bureaucratic monitoring and standards.

Thus we observe that the macro-level features of the current neo-liberal version of the information society or knowledge economy have been stamped and shaped in fundamental ways by political, economic and social shifts rather than by any factors intrinsic to new ICTs or other technical innovations. New technologies may enable and facilitate the proliferation of diverse media outlets. But it is the macro political and economic factors that largely shape and regulate the evolving structures of media markets, including the growth in concentration of media ownership, the increasing sway of intellectual property rights, advertising and public relations services, as well as the enhanced role of commercial criteria and consumerist values in shaping trends in content production. These factors also favour the trends towards quantitative increases in commercial media outlets without accompanying growth in numbers of professional journalists. These developments help define and situate the trends towards soft news, infotainment and the tendencies towards speed-up, cut-and-paste and mouse-minding in newsmaking practices reported earlier.

The neo-liberal turn involves an extended marketisation or commodification of all forms of knowledge, including those related to newsmaking. As a consequence, these political-economic innovations serve to embed and legitimate the macro-level norms and practices which favour growing allocations of specialist knowledge and resources towards public relations, advertising and sporsorship functions engaged in promoting the private and partial interests of those with the ability to pay for their services. At the same time they diminish the shares of newsmaking resources orientated towards the public interest, including those needed by professional journalists interested in investigative reporting or researching stories critical of the economic and political establishment.

This analysis suggests that the neo-liberal turn shapes the contours of the emerging information or knowledge society in ways that are much more fundamental than any ICT-based 'technology effects'. It also poses significant implications for the modern model of professional journalism and newsmaking that emerged in the early twentieth century. It suggests that the news media now operate in an overall environment where economic power, marketisation and commerical logics play a much greater role than before. All forms of knowledge and information, including those related to newsmaking, are now much more subject to economic power and the play of market based, commercial criteria. The spaces for non-marketised knowledge production shaped by specialist professional norms, values and criteria have been eroded by the neo-liberal regime of regulation.

Most accounts suggest that the relative autonomy of the modern model of journalism has been framed around the assertion of professional norms, a certain distancing from both political and economic sources of power, in combination with an internal organisational differentiation from business, management and commercial criteria. The commercial basis of most media organisations was deemed to be compatible with modern professional journalism since it provided an independent source of revenue. At the macro level, the neoliberal turn has changed the balance between economic power and state or formal political authority at the same time that sectoral institutional changes have eroded the boundaries between professional journalistic and business norms in media organisations. This double movement suggests that the news media are now increasingly subject to influences from economic power and criteria, marked by 'a general shift toward the dominance of commercial logic' (Hallin, 2005).

The modern model of journalism has tended to define and protect its autonomy and orientation to the public interest in terms of its distance from the state and the arena of formal political authority and power. Professional journalists have tended to much more readily define their role as that of interrogating the agents of political authority compared to investigating the forms and sources of economic power. This analysis suggests economic and commercial forms and sources of power – not least those impinging on the production of knowledge and discourses related to news and current affairs – require greater attention and reflexive scrutiny by journalism. Economic forms of power and influence must now be recognised as of increasing importance in defining the mission and relative autonomy of any new model of professional journalism orientated to serving the 'public' and its interests in the contemporary neo-liberal knowledge society setting. This applies with equal force to academic domains engaged in the study of journalism and news as well as in the education of journalists.

If 'the revolution will not be televised', will it be online?

Can the Internet (and other new ICTs) be defined as one of the 'resources of hope' in extending the unfinished project of democratisation, not least by playing a key role in enabling or facilitating new modes of investigative, critical, or even 'reflexive' journalism and news cultures? What are the future prospects for a vibrant journalism and news media system dedicated to not merely entertaining consumers but informing and educating the public?

McLuhan became a media darling as he waxed lyrical in the 1960s and 1970s about the powerful role and effects of television and other (then) new electronic media of communication, proposing, inter alia, a radical demise of nationalism and the inauguration of a cosy new global village in its place. The decade when McLuhan's fame was at its peak was also one of multiple social, political and cultural conflicts and challenges to established forms of power and authority. These included the rise of second-age feminism, student uprisings, large-scale strikes and industrial conflicts, mass demonstrations in opposition to the USA's war in Vietnam, and the civil rights and black power movements in the USA.

Most activists engaged in those struggles and their supporters did not share McLuhan's faith in the power or beneficial effects of electronic media, however pious or sincere his assumptions. Indeed, they regarded the media and its news coverage, especially the then relatively new medium of television, as closely allied to the established elites and forms of power to which they were opposed. As musician Gil Scott-Heron (1970) put it, 'the revolution will not be televised'. But, if the essential mission of the progressive social and political movements of the mid-1960s–1970s were not to be 'televised', will their equivalents be 'online' in the early decades of the twenty-first century? Or, more fundamentally, perhaps, is it even valid to pose or frame any such question?

Whether or how the Internet, or other features of the 'new media' landscape, may support new forms of journalism which reinvigorate the occupation's role and self-image as the public's watchdog or independent fourth estate is not pre-configured or encoded in any technological scripts. We emphasise that whether and how professional journalism reinvents itself to better approximate its declared ideals or watchdog role has relatively little to do with any disruptive effects intrinsic to the new technologies. As we know, old media platforms can equally support bad journalism as well as the excellent and merely mediocre, and so much the same applies to the new media. Much depends on how the Internet is appropriated and used in practice by the interplays between the professional, organisational and institutional factors within the newsroom and in its immediate environment. Important influences comprise the interplay of the institutional, organisational, and professional factors surrounding the newsroom and newsmaking practices as well as the broader social, cultural and indeed political factors identified in Chapters 3 through 7. The influences also include the potential role and impacts of broader political currents and social movements quite external to the formal systems of public communication (Preston, 2001).

First, as regards personal and professional factors, any worthwhile project for a renewal of journalism requires cadres of journalists orientated towards an old, but still fundamental and relevant core professional value: serving the public interest in contrast to the centres of power or the mere pursuit of personal fame and fortune. A renewed news culture depends on journalists with the individual dispositions, professional competencies and values orientated towards informing and educating, as well as entertaining their audiences, not least by investigating the uses and abuses of power or other resources. This also implies journalists equipped with the critical and reflexive competencies as well as technical skills required for monitoring and interrogating the hidden or unspoken faces of social and political power, not merely the more familiar or explicit forms. Such a renewed model of journalism will also engage more with its public, addressing its members as citizens as well as mere consumers. It will also need to engage creatively and productively with the various new forms of alternative media, citizen-based journalism and social mobilisations being facilitated by the Internet. Indeed, the latter may be creative partners for a new journalism orientated to more diverse and pluralist sources of news. They may be treated as new resources to assist professional journalists in engaging with powerful sources, in interrogating and decoding the increasing arrays of promotional information and flak orientated towards the interests of the wealthy and powerful in an increasingly monetised 'knowledge' culture.

But if these individual and professional orientations, competencies and values are to have any significant impact on news practices and cultures, they must be complemented by shifts and reforms related to the institutional and organisational influences shaping the news. The essential requirements here include new roles for independent and self-organising collective formations, such as journalists' trade unions or professional associations, capable of exerting pressure at both the news organisation and sector-wide levels. This will not be easy as it runs counter to the pervasive influence of competitive individualism which has long been a marked feature of the media sector. Yet, such collective forms seem essential requirements to foster and assert the role of modern journalism's 'professional' values and norms and to counter the growing power of managerial norms and business aspects of the news media.

This takes us to our second and third clusters of influences on newsmaking. The recent empirical research indicates that the autonomy of professional journalists, whilst always relative or vulnerable, is being further eroded by the new managerial strategies, organisational regimes and industrial routines within newsrooms and their surrounding contexts. For example, the processes of speed-up and increased throughput and time pressures, dependence on machine or screen or mouse-minding have not only reduced time for deliberation and impacted on news content. They also serve to amplify the trends towards individualisation, undermining the older forms of sociability between professionals in the newsrooms which served as an important base for collective resistance to managerial power as well as business and commercial criteria. For sure, these new industrial routines and organisational factors have been enabled by Internet- and other new ICT-based technical innovations, but they have not been determined by them – the latter could just as easily support quite alternative newsmaking routines and arrangements. Rather, the key, influencing factor, as noted earlier, is the relative of power of instrumental, managerial and business norms, alongside commercial criteria and ownership interests, including the pursuit of profit, over those of mere professional values and norms in such settings.

A new or revamped model of professional journalism will also require reforms that engage with the critical issues of resources. Any worthwhile reforms towards a new news culture will require a significant increase in the numbers of journalists, at least in line with the quantitative growth in news outlets and platforms over the past decade. Such an increase seems a necessary condition if the norms for a 'deliberative' journalism or the proclaimed goals of greater diversity in news content and forms are to be realised. A further challenge to be addressed concerns the trend towards increasing use of precarious (part-time and temporary) employment contracts by news media organisations. Such employment practices and managerial policies seem incompatible with the conditions required for journalists' professional autonomy. Any valid twenty-first century model of professional journalism, especially one with pretensions to high quality or 'deliberative' standards, must engage with these and other crucial material resource factors.

We have already indicated a challenging set of professional, institutional and organisational innovations and reforms as necessary conditions for a renewed professional journalism and news paradigm. But it should also be clear by now that these prerequisites may not fully reside within the power and control of professional journalists or news organisations driven by market criteria. The issues and remedies identified immediately above also spill over to, and in part depend upon, wider categories of influences considered in Chapters 6 and 7, including the political-economic, regulatory, cultural and ideological factors. For example, any self-organised efforts by journalists associations to expand the resources for investigative journalism, or to increase the numbers of reporters or to enhance their professional autonomy by reversing managerial trends related to employment contracts and practices, will be much enhanced by matching reforms in public policies and regulatory innovations. The latter in turn will be enhanced to the extent that the political elites can be persuaded or compelled to end their ever-growing dependency relations with the owners and executives of media corporations.

Addressing the matrix of influences on news

We have indicated that there is no technological or other 'quick-fix' path forward towards a renewed or reinvented model of journalism. Rather, we have here identified what is clearly a challenging and interlocking configuration of professional, institutional, organisational, political and regulatory innovations and reforms. These are proposed in light of the matrix of news influences, especially the multi-layered and complementary set of influencing factors discussed in earlier chapters.

Studies of mediatisation underline how the news media's role and power has grown dramatically since the early modern period. But the research evidence also indicates that the dominant norms and values steering the operations of major news organisations tend to be business and commercial in orientation. In contrast, the professional codes of a deliberative journalism orientated to the public now play a minor and diminishing role. Compared to the earlier stages of industrial modernity, the news media must now be 'perceived as a power – not a counter-power, but a power in itself', according to a former editor of the *Financial Times*, citing Alain Minc, chairman of the board at *Le Monde* (Lambert, 2005). This means that the old slogan of 'freedom of the press' must now be subject to fundamental review. In essence, there is a growing realisation that the news media must be opened up to regulation, accountability and scrutiny like all the other institutions of power (e.g. O'Neill, 2002; Gandy, 2003b; Lloyd, 2004; Lambert, 2005). Any such reforms must include critical interrogations of the changing relations between the business and managerial aspects of the media and the main centres of economic and political power. A necessary element in any such package of institutional innovations must be the enhancement of professional norms and values orientated to a deliberative journalism and public sphere. These must be promoted over and above the systemic trends towards news cultures dominated by business, managerial and bureaucratic logics. But any such moves must also be complemented by other movements and initiatives engaging with the institutional, economic and other sets of influential forces impacting on new culture.

We have identified some of the essential preconditions for a robust renewal of the modern model of journalism and its news practices which matches its distinctive professional self-image, norms and roles in the light of contemporary societal conditions. Clearly, we are here speaking of a reform agenda, rather than any more radical platform such as a 1970s form of 'revolution' that dare not be televised. However, if and when the requisite reforms are introduced, we will be more than pleased to learn the news – whether it be televised or online, in print or blogged.

Bibliography

eMEDIATE project reports

Cisarova, Lenka Waschkova (2007a) 'Report on News Cultures in the Czech Republic', eMEDIATE project, WP3 National report.

——(2007b) 'Report on News Cultures in Slovakia', eMEDIATE project, WP3 National report.

Guyot, J., Mattelart, A. and Multigner, G. (2006) 'Editorial Cultures: Report on France and Spain', eMEDIATE project, WP3 National report.

Horgan, John (2006) 'Ireland: Editorial Cultures', eMEDIATE project, WP3 National report.

Kovács, András, Horváth, Anikó and Welker, Árpád (2005) 'Editorial Culture: Country Report – Hungary', eMEDIATE project, WP3 National report.

——(2006) 'Additional Notes to the Hungarian WP3 Country Report and Comments on the Draft WP3 Comparative Report', eMEDIATE project, WP3 National report.

Preston, Paschal (2006a) 'Editorial Culture in Great Britain', eMEDIATE project, WP3 National report.

——(2006b) 'Report on Media Research: Great Britain', eMEDIATE project, WP2 National report.

——(2006c) '"Meta Matters": Strategic Issues and Notes on Comparative Analyses of Editorial Cultures & Media Systems', Mimeo (eMEDIATE project, WP3).

Preston, Paschal and Horgan, John (2006) 'Comparative Report on Newsmaking Cultures and Values', WP3. eMEDIATE project, WP3 National report.

ter Wal, Jessika (2006a) 'Editorial Culture: The Netherlands', eMEDIATE project, WP3 National report.

——(2006b) 'Comments on the Draft WP3 Comparative Report', eMEDIATE project, WP3 National report.

——(2006c) 'Report on Media Research: The Netherlands', eMEDIATE project, WP2 National report.

ter Wal, Jessika and Valeriani, Augusto (2006) 'Editorial Culture in Italy', eMEDIATE project, WP3 National report.

Zagar, I. (2006) 'Report on Media Research: Slovenia', eMEDIATE project, WP2 National report.

Zagar, Igor and Zeljan, Katja (2006a) 'Final Report on Editorial Cultures: Serbia', eMEDIATE project, WP3 National report.

——(2006b) 'Final Report on Editorial Cultures: Slovenia', eMEDIATE project, WP3 National report.

General bibliography

Aksoy, A. and Robins, K. (2003) 'The Enlargement of Meaning: Social Demand in a Transnational Context', *Gazette*, 65 (4–5).

Aldridge, M. (2003) 'The Ties that Divide: Regional Press Campaigns, Community and Populism', *Media, Culture and Society*, 25.

Allan, Stuart (2004) *News Culture – 2nd Edn*, Maidenhead: Open University Press.

——(2005) 'News on the Web: The Emerging Forms and Practices of Online Journalism', ch. 5 (pp. 67–83) in Stuart Allan (ed.) *Journalism: Critical Issues*, Maidenhead: Open University Press.

——(2006) *Online News: Journalism and the Internet*, Maidenhead: Open University Press.

Allan, Stuart (ed.) (2005) *Journalism: Critical Issues*, Maidenhead: Open University Press.

Altheide, D. L. (1976) *Creating Reality: How TV News Distorts Events*, Beverly Hills, CA: Sage.

——(2004) 'Media Logic and Political Communication', *Political Communication*, 21 (3): 293–6.

Altheide, D. L. and Snow, R. P. (1979) *Media Logic*, Beverly Hills, CA and London: Sage.

Ang, I. (1985) *Watching 'Dallas': Soap Opera and the Melodramatic Imagination*, London: Methuen.

Bagdikian, B. (2000) *The Media Monopoly, 6th Edn*, Boston, MA: Beacon Books.

Bantz, Charles R. (1985) 'News Organizations: Conflict as a Crafted Cultural Norm', *Communication*, 8: 225–44.

Barnett, S. and Curry, A. (1994) *The Battle for the BBC*, London: Aurum.

Barnhurst, Kevin G. (2005) 'News Ideology in The Twentieth Century', ch. 18 (pp. 239–62) in Svennik Høyer and Horst Pöttker (eds) *Diffusion of the News Paradigm 1850–2000*, Göteborg: Nordicom.

Bausch, Kenneth C. (1997) 'The Habermas/Luhmann Debate and Subsequent Habermasian Perspectives on Systems Theory', *Systems Research and Behavioural Science*, 14: 315–30.

BBC (2006) 'The BBC's Statements of Programme Policy (SoPPs)', BBC Press Release, 2 May 2006. Last accessed, 18 Dec. 2007 at www.bbc.co.uk/pressoffice/

——(2007a) 'News Viewers Turned to BBC in 2007', BBC Press Release, 17 Dec. 2007. Last accessed, 18 Dec. 2007 at www.bbc.co.uk/pressoffice/

——(2007b) 'Radical Reform to Deliver a More Focused BBC', BBC Press Release, 18 Oct. 2007. Last accessed, 18 Dec. 2007 at www.bbc.co.uk/pressoffice/

Becker, H. S. (1967) 'Whose Side Are We On?' *Social Problems*, 14 (3): 239–47.

Bell, Daniel (1973) *The Coming of Post-Industrial Society*, New York: Basic Books.

Belsey, A. and Chadwick, R. (1995) 'Ethics as a Vehicle for Media Quality', *European Journal of Communication*, 10 (4): 461–73.

Beniger, James R. (1986) *The Control Revolution: Technological and Economic Origins of the Information Society*, Cambridge, MA: Harvard University Press.

Bennett, W. L., Lawrence, R. G. and Livingston, S. (2007) *When the Press Fails: Political Power and the News Media from Iraq to Katrina*, Chicago, IL: University of Chicago Press.

Benson, R. (2004) 'Bringing the Sociology of Media Back In', *Political Communication*, 21 (3): 275–92.

——(2006) 'News Media as a "Journalistic Field": What Bourdieu Adds to New Institutionalism, and Vice Versa', *Political Communication*, 23 (2): 187–202.

Benson, Rodney and Neveu, Eric (eds) (2005) *Bourdieu and the Journalistic Field*, Cambridge: Polity.

Berkowitz, D. and Limor, Y. (2003) 'Professional Confidence and Situational Ethics–Assessing the Social-Professional Dialectic in Journalistic Ethics Decisions', *Journalism and Mass Communication Quarterly*, 80 (4): 783–801.

Blumler, J. G. and Gurevitch, M. (2001) 'The New Media and Our Political Communication Discontents', *Information, Communication and Society*, 4 (3): 435–57.

Blumler, J. G. and Kavanagh, D. (1999) 'The Third Age of Political Communication: Influences and Features', *Political Communication*, 16 (3).

Boczkowski, Pablo J. (2004a) *Digitizing the News: Innovation in Online Newspapers*, Cambridge, MA: MIT Press.

——(2004b) 'The Processes of Adopting Multimedia and Interactivity in Three Online Newsrooms', *Journal of Communication*, 54 (2): 197–213.

Bodnar, C. (2006) 'Taking it to the Streets: French Cultural Worker Resistance and the Creation of a Precariat Movement', *Canadian Journal of Communication*, 31 (3).

Born, Georgina (2003) 'From Reithian Ethic to Managerial Discourse: Accountability and Audit at the BBC', *Javnost – The Public*, 10 (3): 63–81.

Bouquillion, Philippe (2005) *The Formation of Cultural and Communication Industry Poles: Between Financial Coups and the Integration of Industrial Production Lines*, in www.observatoire-omic. org/omic_docsPres.php?theme_doc = 1&docID = 49&type = 1&paraID = -1

Boyd-Barrett, O. and Newbold, C. (eds) (1995) *Approaches to Media: A Reader*, London: Arnold.

Braverman, Harry (1974) *Labor and Monopoly Capital: The Degradation of Work in the Twentieth Century*, New York: Monthly Review Press.

Breed, Warren (1955) 'Social Control in the Newsroom: A Functional Analysis', *Social Forces*, 33 (4): 326–35; reprinted in ch. 34 (pp. 277–83) in O. Boyd-Barrett and C. Newbold (eds) *Approaches to Media: A Reader*, London: Arnold.

Bücher, Karl (1901) *Industrial Evolution*, translated from the third German edition by S. M. Wickett, London: G. Bell & Sons.

Buonanno, M. (1999) *Faction. Soggetti mobili e generi ibridi nel giornalismo italiano degli anni novanta*, Naples: Liguori editore.

Burawoy, Michael (1985) *The Politics of Production: Factory Regimes under Capitalism and Socialism*, London: Verso.

Cammaerts, B. and Van Audenhove, L. (2005) 'Online Political Debate, Unbounded Citizenship, and the Problematic Nature of a Transnational Public Sphere', *Political Communication*, 22 (2): 179–96.

Carey, J. W. (1989) *Communication as Culture*, Boston, MA: Unwin Hyman.

——(2005) 'Historical pragmatism and the Internet', *New Media and Society*, 7 (4): 443–55.

——(2007) 'A Short History of Journalism for Journalists', *The Harvard International Journal of Press/Politics*, 12 (3): 3–16.

Chalaby, Jean (2002) 'Transnational Television in Europe: The Role of Pan-European Channels', *European Journal of Communication*, 17 (2): 183–203.

Chouliaraki, L. and Fairclough, N. (1999) *Discourse in Late Modernity: Rethinking Critical Discourse Analysis*, Edinburgh: Edinburgh University Press.

Cohen, B. (1963) *The Press and Foreign Policy*, Princeton, NJ: Princeton University Press.

Cohen, Stan and Young, Jock (eds) (1973) *The Manufacture of News*, London: Constable.

Corcoran, Farrel and Preston, Paschal (eds) (1995) *Democracy and Communication in the New Europe: Change and Continuity in East and West*, Cresskill, NJ: Hampton Press.

Cottle, S. (ed.) (2000) *Ethnic Minorities and the Media*, Buckingham: Open University Press.

Curran, James (1979) 'Press Freedom as a Property Right: The Crisis of Press Legitimacy', *Media, Culture and Society*, 1.

——(1990) 'The New Revisionism in Mass Communication Research: A Reappraisal', *European Journal of Communication*, 5 (2–3): 135–64.

——(2000) 'Rethinking Media and Democracy', ch. 6 (pp. 120–54) in J. Curran and M. Gurevitch (eds) *Mass Media and Society – 3rd Edn*, London: Arnold.

——(2002) 'Media and the Making of British Society, 1700–2000', *Media History*, 8 (2): 135–55.

Curran, J. and Gurevitch, M. (eds) (1996) *Mass Media and Society – 2nd Edn*, London: Arnold.

——(2000) *Mass Media and Society – 3rd Edn*, London: Arnold.

Curran, James and Seaton, Jean (1997) *Power Without Responsibility*, London: Routledge.

——(2003) *Power Without Responsibility: Press and Broadcasting in Britain*, 6th edn, London: Routledge.

Curran, J., Gabor, I. and Petley, J. (2005) *Culture Wars: Media and the British Left*, Edinburgh: Edinburgh University Press.

Curran, J., Gurevitch, M. and Woollacott, J. (eds) (1977) *Mass Communication and Society*, Beverly Hills, CA: Sage.

Darnton, R. (1975) 'Writing News and Telling Stories', *Daedalus*, 104: 175–94.

Deuze, M. (2002) 'National News Cultures', *Journalism and Mass Communication Quarterly*, 79 (1): 134–49.

——(2005) 'Popular Journalism and Professional Ideology: Tabloid Reporters and Editors Speak Out', *Media, Culture and Society*, 27 (6): 861–82.

Deuze, Mark and Dimoudi, Christina (2002) 'Online Journalists in the Netherlands: Towards a Profile of a New Profession', *Journalism*, 4 (3): 85–100.

Dewey, John (1927/1954) *The Public and Its Problems* (originally published by Henry Holt and Company) reprint edition, Athens: Swallow Press.

Djupsund, G. and Carlson, T. (1998) 'Trivial Stories and Fancy Pictures? Tabloidization Tendencies in Finnish and Swedish Regional and National Newspapers, 1982–1997', *Nordicom*, 19 (1).

Downing, J., McQuail, D., Schlesinger, P. and Wartella, E. (eds) (2004) *Sage Handbook of Media Studies*, Thousand Oaks, CA and London: Sage.

Doyle, Gillian (2002) *Media Ownership*, London: Sage.

Eldridge, J. (ed.) (1995) *Glasgow Media Group Reader: Vol. 1: News Content, Language and Visuals*, London: Routledge.

Eldridge, John (2000) 'The Contribution of the Glasgow Media Group to the Study of Television and Print Journalism', *Journalism Studies*, 1 (1): 113–27.

Eldridge, John and Eldridge, Lizzie (1994) *Raymond Williams: Making Connections*, London: Rouledge.

Elliott, Philip (1972) *The Making of a TV Series: A Case Study in the Production of Culture*, London: Constable.

——(1977) 'Media Organizations and Occupations: An Overview' (pp. 142–73) in J. Curran, M. Gurevitch and J. Woollacott (eds) *Mass Communication and Society*, Beverly Hills, CA: Sage.

Entman, R.M. (1991) 'Framing US Coverage of International News', *Journal of Communication*, 41W: 6–17.

——(1993) 'Framing: Towards Clarification of a Fractured Paradigm', *Journal of Communication*, 43 (4): 51–68.

——(2004) *Projections of Power: Framing News, Public Opinion, and U.S. Foreign Policy*, Chicago, IL: University of Chicago Press.

Epstein, Jay (1973) *News from Nowhere*, New York: Random House.

Erdal, Ivar John (2007a) 'Negotiating Convergence in News Production', ch. 5 (pp. 73–87) in Tanja Torsul and Dagny Steudahl (eds) *Ambivalence Towards Convergence: Digitalization and Media Change*, Göteborg, Sweden: Nordicom.

——(2007b) 'Cross-media (re)production cultures', paper presented to 50th Anniversary Conference of the International Association for Media and Communication Research, held at UNESCO, Paris, 22–25 July 2007.

Erjavec, K. (2004) 'Beyond Advertising and Journalism: Hybrid Promotional News Discourse', *Discourse and Society*, 15 (5): 553–78.

——(2005a) 'Hybrid Public Relations News Discourse', *European Journal of Communication*, 20 (2): 155–79.

——(2005b) 'Beyond Advertising and Journalism: Hybrid Promotional News Discourse', *Discourse and Society*, 15 (5): 553–78.

European Commission (2006) 'White Paper on European Communication Policy', COM 2006, 35 Final.

Fairclough, N. (1989) *Language and Power*, London: Longman.

——(1995) *Media Discourse Analysis*, London: Arnold.

——(1998) 'Political Discourse in the Media: An Analytical Framework', in A. Bell and P. Garrett (eds) *Approaches to Media Discourse*, Oxford: Blackwell.

——(1999) 'Global Capitalism and Critical Awareness of Language', *Language Awareness*, 8 (2): 71–83.

Fishman, M. (1980) *Manufacturing the News*, Austin, TX: University of Texas Press.

Fleury (2006) *Het schitterende scherm. 50 Jaar Journaal*. Documentary, broadcast on NOS television 5 January 2006.

Frenzen, J., Hirsch, P. M. and Zerillo, P. (1994) 'Consumption Preferences and Changing Lifestyles' (pp. 403–25) in N. Smelser and R. Swedberg (eds) *Handbook of Economic Sociology*, Princeton, NJ: Princeton University Press.

Friedman, Andrew (1977) *Industry and Labor: Class Struggles at Work and Monopoly Capitalism*, London: Macmillan.

Friel, Howard and Falk, Richard A. (2007) *The Record of the Paper: How the 'New York Times' Misreports US Foreign Policy*, London and New York: Verso.

Galtung, Johan and Ruge, Mari Holmboe (1965) 'The Structure of Foreign News', *Journal of Peace Research*, 2 (1): 64–91.

Gandy, Oscar H. Jr (1982) *Beyond Agenda Setting: Information Subsidies and Public Policy*, Norwood, NJ: Ablex.

——(2003a) 'Epilogue: Framing at the Horizon – A Retrospective Assessment', ch. 21 (pp. 355–79) in Stephen Reese, Oscar Gandy and August Grant (eds) *Framing Public Life*, Hillsdale, NJ: Erlbaum.

——(2003b) '*The Great Frame Robbery: The Strategic Use of Public Opinion in the Formation of Media Policy*', report to the Ford Foundation, Grant 1025-1178. Last accessed 21 Nov. 2007 from www.asc.upenn.edu/usr/ogandy/

Gandy, Oscar H. Jr and Kenneth Neil Farrall (2007) 'Putting Down Stakes: Exploring the Political Economy of Property in Cyberspace', paper presented to the conference of the International Association for Media and Communication Research, (IAMCR) Paris, France, July 2007.

Gans, H. (1972) 'The Famine in American Mass Communication Research: Comments on Hirsch, Tuchman and Gecas', *The American Journal of Sociology*, 77 (4): 697–705.

——(1979) *Deciding What's News*, New York: Pantheon Books.

——(1985) 'Are US Journalists Dangerously Liberal?', *Columbia Journalism Review*, 24: 29–33.

——(2003) *Democracy and the News*, New York: Oxford University Press.

——(2007) 'Everyday News, Newsworkers, and Professional Journalism', *Political Communication*, 24 (2): 161–6.

Garnham, Nick (1990) *Capitalism and Communication*, London: Sage.

Geens, Davy; Picone, Ike and Vandebrande, Kristel (2007) 'Another Breach in the Wall: Organizational Dynamics of Today's News Ecology', presented at conference on 'The Future of Newspapers', Cardiff Centre for Journalism, Media and Cultural Studies, Cardiff University, 12–13 Sept.

Georgiou, M. (2005) 'Mapping Diasporic Media Cultures: A Transnational Cultural Approach to Exclusion', ch. 2 in R. Silverstone (ed.) *Media Technology and Everyday Life*, Aldershot: Ashgate.

Gieber, W. (1960) 'Two Communicators of the News: A Study of the Roles of Sources and Reporters', *Social Forces*, 39 (1): 76–83.

Gieber, W. and Johnson, W. (1961) 'The City Hall Beat: A Study of Reporter and Source Roles', *Journalism Quarterly*, 38: 289–97.

Gillespie, M. (1995) *Television, Ethnicity and Cultural Change*, London Routledge.

Gitlin, T. (1980/2003) *The Whole World Is Watching: The Role of the Media in the Making and Unmaking of the New Left*, Berkeley, CA: University of California Press.

——(2004) 'Reply to Rodney Benson', *Political Communication*, 21 (3): 309–10.

Glasgow Media Group (1976) *Bad News*, London: Routledge and Kegan Paul.

——(1980) *More Bad News*, London: Routledge and Kegan Paul.

——(1982) Really Bad News, London: Writers and Readers.

Global Media Monitoring Project (GMMP) (2006) *Who Makes the News: Executive Summary*, accessed online from GMMP.

Goffman, E. (1974) *Frame Analysis*, New York: Harper and Row.

Golding, P. and Elliott, P. (1979) *Making the News*, London: Longman.

Golding, P. and Murdock, G. (2000) 'Culture, Communications and Political Economy', ch. 4 (pp. 70–93) in J. Curran and M. Gurevitch (eds) *Mass Media and Society – 3rd Edn*, London: Arnold.

Gollin, A. E. (1980) 'Critiques and Celebrations of the Newsmaking Process: An Expository Review', *The Public Opinion Quarterly*, 44 (2): 276–83.

Graves, W. B. (ed.) (1928) *Readings in Public Opinion: Its Formation and Control*, New York: D. Appleton & Co.

Gronke, Paul and Cook, Timothy E. (2007) 'Disdaining the Media –The American Public's Changing Attitudes Toward the News', *Political Communication*, 24 (3): 259–81.

Gunter, Barrie (2005) 'Trust in the News on Television', *ASLIB Proceedings*, 57 (5): 384–97.

Habermas, J. ([1962] 1989) *The Structural Transformation of the Public Sphere*, Cambridge: Polity Press (originally published in German, 1962. English translation 1989).

——(2001) *The Postnational Constellation*, Cambridge: Polity Press.

——(2006) *The Divided West*, Cambridge: Polity Press.

Habermas, J. and Derrida, J. (2003/2005) 'February 15: Or What Binds Europeans Together: Plea for a Common Foreign Policy, Beginning in Core Europe' (pp. 3–14) in D. Levy, M. Pensky and J. Torpey (eds) (2005) *Old Europe, New Europe, Core Europe*, London: Verso.

Hackett, R. A. and Zhao,Y. (1998) *Sustaining Democracy? Journalism and the Politics of Objectivity*, Toronto: Garamond.

Hafez, K. (2002) 'Journalism Ethics Revisited: A Comparison of Ethics Codes in Europe, North Africa, the Middle East, and Muslim Asia', *Political Communication*, 19 (2): 225–50.

Hall, Peter and Preston, Paschal (1988) *The Carrier Wave: New Information Technology and the Geography of Innovation*, London: Unwin Hyman.

Hall, S. ([1974]1980) 'Encoding and Decoding in Television Discourse' (pp. 128–38) in S. Hall, D. Hobson, A. Lowe and P. Willis (eds) *Culture, media, language*, London: Hutchinson.

Hall, Stuart; Critcher, C., Jefferson, T., Clarke, J. and Roberts, B. (1978) *Policing the Crisis*, London: Macmillan.

Hall, S., Hobson, D., Lowe, A. and Willies, P. (eds) (1980) *Culture, Media, Language*, London: Hutchinson.

Hallin, D. (1986) *The 'Uncensored War': The Media and Vietnam*, Berkeley, CA: University of California Press.

——(1992) 'The Passing of the "High Modernism" of American Journalism', *Journal of Communication*, 42 (3): 14–25.

——(1994) *We Keep America on Top of the World: Television Journalism and the Public Sphere*, London: Routledge.

——(1996) 'Commercialism and Professionalism in the American News Media' (pp. 243–64) in J. Curran and M. Gurevitch (eds) *Mass Media and Society – 2nd Edn*, London: Arnold.

——(2000) 'Commercialism and Professionalism in the American News Media', ch. 10 (pp. 218–38) in J. Curran and M. Gurevitch (eds) *Mass Media and Society – 3rd Edn*, London: Arnold.

——(2005) 'Field Theory, Differentiation Theory and Comparative Media Research', ch. 12 (pp. 224–44) in R. Benson and E. Neveu (eds) *Bourdieu and the Journalistic Field*, Cambridge: Polity Press.

Hallin, Daniel C. and Mancini, Paolo (2004) *Comparing Media Systems: Three Models of Media and Politics*, Cambridge: Cambridge University Press.

Hallin, D. C. and Papathanassopoulos, S. (2002) 'Political Clientelism and the Media: Southern Europe and Latin America in Comparative Perspective', *Media, Culture and Society*, 24 (2): 175–95.

Halloran, James D., Elliott, Phillip and Murdock, Graham (1970) *Demonstrations and Communication: A Case Study*, London: Penguin.

Hanitzsch, T. (2005) 'Comparing Journalism Cross-Culturally; Defining the Core Concepts for Empirical Inquiry', paper to ICA conference, New York, May 2005.

Harcup, Tony and O'Neill, Deirdre (2001) 'What Is News? Galtung and Ruge Revisited', *Journalism Studies*, 2 (2): 261–80.

Hardt, Hanno (1979) *Social Theories of the Press: Early German and American Experiences*, Beverly Hills, CA and London: Sage.

Hartmann, Paul and Husband, Charles (1973) *Mass Media and Racial Conflict in the Manufacture of News*, London: Davis-Poynter.

Herman, Edward S. and Chomsky, Noam (1988) *Manufacturing Consent: The Political Economy of the Mass Media*, New York: Pantheon Books.

Hermida, A. and Thurman, Neil (2007) 'A Clash of Cultures: The Integration of User-Generated Content Within a Professional Journalistic Framework at British Newspaper Websites', presented at conference on 'The Future of Newspapers', Cardiff Centre for Journalism, Media and Cultural Studies, Cardiff University, 12–13 Sept.

Hesmondhalgh, David (2002) *The Cultural Industries*, London: Sage.

Himelboim, Itai and Limor, Yehiel (2005) 'The Journalistic Societal Role – An International Comparative Study of 242 Codes of Ethics', paper to ICA conference, New York, May 2005.

Hirsch, Paul M. (1972) 'Processing Fads and Fashions: An Organization-Set Analysis of Cultural Industry Systems', *American Journal of Sociology*, 77 (4): 639–59.

——(1977) 'Occupational, Organizational and Institutional Models in Mass Media Research: Toward an Integrated Framework' (pp. 13–42) in P. M. Hirsch, P. V. Miller and F. G. Kline (eds) *Strategies for Communication Research*, Beverly Hills, CA: Sage.

——(1978) 'Production and Distribution Roles Among Cultural Organizations: On the Division of Labor Across Intellectual Disciplines', *Social Research*, 45 (2): 315–30.

——(1997) 'Review Article: Sociology Without Social Structure: Neo-Institutional Theory Meets Brave New World', *The American Journal of Sociology*, 102 (6): 1702–23.

——(2000) 'Cultural Industries Revisited', *Organization Science*, 11 (3): 356–63.

Hoggart, Richard (1976) 'Foreword' in Glasgow Media Group, *Bad News*, London: Routledge and Kegan Paul.

Holmes, S. (2004) '"But This Time *You* Choose!": Approaching the "Interactive" Audience in Reality TV', *International Journal of Cultural Studies*, 7 (2).

Hourigan, N. (2001) 'New Social Movement Theory and Minority Language Television Campaigns', *European Journal of Communication*, 16 (1).

Høyer, Svennik and Pöttker, Horst (eds) (2005) *Diffusion of the News Paradigm, 1850–2000*, Göteborg, Sweden: Nordicom.

Hughes, Helen McGill (1940) *News and the Human Interest Story*, Chicago, IL: University of Chicago Press.

Hujanen, J. and Pietikainen, S. (2004) 'Interactive Uses of Journalism: Crossing Between Technological Potential and Young People's News-Using Practices', *New Media and Society*, 6 (3).

IFJ (International Federation of Journalists) and ILO (International Labor Organization) (2006) *The Changing Nature of Work: A Global Survey and Case Study of a Typical Work in the Media Industry'*, Brussels: International Federation of Journalists.

Im, Yung-Ho (1997) 'Towards a Labour Process History of Newsworkers', *Javnost – The Public*, 4 (1).

Jakubowicz, K. (2004) 'Ideas In Our Heads: Introduction of PSB as Part of Media System Change in Central and Eastern Europe', *European Journal of Communication*, 19 (1): 53–74.

Jensen, K. B. and Jankowski, N. W. (eds) (1991) *A Handbook of Qualitative Methodologies for Mass Communication Research*, London: Routledge.

Jochen, Peter; and de Vreese, C. H. (2004) 'In Search of Europe: A Cross-National Comparative Study of the European Union in National Television News', *Harvard International Journal of Press/Politics*, 9 (4): 3–24.

Johnson, Richard (2007) 'Post-Hegemony? I Don't Think So', *Theory, Culture and Society*, 24 (3): 95–120.

Johnstone, John W. C. (1982) 'Who Controls the News: Review', *American Journal of Sociology*, 87 (5): 1174–81.

Josephi, Beate (2005) 'Journalism in the Global Age: Between Normative and Empirical', *Gazette*, 67 (6): 575–90.

Kaitatzi-Whitlock, Sophia (2008) 'The Missing European Public Sphere and the Absence of Imagined European Citizenship: Democratic Deficit as a Function of a Common European Media Deficit', *European Societies*, 9 (5): 685–704.

Kaplan, R. L. (2006) 'The News About New Institutionalism: Journalism's Ethic of Objectivity and Its Political Origins', *Political Communication*, 23 (2): 173–85.

Katz, E. and Szecsko, T. (eds) (1981) *Mass Media and Social Change*, London and New York: Sage.

Keeble, Richard (2005) 'Journalism Ethics: Towards an Orwellian Critique?' (pp. 54–66) in Stuart Allan (ed.) *Journalism: Critical Issues*, Maidenhead: Open University Press.

Klinenberg, Eric (2005a) 'Convergence: News Production in a Digital Age', *The Annals of the American Academy of Political and Social Science*, 597: 48–64.

——(2005b) 'Channeling into the Journalistic Field: Youth Activism and the Media Justice Movement', ch. 9 (pp. 174–94) in R. Benson and E. Neveu (eds) *Bourdieu and the Journalistic Field*, Cambridge: Polity.

Klinenberg, E. and Fayer, H. (2005) 'Quick Read Synopsis: Cultural Production in a Digital Age', *The Annals of the American Academy of Political and Social Science*, 597: 223–44.

Kopper, Gerd G., Kolthoff, Albrecht and Czepek, Andrea (2000) 'Research Review: Online Journalism – A Report on Current and Continuing Research and Major Questions in the International Discussion', *Journalism Studies*; 1 (3): 499–512.

Kuhar, R. (2001) 'Zgrabiti in izgnati', in B. Petkovic (ed.) *Porocilo za spremljanje nestrpnosti 01*, Ljubljana: Mirovni Institut.

Laitila, Tiina (2005) 'Journalistic Codes of Ethics in Europe', ch. 15 (pp. 191–204) in D. McQuail, P. Golding and E. de Bens (eds) *Communication Theory and Research: An EJC Anthology*, London: Sage.

Lambert, Richard (2005) 'The Path Back to Trust, Truth and Integrity', *Guardian*, 17 Jan.

Lang, Kurt (1974) 'Images of Society: Media Research in Germany', *Public Opinion Quarterly*, 38 (3): 335–51.

Laville, Camille (2007) '1945–2005: The Transformations of Journalism Practices. A Case Study of the Foreign Correspondents of the Agence France-Presse', paper presented to 50th Anniversary Conference of the International Association for Media and Communication Research, held at UNESCO, Paris, 22–25 July 2007.

Leurdijk, A. (2006) 'In Search of Common Ground: Strategies of Multicultural Television Producers in Europe', *European Journal of Cultural Studies*, 9 (1).

Levy, D., Pensky, M. and Torpey, J. (eds) (2005) *Old Europe, New Europe, Core Europe*, London: Verso.

Leys, C. (2001) *Market Driven Journalism*, London: Verso.

Lichter, S. R., Rothman, S. and Lichter, L. S. (1986) *The Media Elite*, Bethesda, MD: Adler & Adler.

Lippmann, Walter (1922) *Public Opinion*, New York: Harcourt, Brace & Co.

Livingstone, S. (1998) 'Mediated Childhoods: A Comparative Approach to Young People's Changing Media Environment in Europe', *European Journal of Communication*, 13 (4).

——(2003) 'On the Challenges of Cross-national Comparative Media Research', *European Journal of Communication*, 8 (4): 477–500.

Lloyd, John (2004) *What the Media Are Doing to Our Politics*, London: Constable.

Lowe, G. F. and Hujanen, T. (eds) (2003) *Broadcasting and Convergence: New Articulations of the Public Service Remit*, Göteborg, Sweden: Nordicom.

Luhmann, Niklas (2000) *The Reality of the Mass Media*, Cambridge: Polity Press.

Luther, C. A. and Miller, M. M. (2005) 'Framing of the 2003 US–Iraq War Demonstrations: An Analysis of News and Partisan Texts', *Journalism and Mass Communication Quarterly*, 82 (1): 78–96.

MacBride Report (1980/2004) *Many Voices, One World – Towards a New, More Just, and More Efficient World Information and Communication Order*, International Commission for the Study of Communication Problems (ICSCP). First published by UNESCO, 1980. Re-published 2004, Lanham, MD: Rowman & Littlefield.

MacKinnon, William A. ([1828] 1971) *On the Rise, Progress and Present State of Public Opinion in Great Britain and Other Parts of the World*, Shannon, Ireland: Irish University Press.

McManus, John H. (1994) *Market-Driven Journalism: Let the Citizen Beware*, Thousand Oaks, CA: Sage.

——(1995) 'A Market-based Model of News Production', *Communication Theory*, 5 (4): 301–38.

——(1997) 'Who's Responsible for Journalism?' *Journal of Mass Media Ethics*, 12 (1): 5–17.

McNair, Brian (2006) *Cultural Chaos – Journalism, News and Power in a Globalised World*, London: Routledge.

McQuail, D. (2000) *McQuail's Mass Communication Theory – 4th Edn*, Thousand Oaks, CA: Sage.

——(2003) 'Democracy and the Media', *Political Communication*, 20 (2): 201–4.

——(2005) *McQuail's Mass Communication Theory – 5th Edn*, London and Thousand Oaks, CA: Sage.

McQuail, D. (ed.) (2002) *McQuail's Reader in Mass Communication Theory*, London, Sage.

McQuail, D., Golding, P. and de Bens, E. (eds) (2005) *Communication Theory and Research: An EJC Anthology*, London: Sage.

Mattelart, Armand (1991) *Advertising International: The Privatization of Public Space*, London: Routledge.

——(1994) *Mapping World Communication: War, Progress and Culture*, Minneapolis, MN: University of Minnesota Press.

——(2007) 'Position Statement', presentation to opening session on 'The French Research Landscape', IAMCR 50th Anniversary Conference 2007: 'Media, Communication, Information: Celebrating 50 Years of Theories and Practices', held at UNESCO, Paris, 23–25 July.

Mattelart, Armand (ed.) (2005) *Sur la concentration dans les médias*, Paris: Liris.

Mattelart, Armand and Mattelart, Michèle (1998) *Theories of Communication. A Short Introduction*, London: Sage.

Mayhew, Leon H. (1997) *The New Public: Professional Communication and the Means of Social Influence*, New York: Cambridge University Press.

Mazzoleni, G. (1995) 'Towards a "Videocracy"? Italian Political Communication at a Turning Point', *European Journal of Communication*, 10: 291–319.

Miège, Bernard (2006) *L'information-communication, objet de connaissance*, Brussels: De Boeck/INA.

Mills, C. Wright (1956) *White Collar: The American Middle Classes*, New York: Oxford University Press.

Modleski, T. (1982) *Loving with a Vengeance: Mass-Produced Fantasies for Women*, London: Methuen.

Molotch, Harvey and Lester, Marilyn (1974) 'News as Purposive Behavior: On the Strategic Use of Routine Events, Accidents, and Scandals', *American Sociological Review*, 39 (1): 101–12.

Moores, S. (1996) *Satellite Television and Everyday Life*, Luton: John Libbey Media.

Morley, D. (1980) *The Nationwide Audience*, London: British Film Institute.

——(1992) *Television, Audiences and Cultural Studies*, London: Routledge.

Napoli, P. M. (2003) *Audience Economics: Media Institutions and the Audience Marketplace*, New York: Columbia University Press.

Negrine, R. and Papathanassopoulos, S. (1990) *The Internationalization of Television*, London: Pinter.

Nip, Joyce Y. M. (2006) 'Exploring the Second Phase of Public Journalism', *Journalism Studies*, 7 (2): 212–36.

Nordenstreng, K. and Topuz, H. (eds) (1989) '*Journalist: Status, Rights and Responsibilities*, Prague: International Organization of Journalists.

Noyes, Newbold (1971) Extract from speech to the American Society of Newspaper Editors, Washington, DC, 14 April 1971.

Nygren, Gunnar (2007) 'The Changing Journalistic Work: Changing Professional Roles and Values', presented at conference on 'The Future of Newspapers', Cardiff Centre for Journalism, Media and Cultural Studies, Cardiff University, 12–13 Sept.

Ogden, Rollo (1912) 'Journalism and Public Opinion: An Address before the American Political Science Association', December 1912. Proceedings IX, 194. Reproduced in pp. 317–23 of W. Brooke Graves (ed.) (1928) *Readings in Public Opinion: Its Formation and Control*, New York: D. Appleton & Co.

O'Malley, Tom (1994) *Closedown? The BBC and Government Policy, 1979–92*, London: Pluto.

O'Neill, Deirdre and O'Connor, Catherine (2007) 'The Passive Journalist: How Sources Dominate Local News', presented at conference on 'The Future of Newspapers', Cardiff Centre for Journalism, Media and Cultural Studies, Cardiff University, 12–13 Sept.

O'Neill, Onora (2002) 'On Trust – BBC Radio 4's Reith Lectures 2002', text downloaded 9 Feb. 2008 from BBC website www.bbc.co.uk/radio4/reith2002/

Örnebring, Henrik (2007) 'The Consumer as Producer – of What? User-generated Tabloid Content in *The Sun* (UK) and *Aftonbladet* (Sweden)', presented at conference on 'The Future of Newspapers', Cardiff Centre for Journalism, Media and Cultural Studies, Cardiff University, 12–13 Sept.

Panarese, P. (2005) 'Il racconto dell'immigrazione. Cronaca di un male diffuso', *Problemi dell'informazione*, 30 (1).

Park, Robert E. (1927) 'Topical Summaries of Current Literature – The American Newspaper', *American Journal of Sociology*, 32 (5): 806–13.

——(1940) 'News as a Form of Knowledge: A Chapter in the Sociology of Knowledge', *American Journal of Sociology*, 45 (5): 669–86.

Pavlik, John (2000) 'The Impact of Technology on Journalism'. *Journalism Studies*, 1 (2): 229–37.

——(2001) *Journalism and the New Media: New Edition*, New York: Columbia University Press.

Peiser, Wolfram (2000) 'Setting the Journalist Agenda: Influences from Journalists' Individual Characteristics and from Media Factors', *Journalism and Mass Communication Quarterly*, 77 (2): 243–57.

Petkovic, B (ed.) (2001) *Porocilo za spremljanje nestrpnosti 01*, Ljubljana: Mirovni Institut.

Pew Research Center (2008) 'Internet's Broader Role in Campaign 2008 –Social Networking and Online Videos Take Off', Pew Research Center for the People and the Press, survey conducted in association with The Pew Internet and American Life Project. From www.pewinternet.org/pdfs/Pew_MediaSources_jan08.pdf. Last accessed 22 Feb. 2008.

Picard, Robert G. (2003) 'Assessment of Public Service Broadcasting: Economic and Managerial Performance Criteria', *Javnost – The Public*, 10 (3).

——(2007) 'Shifts in Newspaper Advertising Expenditures and their Implications for the Future of Newspapers', presented at conference on 'The Future of Newspapers', Cardiff Centre for Journalism, Media and Cultural Studies, Cardiff University, 12–13 Sept.

Pleijter, A., Hermans, F. and Tebbe, L. (2002) *Nieuwe journalisten door nieuwe bronnen? Een landelijke inventarisatie van het internetgebruik in de Nederlandse journalistiek*. http://villa.intermax.nl/digiproject/n/nenquetes/onderzoek.pdf

Preston, Paschal (1999) 'Media Coverage of Elections for the European Parliament in 1999: The Case of Ireland', report for EIM project 'Building Bridges Between Cultures', Dublin: COMTEC Centre research paper.

——(2001) *Reshaping Communication: Technology, Information and Social Change*, London and Thousand Oaks, CA: Sage.

——(2003) 'The European Union's ICT Policies: Neglected Social and Cultural Dimensions', ch. 2 (pp. 33–58) in J. Servaes (ed.) *The European Information Society*, Bristol, UK and Portland, OR: Intellect Books.

——(2005) 'ICTs in Everyday Life: Public Policy Implications for "Europe's Way to the Information Society"', ch. 12 (pp. 195–212) in R. Silverstone (ed.) *Media Technology and Everyday Life*, Aldershot: Ashgate.

Preston, Paschal and Grisold, Andrea (1996) 'Unpacking the Concept of Competition in Media Policy Making: The Case of Ireland and Austria', *Democracy and Communication in the New Europe: Change and Continuity in East and West*, Cresskill, NJ: Hampton Press, pp. 67–96.

Preston, Paschal and Kerr, Aphra (2001) 'Digital Media, Nation-states and Local Cultures: The Case of Multimedia "Content" Production', *Media, Culture and Society*, 23: 109–31.

Quinn, S. (2006) *Knowledge Management in the Digital Newsroom*, Oxford: Focal Press.

Reese, S. D. (2001) 'Understanding the Global Journalist: A Hierarchy-of-Influences Approach', *Journalism Studies*, 2 (2): 173–87.

Reese, Stephen D. Jr, Gandy, Oscar H. Jr and Grant, August E. (2003) *Framing Public Life: Perspectives on Media and Our Understanding of the Social World*, London and New York: Routledge.

Reese, Stephen D., Rutigliano, Lou, Hyun, Kideuk and Jeong, Jaekwan (2007) 'Mapping the Blogosphere – Professional and Citizen-based Media in the Global News Arena', *Journalism*, 8: 235–61.

Reich, Z. (2005) 'New Technologies, Old Practices: The Conservative Revolution in Communication Between Reporters and News Sources in the Israeli Press', *Journalism and Mass Communication Quarterly*, 82 (3): 552–70.

Robinson, Susan (2006) 'The Mission of the J-blog: Recapturing Journalistic Authority Online', *Journalism*, 2 (7): 65–83.

Rooney, D. (2000) 'Thirty Years of Competition in the British Tabloid Press', in C. Sparks and J. Tulloch (eds) *Tabloid Tales: Global Debates over Media Standards*, Lanham, MD, Boulder, CO, New York and Oxford: Rowman and Littlefield.

Rosen, Jay (2006) 'The People Formerly Known As The Audience', *Press Think*, 27 June 2006. Last accessed 23 Nov. 2007 at http://journalism.nyu.edu/pubzone/weblogs/pressthink/

Rosten, L. ([1937]1974) *The Washington Correspondents*, New York: Arno.

Rusbridger, Alan (2005) 'Hugo Young Lecture: What Are Newspapers for?', Sheffield University, 9 March 2005. Downloaded from the *Guardian*'s website, last accessed 2 Dec. 2005.

Ruusunoksa, Laura and Kunelius, Risto (2007) 'Professional Imagination and the Future of the Public Service Newspaper: Challenges for Practice and Research', presented at conference on 'The Future of Newspapers', Cardiff Centre for Journalism, Media and Cultural Studies, Cardiff University, 12–13 Sept.

Saltzis, Konstantinos (2007) 'From Single To Multi Media News: How Convergence Affects The Management and the Production of Newspapers', presented at conference on 'The Future of Newspapers', Cardiff Centre for Journalism, Media and Cultural Studies, Cardiff University, 12–13 Sept.

Sampson, Anthony (1996) 'The Crisis at the Heart of Our Media', *British Journalism Review*, 7(3): 42–51.

——(2005) 'The Fourth Estate under Fire', *Guardian*, 10 Jan. 2005.

Sampson, T. and Lugo, J. (2003) 'The Discourse of Convergence: A Neo-liberal Trojan Horse' (pp. 83–93) in G. F. Lowe and T. Hujanen (eds) *Broadcasting and Convergence: New Articulations of the Public Service Remit*, Göteborg, Sweden: Nordicom.

Schiller, Herbert I. (1976) *Communication and Cultural Domination*, New York: Sharpe.

Schlesinger, P. (1978) *Putting 'Reality' Together: BBC News*, London and New York: Methuen.

——(1990) 'The Other Europe', *Media, Culture and Society*, 12 (2): 147–52.

——(1999) 'Changing Spaces of Political Communication: The Case of the European Union', *Political Communication*, 16: 263–79.

Schlesinger, P. and Tumber, H. (1994) *Reporting Crime: The Media Politics of Criminal Justice*, Oxford: Clarendon Press.

Schoenbach, K., de Waal, E. and Lauf, E. (2005) 'Research Note: Online and Print Newspapers: Their Impact on the Extent of the Perceived Public Agenda', *European Journal of Communication*, 20 (2).

Schudson, M. (1978) 'Discovering the News: A Social History of American Newspapers', New York: Basic Books.

——(2000) 'The Sociology of News Production Revisited (Again)' (pp. 175–200) in J. Curran and M. Gurevitch (eds) *Mass Media and Society – 3rd Edn*, London: Arnold.

Scott, W. Richard (1995) 'Institutions and Organisations, Theory and Research', London: Sage. Cited in P. Hirsch (1997) 'Review Article: Sociology Without Social Structure: Neo-Institutional Theory Meets Brave New World', *American Journal of Sociology*, 102 (6): 1702–23.

Scott-Heron, Gil (1970) *Small Talk at 125th & Lenox*, audio recording, New York: Flying Dutchman records, distributed by Mainstream Records/RCA.

Seiter, E., Borchers, H., Kreutzner, G. and Warth, E. (eds) (1989) *Remote Control: Television, Audiences, and Cultural Power*, London: Routledge.

Selznick, P. (1957) *Leadership in Administration*, New York: Harper & Row.

Shoemaker, Pamela and Reese, Stephen D. (1996) *Mediating the Message: Theories of Influence on Mass Media Content – 2nd Edn*, White Plains, NY: Longman.

Sigelman, Lee (1973) 'Reporting the News: An Organizational Analysis', *American Journal of Sociology*, 79 (1): 132–51.

Silverstone, Roger (ed.) (2005) *Media, Technology, and Everyday Life in Europe: From Information to Communication*, Burlington, VT and Aldershot: Ashgate.

Silverstone, R. and Hirsch, E. (eds) (1992) *Consuming Technologies: Media and Information in Domestic Spaces*, London: Routledge.

Simmonds, P. L. (1841) 'Statistics of Newspapers in Various Countries', *Journal of the Statistical Society of London*, 4 (2): 111–36.

Singer, Jane B. (2003) 'Who Are These Guys? The Online Challenge to the Notion of Journalistic Professionalism', *Journalism*, 5 (4): 139–63.

——(2005) 'The Political J-blogger: "Normalizing" a New Media Form to Fit Old Norms and Practices', *Journalism*, 5 (6): 173–98.

Smith, Adam (1776) *An Inquiry into the Nature and Causes of the Wealth of Nations*.

Soloski, John (1989) 'News Reporting and Professionalism: Some Constraints on the Reporting of the News', *Media, Culture and Society*, 11 (2): 207–28.

Sparks, C. and Tulloch, J. (eds) (2000) *Tabloid Tales: Global Debates over Media Standards*, Lanham, MD: Rowman and Littlefield.

Sparrow, B. H. (2006) 'A Research Agenda for an Institutional Media', *Political Communication*, 23 (2): 145–57.

Speed, J. G. (1893) 'Do Newspapers Now Give the News?', *Forum* (August 1893): 705–11. Cited in D. C. Whitney, R. S. Sumpter and D. McQuail (2004) 'News Media Production: Individuals, Organizations and Institutions', ch. 19 (pp. 393–410) in J. Downing, D. McQuail, P. Schlesinger and E. Wartella (eds) *Sage Handbook of Media Studies*, Thousand Oaks, CA and London: Sage; and also in R. S. Sumpter (2001) 'News about News: John G. Speed and the First Newspaper Content Analysis', *Journalism History*, 27 (2): 64–72.

Splichal, Slavko (1999) *Public Opinion: Developments and Controversies in the Twentieth Century*, Lanham, MD: Rowman and Littlefield.

——(2002) *Principles of Publicity and Press Freedom*, Lanham, MD and Oxford: Rowman and Littlefield.

——(2006) 'In Search of a Strong European Public Sphere: Some Critical Observations on Conceptualizations of Publicness and the (European) Public Sphere', *Media, Culture and Society*, 28 (5): 695–714.

Staats, J. L. (2005) 'Habermas and Democratic Theory: The Threat to Democracy of Unchecked Corporate Power', *Political Research Quarterly*, 57 (4): 585–94.

Stark, Rodney W. (1962) 'Policy and the Pros: An Organisational Analysis of a Metropolitan Newspaper'. *Berkeley Journal of Sociology*, 7 (1): 11–31.

Sumpter, R. S. (2001) 'News About News: John G. Speed and the First Newspaper Content Analysis', *Journalism History*, 27 (2): 64–72.

Taylor, P. (1997) *Global Communications: International Affairs and the Media Since 1945*, London: Routledge.

Thrall, A. Trevor (2006) 'The Myth of the Outside Strategy: Mass Media News Coverage of Interest Groups', *Political Communication*, 23 (4): 407–20.

——(2007) 'Review Essay', *Political Communication*, 24 (2): 202–8.

Thurman, Neil (2007) 'The Globalization of Journalism Online: A Transatlantic Study of News Websites and Their International Readers', *Journalism*, 8 (8): 285–307.

Torsul, Tanja and Steudahl, Dagny (eds) (2007) *Ambivalence Towards Convergence: Digitalization and Media Change*, Göteborg, Sweden: Nordicom.

Tuchman, Gaye (1972) 'Objectivity as Strategic Ritual: An Examination of Newsmen's Notions of Objectivity', *American Journal of Sociology*, 77 (4): 660–79.

——(1973) 'Making News by Doing Work: Routinizing the Unexpected', *American Journal of Sociology*, 79 (1): 110–31.

——(1976) 'The News' Manufacture of Sociological Data: Comment on Danzger', *American Sociological Review*, 41 (6): 1065–67.

——(1978) *Making News: A Study in the Construction of Reality*, New York: Free Press.

Tumber, Howard (ed.) (1999) *News: A Reader*, Oxford: Oxford University Press.

Tunstall, Jeremy (1971) *Journalists At Work*, London: Constable.

Tunstall, Jeremy and Palmer, Michael (1991) *Media Moguls*, London: Routledge.

Turner, G. (1999) 'Tabloidization, Journalism and the Possibility of Critique', *International Journal of Culture Studies*, 2 (1): 59–76.

Ugille, Peter and Paulussen, Steve (2007) 'Moderation, Conversation and Collaboration? Organisational Implications of Citizen Journalism Projects in Professional Newsrooms', presented at conference on 'The Future of Newspapers', Cardiff Centre for Journalism, Media and Cultural Studies, Cardiff University, 12–13 Sept.

Uribe, G. and Gunter, B. (2004) 'Research Note: The Tabloidization of British Tabloids', *European Journal of Communication*, 19 (3).

Ursell, Gillian (2001) 'Dumbing Down or Shaping Up? New Technologies, New Media, New Journalism', *Journalism*, 8 (2): 175–96.

Van Dijk, T. A. (1991) *Racism and the Press*, London: Routledge.

Van Zoonen, L. (1994/2002) 'A New Paradigm?' *Feminist Media Studies*, London: Sage. Reprinted as ch. 3 (pp. 46–59) in D. McQuail (ed.) (2002) *McQuail's Reader in Mass Communication Theory*, London: Sage.

Wahl-Jorgensen, Karin (2007) 'The Future of Local Journalism: A Digital Divide between News Organizations?', presented at conference on 'The Future of Newspapers', Cardiff Centre for Journalism, Media and Cultural Studies, Cardiff University, 12–13 Sept.

Weaver, David H. (ed.) (1998) *The Global Journalist: News People Around the World*, Cresskill, NJ: Hampton Press.

Weaver, David H. and Wilhoit, G. Cleveland (1996) *The American Journalist in the 1990s*, Bloomington, IN: Indiana University Press.

White, D.M. (1950/1999) 'The "Gate Keeper": A Case Study in the Selection of News', *Journalism Quarterly*, 27 (4): 383–90. See also extract reproduced as ch. 8 (pp. 66–73) in H. Tumber (ed.) (1999) *News: A Reader*, Oxford: Oxford University Press.

Whitney, D. C., Sumpter, R. S. and McQuail, D. (2004) 'News Media Production: Individuals, Organizations and Institutions', ch. 19 (pp. 393–410) in J. Downing, D. McQuail, P. Schlesinger and E. Wartella (eds) *Sage Handbook of Media Studies*, Thousand Oaks, CA and London: Sage.

Wilcox, D. F. (1900) 'The American Newspapers: A Study in Social Psychology', *Annals of the American Academy of Political and Social Science*, 16: 56–92.

Williams, Andrew and Franklin, Bob (2007) '"Turning Around the Tanker": Regional Journalists' Perceptions about Multiple Platform Working – A Case Study', presented at conference on 'The Future of Newspapers', Cardiff Centre for Journalism, Media and Cultural Studies, Cardiff University, 12–13 Sept.

Williams, Raymond (1961/1965) *The Long Revolution*, Harmondsworth: Penguin.

——(1976/1988) *Key Words: A Vocabulary of Culture and Society – Revised Edition*, London: Fontana Press.

——(1958/1989) 'Culture is Ordinary', in *Resources of Hope: Culture, Democracy, Socialism*, London: Verso.

Winston, B. (2002) 'The Tabloidisation of Television: 1975–2001', *Journalism Studies*, 3 (1).

Wodak, Ruth (1996) *Disorders of Discourse*, New York and London: Longman.

Wodak, Ruth; de Cillia, F. R., Reisgl, M. and Liebhart, K. (1999) *The Discursive Construction of National Identity*, Edinburgh: Edinburgh University Press.

Zavratnik Zimic, Simona (2001) 'Perspektiva konstriranja schengenske "emeje": Slovenija', in A. Milohnic (ed.) *Evropski vratarji: migracijske in azilne politike v Vzhodni Evropi*, Ljubljana: Mirovni Institut.

Zelizer, Barbie (2004) *Taking Journalism Seriously: News and the Academy*, London: Sage.

Index

Page spans may indicate separate mentions rather than continuous discussion. Italic page numbers indicate figures.